BIRMINGHAM
and the Black Country's
CANALSIDE INDUSTRIES

BIRMINGHAM
and the Black Country's
CANALSIDE INDUSTRIES

Ray Shill

TEMPUS

First published 2005

Tempus Publishing Limited
The Mill, Brimscombe Port,
Stroud, Gloucestershire, GL5 2QG
www.tempus-publishing.com

British Library Cataloguing in Publication Data.
A catalogue record for this book is available from the British Library.

ISBN 0 7524 3262 1

Typesetting and origination by Tempus Publishing Limited
Printed in Great Britain

CONTENTS

Acknowledgements — has none!!

INTRODUCTION

Industry made Britain great. British people, through skill and innovation, developed many new ideas that have become the cornerstones of our modern world. Industry has been part of society ever since people started to manufacture, and integral to this development was the ability to work with clay, metals and wood.

Britain was fortunate to have deposits of copper, iron, lead and tin ores and these were worked for generations in a basic, but effective, manner. The ores were dug out and refined through sheer hard work. Scattered throughout the country were pockets of industry where ores were processed with the aid of water and fire to extract the metal for working up into useful goods.

It has been said that Shropshire was the cradle of the iron industry, but the West Midlands became a cradle for science and innovation. New and different methods of working with chemicals and metals frequently had their trials conducted in the West Midlands where a reservoir of skilled workmen existed. It is with metalworking that the area became best known. Reserves of coal, iron and limestone were all exploited to this end. Essential to this development was an efficient transport system. The West Midlands comprised a range of low hills and river valleys. The principal mineral reserves were located under land, which was over 400ft above sea level. The streams and rivers that flowed from this district were narrow and at times fast flowing. In their existing unmodified form local waterways were unsuitable for navigation, but the power of water was, however, harnessed to drive a host of mills.

The only means of transport was rough roads and packhorse tracks. New turnpike roads came into existence during the eighteenth century, striking out to link centres of industry. Towns like Birmingham and Wolverhampton came to be served by an embryonic network of roads that crossed the intervening district to reach existing coal and iron mines around Bilston, Tipton and Wednesbury. Others extended across to Bewdley on the River Severn, which became an important river port. Upkeep for the turnpike roads was achieved through the charging of tolls. But turnpike owners also profited from their roads and only a portion of the revenue was channelled back into maintenance and improvement.

By 1760 a growing dissatisfaction was felt with the existing transport links. Local businessmen looked for means of improvement. The solution came in the form of building artificial waterway links, or canals. A network of inland waterways came to be built, which linked the West Midlands with the Mersey, Severn, Thames and Trent.

Coal mining and iron working prospered. Such was the concentration of works around Dudley, Tipton and Wednesbury that this area, and that adjacent, became known as the Black Country. People flocked into the area to find work. They came from all walks of life and trades. There was a special demand for experienced miners, many of whom came from existing mines in East Shropshire and South Wales, and these moved to the Black Country with the promise of paid work. Many others were drawn to the district in the hope of employment as labourers. They came from different parts of the country bringing their own ways of speaking, customs and culture. As local mineral resources were depleted local waterways continued to play an important part with the moving of raw material and produce. Even when, from 1850, an integrated public railway network was constructed, canals still retained an essential role.

The West Midlands iron industry was at its peak during the nineteenth century. As engineering skills were perfected new methods of dealing with metals led to the establishment of firms engaged in the production of galvanised sheets, iron tubes, steel and structural ironwork. The working of non-ferrous metal, such as copper and brass, produced articles for the gas and water industry, and metallic bedstead trades. Metalworking also stimulated the growth of a local chemical industry where acids and alkalis were produced. This in turn led to the making of pure chemicals, which assisted the local paint and varnish industry. All these varied works became canalside features. Other needs led to building of brickyards, flourmills, glassworks and timber yards beside the water's edge.

During the early years of the twentieth century canalside industry remained dependent on water carriage for coal from nearby pits. A series of bad trading years had led to a considerable decline in the local iron and steel trades. Engineering also suffered and as traditional means of employment dwindled in the metal trades, new firms moved in to fill the vacuum. Several were engaged as suppliers to the automotive trade and utilised the power of electricity or gas rather than coal.

These were changing times for the waterways. There was still a demand for coal by boat to serve certain works as well as a continuing domestic requirement at the coal merchant's yard. A new user was the growing number of power stations that generated electricity for public tramways, public lighting, industry and domestic use.

Closure, competition, merger and rationalisation are words commonly associated with the fate of West Midlands industry. Factory closures became more prevalent after 1920, particularly during the depression that followed in the years 1922–1926. Throughout these times coal remained the most important traffic on the waterways, but even this dwindled through mine closures. Eventually all the local mines either closed or diverted their traffic to the railways or roads.

The last canal traffic included power station coal, gas works by-products and salvage to tips during the 1960s. Nationalisation had led to the restructuring of several industries, which included the electricity industry, gas industry and even the waterways. The electricity industry when nationalised closed down smaller works and enlarged others. Power stations at Birchills (Walsall), Nechells (Birmingham), Ocker Hill (Tipton) and Wolverhampton were supplied by canal through to the mid-1960s when a decision was made to end boat traffic. Nationalisation of the gas industry also led to changes in the way gas was made. Certain works were closed or converted to water gas plants. Eventually the adoption of natural gas spelled an end to coal carbonisation and the closure of the remaining gas works put an end to the by-product traffic.

The last canal traffic ceased about 1970. Although a few working boats pass through the district from time to time, their duty is more for pleasure than as a cargo carrier. Yet the odd load still occasionally turns up. Local industry continues to decline as the demand for cheap goods is directed to Asia where low wages and lesser production costs more than compensate for the transport of goods from those parts. Every month, every day some local firm decides to shut its doors for the last time. It is a sad legacy for the future.

The main purpose of this book is to investigate the rise, development and metamorphosis of West Midlands industry with particular respect to those dependent on local canals as well as the role of canals in encouraging further industry. There were some 200 years of canal transport in the Midlands and any description of the trade would fill more than one book, such was the diversity. The text concentrates on the metal and related trades, as these often required the movement of bulk goods. A canal narrow boat had the capacity to carry up to 25 tons of goods or minerals in its hold. Works located on the canal would receive and despatch loads by boat and through the canal network could reach different parts of the country as well as some the country's major ports. It was an asset, which businessmen found essential to the success of their trade. Traffic and trade started to increase. And that is where the description begins.

one

CANAL GENESIS

Canals are a living heritage. They are to be found throughout the country, in England, Northern Ireland, Scotland and Wales, where they improved the carriage of goods and led to the industrial growth of many a town and city. West Midland waterways came to prominence during the eighteenth century when the first canal routes were constructed. These formed the basic fabric of a network that would aid the development of local industry, and in particular promote the chemical, glass and metal trades.

Navigable rivers provided the earliest types of water communications. The River Severn, Sabrina, had long been used as a navigable waterway. Barges and trows carried goods and minerals along this waterway from estuary ports to Gloucester, Worcester, Bewdley and Bridgnorth. Midland towns benefited through this traffic, albeit via the muddy tracks, packhorse ways and early turnpiked roads that brought their traffic to the banks of the Severn. The merchants of Bewdley amassed fortunes through the rights of free passage along this river, which Royal Charter afforded them.

The Severn, above Worcester, had shallow sections that restricted navigation to times of high water called 'springs', which provided a natural limit to the carrying of trade. Yet despite these restrictions, boats were able to reach Shrewsbury and beyond. People seemed content with these restrictions until the middle of the eighteenth century, when plans for artificial waterways to existing manufacturing centres were considered.

Elsewhere in the country unnavigable rivers had been made navigable through the building of locks and short canals that avoided rapids and other hindrances to navigation. Such works enabled boats to reach far beyond the navigable limits of the River Thames, pass up the Irwell to Manchester and reach Leeds via the Aire & Calder Navigation. Here in the Midlands, the Warwickshire Avon had been made navigable as far as Stratford and for a period the Dick Brook, Salwarpe and Stour had locks provided to assist navigation.

Andrew Yarranton (1619–1684) was associated with several Midlands navigation improvements. Andrew was born at Larford in the parish of Astley. His family were staunch Presbyterians and Yarranton followed the strict doctrines of the Presbyterian Church, as his parents had done before him. Andrew joined the Parliamentary Army and rose to the rank of Captain. He fought throughout the years of civil conflict and his military career only came to an end in 1652. Yarranton developed an entrepreneurial spirit and gained skills in dealing with men during his time in the army, and both would stand in him in good stead for his subsequent varied careers. Andrew left the army to start an iron furnace near where he was born and where was still his home. The furnace was placed near the Dick Brook, a section of which was made navigable from the Severn through the provision of two locks. Barges carrying ironstone were brought up the brook for unloading.

Yarranton was associated with work on the Avon, Salwarpe and Stour. In 1666 an act was granted to make the River Stour navigable. Andrew eventually undertook the work. In his own words he

made it completely navigable from Stourbridge to Kidderminster and carried down many hundred tuns of coales…

He and his son made improvements to the river, which included locks and new channels, and navigation was possible at times through to Stourport.

The borderland of the counties of Staffordshire and Worcestershire became a place of significant industrial development that took years to nurture. Long before the Industrial Revolution took hold of this district, water mills had been adapted for metalworking. The skills of the nameless engineers who diverted the courses of rivers and streams to make millraces and mill pools, are all but forgotten, but their legacy was the foundation of industry in the region. The Rea, Stour, Tame and many brooks and streams were adapted to capture the precious water and impound it so that its power could be harnessed to drive a water wheel. The power was enough when conveyed through wooden gears and shafting to turn a millstone, raise a hammer, roll and split metal or work bellows for a blast furnace.

Hidden below the surface of what became known as the Black Country, were layers of coal, ironstone, limestone and clay, all of which were to be developed for commercial gain. Yet integral to the success of the district was the smelting of ironstone and iron ore to produce iron. Wood had long provided the source of charcoal for the limited production of pig iron. Supplies of wood, though sustainable, were a dwindling resource through increased demand. Coal eventually came to supersede it once the method had been perfected for this to be done. Many coals contained a variety of other elements, including sulphur, and it was the sulphur content that handicapped the direct smelting of coal with the ores. Some success was achieved when low-sulphur coal was used, but it was not until coke was adopted that iron production was materially increased. Various people deserve the credit for the inception of the coke smelting process and even now historians labour to discover the true history. But an important share of the credit still lies with the Darby family at Ironbridge, who built the coke smelting furnaces at Coalbroodale. Iron making blossomed along the banks of the Severn and throughout East Shropshire, where local supplies of coal, ironstone and limestone (used as the flux) were utilised to best advantage.

The Black Country received lesser recognition for these early improvements, yet here too mines existed for the coal, ironstone and limestone, and the water mills played their part in the metalworking process. One Shropshire ironmaster, John Wilkinson, was inspired to work an estate at Bradley, Near Bilston and it was on this mining estate that he arranged for a blast furnace to be erected in about the year 1757.

Iron was not the only metal worked. There was particular interest in brass casting in Birmingham, which rose to prominence during the eighteenth century. Brass was then made by the combination of copper with calamine, a zinc ore. It was a method that was both time-consuming and wasteful. Yet Birmingham manufacturers used it to make buttons, trinkets, ormolu decorations and cabinet fittings for furniture. The decorative nature of brass was particularly appreciated by the wealthy whose purse could then afford the high cost of production. Some Birmingham manufacturers were also early workers in steel for military and domestic uses. Their products included 'toys', swords, bayonets and edge tools. The need for cleaning and treating metals also led to a chemical works being established for the production of acid.

With each new trade came a proportionate demand for coal. Fires, fuelled by coal, were used to melt and temper metal, and they were needed to assist the chemical reactions that first produced sulphuric acid in the lead vats in Steelhouse Lane. Coal was readily available in the Black Country and was already being mined around Bilston, Dudley, Stourbridge, Tipton, Wednesbury, Walsall and Wolverhampton.

Resources of coal and fireclay in the Stourbridge area proved an invaluable supply for the glass-making industry established in this area during the seventeenth century, when coal was first used to heat glass furnaces. In 1696 seventeen glasshouses were recorded in the Stourbridge and Brierley Hill district. Best quality fireclay was formed into the pots used to melt the ingredients of glass for the glass blowers to work upon. These glassworks came to specialise in the making of flint glass, often made to a fine quality. It is a reputation that has been passed down to the present day. A lesser-known glassworks was located at Bilston, near Bradley, which was in existence by the middle of the eighteenth century.

To be sold or Lett
At Bulls-Head at Bilston, on Tuesday the 5th of March 1765,
The Glasshouse at Glassborough, near Bilston, with house adjoining, and also the possession of a farm house, and land, with the Barns and Stables belonging to it, and a Contract for Coal for supplying the said Glasshouse; all of which Premises are held by Lease under Thomas Hoo, Esq; for a Term of Years yet to come and unexpired.
At the same time will be sold, to the purchaser of the said Glasshouse, the Materials and Utensils now upon the Spot for working the same
And also several very good Waggon Horses, with Gearing and Accoutrements, and two Broad Wheel Waggons, one Narrow Wheel Waggon, with several other utensils in Husbandry

Other clays were adapted for brick making, tile making and pottery manufacture. Surface brick clays were encountered throughout the region and proved a useful resource for the canal builders when material was required for bridges, locks, offices and other structures.

An early eighteenth-century development was the Newcomen engine, which contemporary texts call a fire engine. These basic engines were first employed in 1712 when Thomas Newcomen and Captain Savery provided an engine to drain the mines near Dudley Castle. Fire engines came to be erected across the coalfield and assisted in keeping the mines dry. These early engines were simple affairs that essentially comprised a cylinder, which sat on top of the boiler that provided the steam. The movement of the piston in the cylinder moved a wooden beam up and down, which in turn raised and lowered the pump rods to drain the mine. It was an action that kept the mine relatively free from water and enabled the miners to reach deeper coal measures.

To be SOLD, a fire engine consisting of a Cast Metal Cylinder, 25 inches diameter, a wrought iron boyler with lead top, one complete lift of between 30 and 40 yards of cast-iron pipes, and wood tubes, 27 yards of cast-iron pipes, the working barrel about 9 inches and a half diameter, Jackhead, Lift compleat, with a brass working barrel, regulator beam, plug and gears, wrought iron chains, rods, buckets, clacks, and brass cocks and clacks, and all the implements in working conditions, and four coal pit gins – for further particulars enquire Thomas Hateley, of Wednesbury, the seller
(*Aris's Gazette*, 7 September 1772).

Coal mining was long established in the district by the time a canal was contemplated to move the coal. Amongst the eighteenth century coalmasters were John Sparrow, Thomas Tomkys and John Bickley. These men were mine owners, but employed contractors to actually get the coal. The chief object of their attentions was the 'thick coal', which was a seam of coal that could be up to 30 yards deep. Miners worked this coal by the rib and pillar method, digging out the coal, but leaving thick pillars of coal to support the roof. These miners included the pikemen and loaders who brought down the coal and then placed the coal on small-wheeled skips. The coal was taken away in long and heavy lumps that were stacked on the skip and banded together before being raised to the surface by a horse-gin. The mouth of the pit was known as the bank and it was here that coal was sold to the customers to cart away by wagon.

Mining was a precarious occupation, even in these times. Water could drown out a mine, even with the assistance of pumping. Falls of rock and coal could injure or kill, and another danger was methane gas that could suffocate the unwary or explode into a serious fire with equally devastating results. During this period, when pumping machinery was relatively basic, flooding would often stop a mine's operation. Those who were not affected were quick to capitalise on their neighbour's misfortunes. Tomkys was a man who evidently did not share this view:

Whereas a false and malicious report has been raised that the coal-works at Wednesbury being drowned out, will make a total stagnation of getting the coal, and that the price of coal upon the coal-pit bank, will thereby enhanced to a very extravagant price. Notice is hereby given that the public may be supplied with any quantity of coals at my works at Bilstone for 8.d a skip (about 500 lb) and that during the scarcity (others raise them as they please, and oppress the country) they shall not be raised at any more at any of my works upon any account whatever.
Thomas Tomkys
(*Aris's Gazette*, 23 July 1759).

During this period, production of coal remained limited and any thoughts of export to a wider market were discouraged. The location of most were above the 400ft contour and many miles from the nearest navigable waterway.

Coal mined around Wednesbury and Bilston was regularly conveyed along the turnpike to Birmingham, but again at a cost. Water travel was cheaper, but local rivers were either too shallow or swift to entertain a regular traffic. Most had been adapted to power mills whose owners would have been a potent force to contend with should anyone wish to do so.

When the Bridgewater Canal was constructed to serve the Worsley mines, new hope for inland navigation was generated. Canal schemes were proposed to unite important towns across the country. The routes of these schemes were prone to alteration and one early proposal made in January 1766 was to make a canal from Tern Bridge, Shropshire, by Crushington Bridge and Chetwyn Park through to Bridgeford on the River Sow, Staffordshire and then onto Winsford Bridge on the River Weaver. A second canal was to run from Bridgeford, Staffordshire through to Wilden Ferry on the River Trent. A meeting was held at the Raven, Shrewsbury on 5 February 1766, where the local manufacturers were invited to attend.

It is desired that the masters of the Great Forges and other works of Kineton, Tibberton, Upton under Haymon, Coalbrook Dale, Ketley, Horsley, Witheyford, Moreton, Willey, Pitchford, Sutton and Longnor, and all the various large manufacturers lying upon the intended Navigation, or Severn, will then and there give their attendance.
(*Aris's Gazette*, 7 January 1766).

Had this route been made the canal map would have been dramatically altered within the West Midlands, for the line would have avoided the Black Country. The Severn Navigation would have been utilised north through Ironbridge to near Atcham before the canal diverged off across the countryside towards Stafford. As it was other routes were considered and it was the 'Wolverhampton' canal that joined the Severn at Mitton, which was finally approved. It was a decision that was to materially affect the future prospects of the East Shropshire ironmasters, who no doubt would have benefited by a direct route to the ports of Liverpool and Hull. Instead the Birmingham and Black Country manufacturers were handed a golden opportunity for development. Through this simple act an irresistible process was set in motion that would forever place the West Midlands at the heart of the canal network.

Early in 1767 several prominent Birmingham businessmen came together to examine a proposal to build a canal to the coalmines. This scheme soon became a concrete determination to make a waterway to Bilston and thereafter to join with the Wolverhampton Canal at Aldersley.

The Wolverhampton Canal quickly became better known as the Staffordshire & Worcestershire Canal and it is by this name that a company of proprietors was formed during 1766. A well-attended meeting was held at Wolverhampton during March 1766 where those who attended considered the wording of the application to be made to Parliament for a navigable canal from the River Severn, at or near a place called Stours Mouth, to join up with another proposed canal to link the Trent with the Mersey. The route was planned to pass near Kidderminster, to, or near, Kinver (Kinfare), Prestwood, Orton, Tettenhall, Coven, Brewood and Penkridge, then to, or near, Shutborough, there to join the intended canal to be made between Wilden Ferry and the River Mersey. The closest it came to the industrial Black Country was the section between Kinver and Coven.

Wolverhampton was a midway point on the Staffordshire & Worcestershire Canal. Although the town centre was placed a couple of miles away, the turnpike road to Tettenhall enabled transport of goods between the two places. A similar arrangement existed at Stewponey where a warehouse was established to receive goods from and send goods to Stourbridge.

Birmingham developed rapidly during the seventeenth and eighteenth centuries. A major restriction to development, however, was the primitive transport arrangements that then existed. Being a manufacturing town, but lacking local resources, Birmingham required materials and components to be transported to it. This was often done at a cost. Poor roads led to constant delays in securing goods.

During the eighteenth century a number of new turnpike roads were constructed from the south and the north. A turnpike was made through to Wednesbury in 1727 and further extensions took this turnpike route through Wolverhampton to Bridgnorth by 1748. In this fashion Birmingham was united with the River Severn, an important highway for the transport of goods.

Construction of what was to become the Birmingham Canal Navigation was carried out in stages. The first section opened between Hill Top, West Bromwich and Birmingham in November 1769. Gradually, the main canal took shape as it wound through Oldbury, Tipton, Bilston and Wolverhampton, finally reaching Aldersley in 1772. This canal was the first of many waterways that came to serve the town of Birmingham – others soon followed. The making of the Birmingham Canal deserves discussion, as a number of factors influenced the construction. This first waterway was far from suitable for the purposes for which it was made and many alterations and improvements were required to make the valuable waterway link, which it finally became.

If a count were made of all the different trades carried out in Birmingham during the nineteenth and twentieth centuries, the accepted figure of 1,000 would fall short. The centre of Birmingham then teamed with life. Over a million people were crammed into a relatively small area. Back-to-back houses were in abundance and backyard workshops mixed with the houses. In the dark recesses, often hidden from the busy streets, a multitude of trades were carried on. Whether a business was small or large, it relied on the transport system of the day for its material and produce. Both canals and railways were to play their part in the development of Birmingham's industry. But it is the canal that deserves the greatest honour.

Industry flourished in Birmingham, encouraged through the lack of an organised Guild system that was often a stranglehold on innovation. Men of vision such as Matthew Boulton and James Watt would have been hampered elsewhere. People came to Birmingham because of this freedom. They set up their own small trades in the town. All goods came in and out by road. Transport was in the hands of the stage-wagon proprietor. During the eighteenth and early nineteenth centuries the covered stage wagon was just as common on the streets of Birmingham as it was in America. The roads were generally poor and the service was, consequentially, poor.

The carriers were limited to what they could carry and would charge what they liked for their services. Some road carriers even operated on the principle of what their customers could stand rather than a regular set of rates. When the Birmingham Canal was first proposed many businessmen became subscribers because of the possibility of cheaper transport rates. It even took precedence over the new proposed hospital, such was the need for cheap rates of commodities such as coal.

Coal was important to Birmingham. It quite literally fuelled the fires of Birmingham's industry. Those who provided the means for cheaper coal also provided the impetus for the town's development. Those who owned coalmines were therefore mindful of this fact. A canal was suggested to bring coal into Birmingham at a cheaper rate. Thomas Tomkys wrote to Matthew Boulton in January 1767. He had heard about a canal that was to serve Birmingham and was keen to be involved with its promotion.

I think you know the level between Birmingham and Great Bridge is already known, if there is a level taken between Great Bridge and Bickley's Mill at Bilston it most certainly will show you how far the Bilstone water will run towards Birmingham for it seems to me that you will have a dead canal from Birmingham to Bilstone and the only difficulty you will have to surmount will be to get over a small brook at Bilstone and the other at Hampton and it may soon be supplied with water upon the summit at a small expense by a Fire Engine to lift it about 5 or 6 yards and the expense of working that engine will cost only a workman, the coalmasters will let you have the small to work it for a small price for getting to colliery and boats might carry gratis.

Tomkys also mentioned a possible branch to Tipton, which could supply coal sold at the pit bank at 3*s* per ton. Evidently, there were people such as Thomas Tomkys who already believed that a canal from Birmingham to Bilston was possible.

On 4 June 1767, the Swan Inn in High Street, Birmingham was unusually busy. The members of its normal clientele had been swelled by a group of people attending the inn for the canal meeting. Some prominent Birmingham residents were present. Attorneys, merchants and medical men had arrived and now all had a part in shaping Birmingham's destiny. Now they were congregated together at the Swan to make a little history. It had become their purpose to build a navigable waterway from Birmingham to Wolverhampton and to link up with other canals then under construction. Those present listened eagerly to the proposals. It was a bold scheme – few canals had been built before, but those at the Swan, that day, were determined to accomplish it. The road system which then existed had the monopoly of the traffic. Roads were then a mixture of tracks and turnpike roads. The turnpikes were maintained by trusts, which collected tolls for maintenance and profit. They were the means of bringing coal, metals and merchandise to Birmingham. Local businessmen looked for alternatives and, thanks to the vision of the Duke of Bridgewater and Josiah Wedgewood, the concept of a man-made waterway was already a reality.

The carriage of goods by road was slow and expensive. For business to flourish in Birmingham a cheaper alternative was sought. Two canal schemes had been proposed the previous year, which when completed would link the Humber, Mersey and Severn. Those in Birmingham saw that they might link up with these schemes and the idea of the Birmingham Canal was born. Supporters of this canal included Dr John Ash, Matthew Boulton, Samuel Galton, Samuel Garbett, Dr William Small and John Wilkinson.

There were few engineers capable of building a canal at that time. But one man had risen to a position of eminence in this field. His work on the Bridgewater Canal had established his reputation and, now in the last years of his life, he was to embark upon a fantastic canal-building programme. Brindley was already engineer to the Grand Trunk and Wolverhampton Canals when he was approached by the Birmingham Canal group. He was to survey two possible routes to link Birmingham with the Wolverhampton Canal. On 4 June he presided over the meeting at the Swan to explain both routes. It was up to those present to decide.

James Brindley produced plans and estimates and his opinion was sought for the better of the two routes. The option from New Hall over Birmingham Heath through the coal works at Bilstone to Wolverhampton and a junction with the Staffordshire and Worcestershire Canal (Wolverhampton Canal) was chosen. Branches were contemplated to other coal works en route.

Having decided on the route the next step was to raise the money for the Bill to pass through Parliament and arrange for construction of the waterway. Another meeting was arranged for 12 June at the Swan, where a public subscription was raised. The initial response was quite high and £35,000 had been pledged by July. The minutes of the proprietors' meetings were recorded after the June 1767 gathering. They form an informative record of the building and operation of the company. On the first page is written in best hand:

A Journal of the Meetings and Proceedings respecting the Navigation

Whereas the utility of a Navigation Cut or Canal from this town through the coal works, setting for the great advantage the inhabitants would receive not only by reducing the price of the carriage of the coals and other commodities, but also the price of provisions, oats, beans etc. by reducing and rendering useless the great number of horses that are now kept employed for such purpose, having been made to appear and offered to the consideration of the publick papers soliciting the attendance at the Swan Inn for consideration of such proposals and if the same should be approved that a proper person might be approached to take a survey and give estimates and expenses.

A list of subscribers to the canal was then given. They included a number of prominent names including the printer John Baskerville and several coalmasters such as John Sparrow and Thomas Tomkys.

At the next meeting held at the Swan on 12 June a committee was appointed for the difficult job of starting the work. As this was a totally new experience, they had to sit down with a blank sheet of paper and effectively draw up the way to do it. The committee comprised the following: Henry Carver, Samuel Garbett, Samuel Galton, John Wilkinson, Matthew Boulton, Dr John Ash, Thomas Salt and John Baskerville. Another two gentlemen, William Bentley and George Holloway, were given the task of contacting the landowners and obtaining their consent to build the canal through their property.

There was a lot to be done even before the canal could be started. A system or organisation had to be created to run the canal and its finances. An Act of Parliament had to be sought and land had to be compulsorily purchased. Those on this first committee were quite capable businessmen. Samuel Garbett was a chemical manufacturer and one of the founders of the Carron Ironworks at Falkirk. Samuel Galton was a Birmingham gunmaker. John Wilkinson had various ironworks and furnaces in Shropshire and Staffordshire. Matthew Boulton was already famous for his Soho Factory, which he had created from virtually nothing on a barren heath. John Ash was a man of science and dedicated to the care of the sick. The man given the task of supervising the subscription was John Meridith, a Birmingham solicitor.

Monthly, and sometimes twice monthly, meetings were held at the Swan Inn where the initial policy decisions were taken which would form the substance of the Bill. John Lane was recruited in July to conduct the intended Act through Parliament. Henry Davidson, a parliamentary solicitor, also joined the team. At a General Meeting of the proprietors held at the Swan on 13 November 1767, the select committee was reconstituted to include nine members. They now had quorum powers to spend the proprietors' money as long as any sum did not exceed £1,000. The new committee comprised: Dr John Ash, Dr William Small, Henry Carver, Samuel Garbett, John Kettle, William Bentley, Matthew Boulton, Joseph Wilkinson and William Welch.

The wording of the Bill took several months to prepare. Rates had to be decided and various clauses were added as different implications were discussed. The committee were careful to take in the needs of the coalmasters, but were insistent that coal should not be worked under the line of the canal. On 26 February 1768 the Bill before Parliament became law, and work could now start on the construction.

When the Bill received the royal assent and became law, it proved to be quite a lengthy tome. Every possible consideration appears to have been attended to. The intended route was carefully described and every possible landowner mentioned. Yet despite their attention to detail, those who prepared the Bill omitted a simple fact. Part of the canal passed through detached portions of the county of Shropshire, but this was not mentioned in the Bill. Thus another Act had to be made the following year to rectify the mistake and clarify the fact that a part of Oldbury was then in Shropshire! Furthermore, despite the verbose description of the route, no specific course was stated. In fact, it may be described as vague. From Newhall Ring to the Staffordshire and Worcestershire Canal it was, by, near, or to. Thus it was to or near Smethwick, Oldbury, Tipton Green and Bilston, and by, or near, the several coalmines and limestone quarries. Even the junction with the other canal was in doubt. The Act stated this intended junction was to, or near, Autherley otherwise Aldersley, which would suggest that the junction could have been either at Autherley or Aldersley.

The first General Meeting of the proprietors was arranged for 24 March 1768 at the Swan Inn. With purpose now firmly in their sights, decisions now had to be made as to the way forward. Appointments for various BCN officers were ratified during the proprietors' meeting held on 18 March 1768.

Name	Position
John Meredith	Clerk to the Company
John Kettle	Treasurer
James Brindley	Engineer and Surveyor
George Holloway	Clerk
Joseph Dalloway	Writing Clerk
William Wright	Under Clerk

Although James Brindley was appointed to the post of engineer and surveyor, he was working on several other canal projects at the same time. A number of assistants helped him with the everyday tasks. In particular Robert Whitworth and Samuel Simcox were his able lieutenants. Whitworth and Brindley were involved in progressing the Birmingham Canal Bill through Parliament, but Samuel Simcox was Brindley's agent on the Birmingham Canal responsible for the day to day running of the project. In this role, Simcox came into contact with William Bentley, who had masterminded the constructed project for the proprietors from the start.

On 4 April 1768 an advertisement was placed in the Birmingham paper, *Aris's Gazette*, requesting contractors to build the canal:

Wanted for the execution of this design several foremen or undertakers who particularly understand the nature of the navigation business and can bring with them sufficient numbers of workmen to whom the proprietors will let the cutting of the canal in parcels.

Work on the canal started in April 1768. During that month John Wall of West Bromwich supplied 200,000 bricks and Mr Iddins supplied deals. Hopes were high for an early completion date. *Aris's Gazette* for 17 October 1768 announced that the canal was in a state of great forwardness and upwards of five miles were completed. At this rate it was expected to meet the Worcestershire and Staffordshire Canal within a year. Unfortunately, this smooth progress received a serious setback during October 1768. Problems were encountered at Smethwick where the original tunnel scheme was quickly abandoned. A start had been made on this tunnel. Gins and mining equipment were obtained and a shaft was sunk. Unfortunately, quicksand was encountered, which halted any further work. A meeting was held in West Bromwich and it was decided to build a flight of locks over the hill instead of going through it. This new proposal created a very short summit, which was to impede the operation of the canal for many years.

The inability to build the Smethwick tunnel was to prove to have a far-reaching effect on canal affairs and also considerably delayed the completion of the canal through to Wolverhampton. New levels had to be surveyed, which eventually led the proprietors to choose an alternate route to Wolverhampton. Information concerning this state of affairs can be gleaned not only from the minute books of the time, but also documents in the Boulton & Watt collection and advertisements in *Aris's Gazette*. Later evidence is derived from notes written in 1824 by John Freeth, the then Clerk, and son of the Birmingham poet of the same name.

The revised line incorporated a flight of six locks at Smethwick and six locks at Spon Lane. Boats navigating the canal onto the Wednesbury Canal had to negotiate all twelve locks, whilst those following the main line through to Wolverhampton passed through nine. The canal from Bilston and Wolverhampton joined above the tenth lock. The changes were a deviation from Brindley's original scheme where the Wednesbury Canal deviated from the main line west of the Smethwick Tunnel and turned north by Mr Abney's Mill.

It was a decision that led to the main canal diverging from the Wednesbury Canal after the ninth lock at Smethwick, and was not lightly taken. Old mine shafts had been discovered across the intended route at Bilston, and it had been considered unwise to cross them. However, once the decision had been taken to vary the route, a complete new line had to be surveyed 18ft above Brindley's suggested route.

Water supply became an immediate problem. The short summit restricted the amount of water available to the navigation. A proprietors' meeting held on 1 July 1768 reported that Mr Simcox had been given the job of surveying the country adjacent to the summit to assess what springs and brooks might be brought into the new canal. Seven likely sources were investigated. By November 1768 work on the Smethwick Locks was well under way. Mr Simcox had surveyed the third lock and work was to start on the construction of that lock.

A decision was also taken amongst the proprietors first to proceed with the completion of the Wednesbury Canal. This, at least, would ensure a supply of coal for Birmingham. It was a decision that was to cause friction amongst the proprietors. The mine owners of Wednesbury would be favoured, as they would be reached first. Messrs Fownes and Aston were particularly critical of this state of affairs, as they wanted the canal to be extended first to their mines at Tipton. It is indeed possible that building the canal to Tipton may have proved cheaper than Wednesbury, but it is difficult to judge such a decision with the benefit of hindsight.

In every undertaking, differing opinions encourage dissent and a rift was slowly forming amongst the proprietors of the Birmingham Canal undertaking. Peter Capper and Samuel Garbett were critical of company policy. Samuel Garbett, in particular, wanted the poor to benefit from cheap coal in preference to the more affluent townspeople. Garbett and William Bentley, the company chairman, clearly differed on how the canal should operate. Matters came to a head at the proprietors' meeting on 1 December 1769 when Bentley received a gold medal for his service to the company.

Bentley obviously thought that it was a good time to tackle Garbett and hopefully curtail his influence. Garbett made allegations that Bentley had received a constant supply of 3 tons of coal per day for his brass works. This allegation was retracted, but Garbett's other views regarding supplying coal to the poor were recorded in the minutes and, two days later, published in *Aris's Gazette*. Garbett resigned from the committee, but was later to conduct an attack through published papers and the press on BCN policy.

Part of the canal was completed within eighteen months. It comprised a section of the main line through to Oldbury and the Wednesbury Canal through West Bromwich to the collieries of John Wood. The first boatload of coal was delivered to the wharf at the temporary terminus on 6 November 1769. Bells are said to have rung out throughout the town, when the boat docked. The occasion was celebrated by Freeth, one of the proprietors, who penned a few lines, which included:

There never in war was for victory won
A cause that desrv'd such respect from the Town;
Then revel in gladness let harmony flow,
From the district of Bordesley to Paradise Row,
For true feeling joy in each breast must be wrought
When coals under Five-pence per hundred are bought.

The Birmingham Canal actually determined to bring coal in by boat and sell it at 4½d per hundred (that is, long weight equal to 120lbs). They intended to fix the price at every street through establishing coal yards about the town, and also sought to gain as much control as possible by using their own boats and restricting access to the waterway. Traders and coalmasters alike rigidly fought this new policy.

Gradually, the main canal was extended through Tipton and Bilston, and much of the work appears to have been conducted by the canal company itself. The collieries of Thomas Tomkys and Bickley were reached towards the end of 1770. By October 1770 Fownes & Aston of Tipton, and Mr Dixon and Mr Nock of Oldbury were carrying coals on the waterway. On 21 October, Mr Meredith was requested to write to them to pay tonnage on their coals and to threaten prosecution if they did not.

The route continued to vary and during 1769 and 1770 some mine owners were certainly favoured when the line of canal was altered to pass closer to their works. From Brindley's original route of 16 miles and 4 furlongs, the main canal had lengthened by exactly 4 miles in 1771 according to a plan published in the *Gentleman's Magazine*. Even then, that was not the end of the variation. A further deviation to Coseley led to another increase in length. The final canal from Birmingham to Autherley was 22 miles and 5 furlongs, 6 miles and 1 furlong more than Brindley suggested. Samuel Simcox seems to have engineered most of the deviations and perhaps it would be fairer to describe the old BCN as a Simcox Canal rather than a Brindley Canal!

By November 1770 there were many who were dissatisfied, not only with the progress of the Birmingham Canal but also with the way the committee handled matters. Charges of extortion, favouritism, oppression and hard dealings were common. In building the canal, several important issues had been neglected by the proprietors. Whether it was through lack of experience or by determined gain, the Birmingham Canal was cast in a poor light. The first of two public meetings concerning these subjects was held at the Swan Inn, near West Bromwich on 23 November. A second meeting was arranged for the next week. The following notice was published in *Aris's Gazette* for 26 November:

There will be a meeting at the Swan Inn in West Bromwich on Friday next at Ten O'clock in the forenoon to consider the Methods to obtain a Free Navigation and a proper use of the banks on the Birmingham Canal, together with free access thereto from the neighbouring collieries, independent of the Canal Company and likewise for the liberty to make basons or bye roads for boats to load or unload and also to make collateral cuts from the coal pits to the banks of the canal and into the canal when the same can be done without injury to the proprietors thereof and to obtain proper wharfs at Birmingham where stocks of coal may be kept in winter – And to consider upon an application to Parliament for all possible accommodation to coalmasters, navigators and dealers in coal, that it may in every respect be free of monopolies and meet with no unnecessary obstruction in the conveyance from the coal pits to the consumer.

The views expressed at both meetings concurred with the views of Samuel Garbett, indeed, he seems to have attended them and no doubt contributed to their proceedings. On 3 December 1770 Samuel wrote to the Earl of Dartmouth:

I have lately been at two meetings in the country of Landowner – Coalowners – & Navigators & Dealers in Coal in order to know with certainty whether the Representations which had been made respecting the conduct of the Birmingham Canal Company & their agents were well founded – and they appear to me so material that I should think myself inexcusable not to lay them before the Town. I have therefore this day put an advertisement in the public papers and in strong terms with a view of exciting Gentlemen's attention or to show that hearty attempts will be made to induce the Canal Company to permit reasonable plans to be established for the accommodation of the Town & Country, as a matter of rights & not favour, as there are many points which examples will now show are unfit to remain at the discretion of the company – If your Lordship is inclined to be acquainted with the particulars of what I intend to lay before the public and which I have not yet acquainted anybody with, I should be glad to wait of you at Sandwell any morning this week you may please to appoint except to morrow.

A third public meeting to discuss the matter of collateral cuts (side branches) to be held at the Chamber over the Old Cross arranged for Tuesday 11 December was deferred when the Birmingham Canal Committee gave assurances that such cuts would be allowed, provided security was given that no damage would be made to the banks. Coalmasters not connected with the canal company were thus more able to open up communications for their trade.

There was a general feeling that the canal company had taken land without arranging payment. In order to redress this issue, the company published an official notice on 8 December 1770 inviting all those with cause of complaint to deliver accounts of their damages to their office in Newhall Street.

If the proprietors did not have enough trouble on their plate, a new problem came to the surface. The proprietors of the Staffordshire & Worcestershire Canal were pushing forward with their waterway. They insisted that the Birmingham Canal should be speedily constructed to 'Autherley', and were determined to go to Parliament to make them complete the canal or they would themselves finish the job. At the time of this notice the Birmingham Canal had not even started work on the Bilston to Wolverhampton section.

The pressure on the Canal Committee continued when a damning statement as to the affairs of the Birmingham Canal was printed in *Aris's Gazette* on 22 January 1771. In a letter addressed to Mr Brindley, an unknown correspondent (presumably Garbett) raised various points of censure. It referred to Brindley's quarrel with Bentley and the lengthy route of the navigation. It was stated that more money would accrue from tolls because of this. The delay in proceeding to the mines of Fownes & Aston was particularly mentioned. S. Aris, despairing of the amount of published dissent in his paper and elsewhere, finally put an end to the dispute and declined to publish any further correspondence or advertisements. The Birmingham Canal proprietors were then left to complete their navigation in relative peace.

Meetings continued to be held at the Old Cross where groups of people met to express their concern over the conduct of the canal company. On 31 January 1771, a petition was placed before Parliament:

The humble petition of proprietors of land and of coal mines near and adjoining the Birmingham Canal, of navigators and dealers in coal, and of others who are interested in the proper conduct of the said canal:

SHEWETH,

THAT in the exercise of the powers granted to the Birmingham Canal Company by Act of Parliament, your petitioners apprehend the said company have done many acts contrary to the intention of Parliament, and in the public good, yet in such matter as to render proceedings for redress before the Courts of Law precarious and uncertain.

THAT the said Company, by the united powers they possess, are enable to exercise partiality to proprietors of land, and of coal, in many instances; and form a dangerous monopoly; they being not only the sole proprietors of the Canal, with its locks and reservoir, but also navigators and buyers and sellers of coal, having upwards of 20 boats employed of about 25 ton each.

THAT they are endeavouring to become Proprietors of the banks and wharfs, in opposition to the proprietors of land; and have prevented an extensive coal mine having access to the canal, because the Proprietors would not sell the mine to them.

Wherefore your petitioners most humbly pray,

THAT this Honourable House will take these premises into consideration, and grant such powers that may effectually prevent the Birmingham Canal Company exercising partiality to the great injury of the proprietors of land, and of coal mines: And also their forming dangerous monopolies by their being at the same time proprietors of the canals and locks, of the wharfs and banks, and the navigators and dealers in coals, and the proprietors of coal mines; or grant such other relief in the premises as to this Honourable House seems meet.

The petition reached Parliament, but was not dealt with until April. Parliament had set up a committee to investigate the Staffordshire & Worcestershire Canal's complaint against the Birmingham Canal. Fortunately a compromise was achieved, which enabled the Birmingham Canal to continue the line to Aldersley. Construction of the final section to Aldersley was authorised by this committee on 11 January 1771. Mr Beswick was given the contract to cut the remaining part. Later Thomas Tomkys offered to make bricks at 11/6 per ton delivered from the kiln.

Those who met at the Old Cross included Samuel Garbett, Joseph Smith, Robert Moore, John Turner, Thomas Faulconbridge and John Ford. Garbett became their chief spokesman. Pamphlets bearing Samuel Garbett's name were published stating their views. The canal proprietors, concerned about such adverse publicity appointed the Earl of Dartmouth to adjudicate in these matters. It was a clever, and well-timed political move. A House of Commons select committee debated the issue on 18 and 19 April 1771. They decided that as the Earl of Dartmouth had been invested with powers to give satisfaction to the country, it was unnecessary for them to examine the allegation of the petition. Thus the petitioner's complaints were never heard.

Samuel Garbett and his associates tenaciously continued the fight and wrote several letters to the Earl of Dartmouth in order to further their cause. There were twelve issues, which were commonly raised:

I. That the canal is made 6 miles longer than the plan laid before Parliament.
II. That the company have varied the line of the canal for 10 miles together, and on some places at a great distance, without going through one piece of ground proposed by the plan to Parliament, the landowners and the country.

III. That they have required money of individuals to vary the course of the canal; and when that could not be obtained, have made the line longer, and thereby taxed the Country at their pleasure.

IV. That the company have entirely deserted large mines of coal in the line held out by plans to Parliament and the neighbourhood, which for many miles contains one of the most valuable fields of coal in this part of the kingdom, and where they had previously obtained the consent of the land-owner, and have arbitrarily carried it into another country, where they had not obtained the consent of a single land-owner.

V. That they may proceed to the coal mines Ocker Hill, or not, as best suits their private interest.

VI. That they carry, or forbear to carry, the canal to neighbouring coal mines according as they may succeed in advantageous contracts for themselves with the owners of the coals.

VII. That they have refused proprietors of land having free access to the canal over the banks and wharfs.

VIII. That they have obtained and possess a title to private roads to distant coal mines which may be used, or not, to the benefit or injury of the country, as the private interest of the company, or as their passions may dictate.

IX. That the Company have the sole power of granting or refusing land-owners to make collateral cuts into the canal independent of commissioners, a jury and even the Courts of Law.

X. That they have entered lands without consent and in defiance of the owners, and without paying for the same, though in some instances often demanded.

XI. That the company have a power of proceeding to the lands of Sir Tho. Gooch, or not, as they may succeed in securing from him the possession of the most convenient spot for wharfs &c. and be enabled to make such a contract, with him, as should prevent access to this canal, from adjoining lands, whoever may possess them in future, and thereby prevent an important establishment being made for this parish, though calculated to check monopolies or any other unreasonable, lucrative advantages, which the company might attempt to make.

XII That the company have the sole power of disposal of water from the reservoirs, the sole command of locks, and the making of Bye-Laws to inflict penalties on the other traders – In the exercise of all which powers they may materially shew partiality to the trade of the Company, or of their leading members, and be enabled to advance the price of coal whenever, it proves their interest.

The canal proprietors produced their own four-page document to answer all twelve points. Published in October 1771, this document disclaimed all of Garbett's statements as either misinterpretation, surmise without foundation, confused and unintelligible, or illiberal and unjust accusation. In our modern society the announcements and publicity statements that enabled the BCN proprietors to colour events to their own advantage would be described as 'spin' and it was by spin that the proprietors' views prevailed on this occasion. In future times they would be less lucky.

Garbett was soon to face other problems. His son-in-law, Charles Gascoigne, through his activities at the Carron Ironworks was to bankrupt Samuel in 1772. This sad turn of events was to take much of Garbett's time, however, through diligence he was able to pay all his debts. Thus it was that Samuel Garbett ceased to be a thorn in the side of the proprietors. There were, however, others equally discontented with matters as they were. Charles Colmore had reason to challenge the BCN way of operation when he became involved in the final decision for the choice of the canal terminus in Birmingham.

Brindley's original plan provided for a terminus at Newhall Ring, but later a rival terminus was proposed in Brick Kiln Croft.

The original line passed through and terminated in the lands of Charles Colmore. Fearing that the Birmingham Canal would by-pass his property, Colmore sought to compel the BCN in the courts to complete their line to Newhall Ring. Finally, in 1771, Charles obtained an Act of Parliament to make them do so. Even with this assistance, Colmore found the BCN still recalcitrant and employed a tactic that delayed construction. The value of the land involved was called into question.

Birmingham Canal Co requests a jury to determine the value of the land taken and to be taken from the said Charles Colmore who refuseth to take and accept as a recompense for the same the annual sum or rent of four pounds/clear of all parliamentary or parochial payments/which the said Birmingham Canal Co have offered him. But insists on a large recompense for the lands so taken and yet remaining to be taken.

A jury was thus formed which met on 16 August 1771 at the Swan Inn, Birmingham. Present were eight commissioners and twelve jurors. Richard Guest was council for the canal company whilst Francis Wheeler represented Charles Colmore.

Mr Guest opened the case. He stated that the land wanted by the Birmingham Canal comprised three parcels of land. Two acres one rood and thirteen perches had been taken to cut the existing canal. There was another parcel, which amounted to two roods and thirty-one perches, which had not been cut but was part of the intended line to Brick Kiln Field. The third parcel totalled one acre, thirty-seven and a half perches. This also had not been cut but comprised the remainder of the canal from Dudley Road to New Hall Ring.

Charles Colmore's claim was that in December 1769 he offered these lands to the BCN at an annual rent of £4 per acre for the use of the canal and towing path. For an additional £30 an acre annual rent, the BCN could erect warehouses on his land. Various witnesses were called and after much discussion the jurors decided that the first two lots were worth £4 10s an acre whilst the third lot was worth £21. The jury may have determined the value of the land, but did little to induce the Birmingham Canal to extend the waterway from the Aqueduct to New Hall Ring. Charles Colmore wrote to the Earl of Dartmouth in December 1771 with the hope that he might speed up the process. The canal was eventually extended to the New Hall terminus in 1772.

Work on the Wolverhampton flight of twenty locks continued through 1771 until the autumn of 1772. On 21 September 1772, the canal was declared officially opened. Traffic could then flow from Birmingham through the coalfield to Autherley and reach Worcester, Gloucester and Bristol by canal and river navigation.

Another jury was called to establish any claims against the canal to Brick Kiln Croft. Two possible routes were available and tunnelling was at one time considered. Work then went ahead with the construction of the branch chiefly through the lands of King Edward's School into the lands of Thomas Gooch. In 1773 the Paradise Street branch and wharf was completed and new offices were built facing Paradise Row (later Paradise Street).

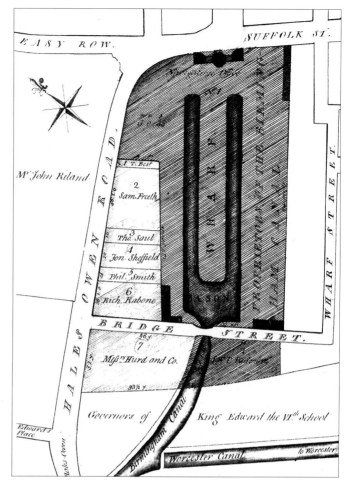

Old Wharf, Birmingham, 1796. John Snape produced a book of plans and rentals for the estate of Thomas Gooch in 1796. The page reproduced shows the Birmingham Canal Wharf and Navigation Offices that faced Paradise Street. (Local Studies Department, Birmingham Library)

Brindley's intended route had carried on through Puppy Green and passed close by Tipton Hall, Bradley Hall, Bilston Glasshouse, Wilkinson's Furnace and east of the town of Bilston before turning west towards Wolverhampton. A branch from Tipton was contemplated to Ocker Hill, but these plans required considerable revision when the main canal to Aldersley came to be built. Doubts were raised as to the need for a branch to Ocker Hill.

Despite uncertainty concerning the building of the Ocker Hill branch, a new course for this branch had been surveyed in September 1771. At the end January 1772 permission was given to build this canal, work started and the Ocker Hill Canal was finished in 1773. This short branch terminated at a wharf beside the old turnpike road. The Birmingham Canal was now complete. Eight years were to elapse before any serious competition was presented.

Samuel Garbett was not the only person who believed in healthy competition. By 1781 there was a group of individuals who sought better communications with London. Garbett became, in fact, a supporter of this new group who wanted to build a new line of canal to part of the coalfield not served by the Birmingham Canal.

two

FIRST CANAL LINKS

The Birmingham Canal Navigation and the Staffordshire & Worcestershire Canal created the first inland navigation links across the plateau land where Birmingham and the Black Country were located. Through locks, cuttings and embankments these first navigable links were achieved. The principal cargo was then coal, but limestone, building stone, road stone and assorted merchandise were also carried.

From Birmingham to Wolverhampton the meandering waterway endeavoured to serve a significant part of the working coalfield. Pits lined the waterway at selected places from Oldbury through to Bilston, but there were still many areas devoted to agriculture or pasture. Several mines were concentrated around Tipton Green, Bradley and Bilston. The route of the main line, at Tipton Green, passed the pits of the Old Park Colliery and mines belonging to Mr Brindley and Richmond Aston. The name Tipton Green originated from the open space that was the village green, and a plan, which dates from about 1788, shows the canal crossing diagonally across it. Houses and other buildings lined the perimeter and beyond the dwellings were the mineshafts and collieries that provided employment for many families.

Tipton has changed considerably since those times. The old green was lost in redevelopment, although rate books continued to use the distinction Low Green and High Green for a number of years thereafter. The route then turned northwards and passed under the bridge that carried Hurst Lane over the waterway. It then crossed a small stream near Bloomfield. Here there was a pair of mill pools and the Bloomsmithy Mill. The line of the canal then turned east towards the Moat Colliery and Gospel Oak. The Moat Colliery was a large estate that surrounded the canal around the junction with the Ocker Hill Branch. This whole district was heavily mined and the resulting subsidence was to create problems in later years for canal engineers. Whole sections of the waterway had to be built up to maintain the level and this long section, originally built on level ground, came to be supported on a high embankment.

From Gospel Oak the canal continued northwards to Wednesbury Oak and then Bradley. It was here that John Wilkinson had established his furnace and ironworks. The furnaces were located at a distance from the waterway, but Mr Wilkinson's foundry and water engine were canalside features. The line then passed back to Mr Tomkys' colliery at Pothouse Bridge and then turned west again through Caponfield to John Bickley's colliery wharf, Penn and Pearsall's colliery and the mines at Catchems Corner.

During these early days, the Birmingham Canal had a single towpath lined with a quick (hawthorn) hedge, which separated the waterway from the adjacent fields. Bridges of brick, capped with stone, crossed the waterway at places to convey turnpikes and lesser tracks, but there were also several wooden swing and swivel bridges provided where economy overruled extravagance.

Exploitation of minerals lying below the surface became easier once the web of canals had been constructed across the Black Country. The useful minerals were found at different depths. Coal was frequently plentiful, but occurred in several layers interspersed with rock and rubbish. Layers of clay and ironstone might be also present and working of different minerals would take place. There was tremendous variation throughout the district, some measures were productive, others were not. Mining was handicapped through faulting that made extraction difficult, or uneconomic in places. Not all seams were worth the expense of mining. Within the Black Country the middle coal measures were the most productive. These had names such as brooch coal, herring coal, thick, main or ten yard coal, heathen coal, sulphur coal, new mine coal, fireclay coal and bottom coal.

Shafts were principally sunk to the thick coal and the accessible ironstone measure and the mines were opened up through the making of headings to the extent of the property. Each mine was kept dry by the atmospheric, or Newcomen, type of engine, whose houses were landmark features amongst the pit mounds, tramway tracks and horse gins.

The role of the Newcomen engine was restricted to pumping water, with a single cylinder and piston assembly raising and lowering a wooden beam, which raised and lowered sets of pump trees in a shaft. With every fall of the piston, a quantity of water was drawn out of the shaft. Engineers had yet to find a way to rotate the wheels and drums used to draw minerals out of the mine and the gin provided the principal means of getting coal and ironstone to the surface. Gins were large-diameter circular drums, which were placed over the pit mouth. Horses and sometimes donkeys, or mules, were employed to turn the drum, which let down, or wound back the chain or rope. Mines of this period were coalfields rather than collieries. It was common to sink a shaft, raise the minerals underground within a defined area and then go on to sink another shaft nearby.

Whilst coal and ironstone mining in the Black Country had a long and established history before the canals, the cutting of these artificial waterways reached untapped mineral resources for commercial exploitation on a grand scale, and many new coal and ironstone workings came to be opened up along the banks of the waterway. Advertisements for sale of land frequently mentioned mines proved nearby to encourage coalmasters and ironmasters to exploit the minerals below. It was a risky business, to a degree. Seams of coal and ironstone might be thin and not worth exploiting, faulting could also depress these measures for a considerable distance downward or raise them to the surface where weathering had obliterated their existence.

Underground within the mine was a completely different world to the surface worker who might labour in the mill or factory. Miners were employed in a range of roles. There were pike men who helped bring down the coal and loaders who stacked the large pieces of coal on skips to be taken away by the horse driver. Coal was extracted over a given area and the thick coal was usually taken first. The thick coal existed in vast seams, which could be up to 30ft in thickness. These seams were not strictly uniform pieces of coal but layers subdivided by thin partings of waste. Miners started at the bottom then worked their way up, often standing on ladders to the get the top part of the thick coal. They left columns of coal, known as ribs and pillars, to support the roof, and often took away the coal in long large pieces, which were loaded on the skip. Other seams were worked under more cramped circumstances. The miners who worked the brooch, herring, heathen and new mine coal worked in thinner seams, with headroom frequently less than 4ft. Each worker had to stoop or lie down to get the coal out.

The skip was raised to the surface and the coal sorted on the pit bank and prepared for despatch by the banksman and his assistants. Fragments of coal from the large coals down to slack had different values, as did the seam from which the coal was taken. Coal might be sent away by road wagon as land sale, or taken down to a canal wharf in a tramway wagon, where the segregated coal was loaded and stacked in the hold.

Customers for the coal usually provided their own transport, whether it was a cart or canal boat. Those who had the fortune to live near the mine could collect by cart, but canal boat transport became a useful means of moving coal longer distances. Coal output increased to serve the growing demands of industry, which came to rely more and more on this commodity to provide heat for boilers to drive steam engines, or furnaces to treat metals.

There was also an increasing requirement as a fuel for domestic purposes. Coal merchants found a lucrative living collecting coal from the pits and delivering it to the centres of population. Paradise Street Wharf, later known as the Old Wharf, in Birmingham, was segregated into plots, for the stacking and sorting of coal. Here merchants rented a space and distributed the coal to domestic and business customers. Some merchants chose to establish their own wharves and operated a number of boats. The largest operator was the Birmingham Coal Co., who had a fleet of boats that brought coal to their wharf on the Newhall Branch. Wolverhampton also received a share of the trade particularly from the Bilston mines that sent coal to Prices Wharf (near Corn Hill) and another at Rotten Row, which became the Birmingham Canal Proprietors Wharf.

Other types of traffic included limestone and other forms of stone. Limestone was both mined and quarried around Dudley and Walsall, where the stone was broken down to a flux for iron making or burnt to make lime for cement or mortar. The Dudley limestone mines occupied a strip of land from Dudley Port through Wrens Nest to Cinderhill. Transport of limestone from these mines provided an essential traffic for the waterways from the earliest days of the Birmingham Canal. Lord Dudley and Ward owned much of the land where the limestone existed and his agents were instrumental in the construction of two private canals into the limestone rock. The best known was Lord Ward's Canal, completed between 1776 and 1778, which joined with the Birmingham Canal at Tipton Green. This waterway divided into two branches, one served Tipton Colliery whilst the other passed into the hillside. Narrow canal tunnels linked with caverns created through the getting of the rock at the East Castle and Wrens Nest Mines.

Limestone miners worked with picks and gunpowder. It was a heavy task bringing down and breaking up the rock, which was then loaded into tramway wagons to be taken down to a subterranean wharf and loaded in boats. Many of the craft employed in the tunnel system were small and narrow, and very unlike the traditional narrowboats that were used on the main waterway. The other canal tunnel was located at Mons Hill, where another canal crossed the Foxyards Colliery to reach the mine. The Foxyards and Roundshill Canal was a private waterway, constructed during 1789, which connected with the Birmingham Canal at Bloomfield and rose through four locks to reach the level for the limestone mines.

Walsall was somewhat isolated from the canal at these times, but seams of useful stone existed to the north and east of the town around Wolverhampton Street, Birchills and the Butts. Other important mines were located further east towards Rushall and Daw End. Mining was already being carried out around Moss Close and Hay Head with stone being distributed by road.

Limestone was carried by boat to canalside limekilns. Kilns were located in Bridge Street, Birmingham on a wharf that belonged to John Wall, canal carrier, and at Farmers Wharf alongside the Newhall Branch. A typical limekiln was brick lined and when viewed from above was oval shaped. There was a single entrance, through which the limestone was fed and vents were provided for the escape of gases. Layers of limestone and coal were placed inside the kiln, a fire lit and the entrance sealed up. Combustion was allowed to proceed for several days. The entrance was then opened up and the lime raked out. Those who worked at the kiln had to contend with the lime that burnt and corroded their clothes and damaged their skin. It was an extremely unhealthy occupation for those who did this task regularly.

Limestone Mines, Sedgley, 1905.
The mining and quarrying of limestone became an important local industry and the carriage of limestone a useful cargo for the canal carriers. (E. Blocksidge)

Limekiln labourers often had shortened lives as a result. The kilns at Farmers Wharf were constructed in 1789 for May & Norton, who brought limestone there by boat from the Dudley area. Wall's Wharf was long associated with the limestone and cement trade, having a succession of owners in future times. The site now forms part of the James Brindley Public House.

The Rowley Hills provided ragstone suitable for road making. Bilston and Pouk Hill, near Walsall, also had outcrops of hard rock. During March 1773 Peter Winstanley, a stone mason of New Hall Walk, opened a white hardstone quarry at Bilston, on an estate belonging to John Bickley, and within half a mile of the Birmingham Canal. This stone, sometimes described as freestone, was the principal stone for blade mills and grinding stone for cutlers, but was also well adapted for making chimneypieces and hearthstones.

Another increasing traffic was the movement of merchandise along the waterway. Merchandise carriage was generally the preserve of the professional carrier who contracted to carry goods in their boats for a charge. Some firms already existed as road carriers, but with the completion of the basic canal network, other entrepreneurs were encouraged to enter the trade. Some did well, others like the firms they served went out of business through competition and costs of operation.

Merchandise carriers set up at specific wharves and provided a service that ran to a timetable with boats running to named destinations on the canal network either daily or weekly, depending on the level of service required. They also frequently provided a collection and delivery service to their wharves.

The original extent of the Birmingham Canal Navigation was limited to a waterway of some 30 miles in length. The greater amount of property remained outside the reach of the navigation.

It was not long before other canal schemes were proposed to link up with the existing waterways and reach districts not served by inland navigation. New waterway schemes included the Stourbridge Canal and the Dudley Canal that struck into the heart of the Black Country to serve important coal and ironstone mines as well as the long-established glass and fireclay works.

A third canal scheme was the Birmingham & Fazeley Canal, which was originally intended to serve the coalmines of Wednesbury and take these coals onto the Coventry and Oxford Canals, where there was a ready market, especially with the hatters of Atherstone and the ribbon makers of Coventry. It was a decision that was to have a tremendous influence on trade, and especially the inland carriage of goods to London. The line of this waterway was intended to run through Coleshill and Minworth to a spot near Salford Bridge and then through Lozells and West Bromwich to Wednesbury, principally to reach mineral estates on a lower level than the Birmingham Canal. Here a set of short connecting canals would extend out from the main waterway to tap the rich coal and ironstone resources, which existed there. Another branch was to be built from a junction with the main canal near Nechells to serve the lower part of Birmingham at Deritend and in this way serve a very busy industrial district.

In essence the canal from Wednesbury to Fazeley was to be a competitor to the Birmingham Canal Navigation. Support for the venture came from the Earl of Dudley who had property near Broadwaters. Opposition to the scheme came from the Earl of

Dartmouth across whose land the new canal would run. Fearing the loss of access to some of the most productive Wednesbury mines, the Birmingham Canal proposed an alternative where branches would be made from their Wednesbury Canal to some of the mineral estates intended to be served by the Birmingham & Fazeley Canal.

The rival proposals were finally resolved by Parliament. In 1783 the Birmingham & Fazeley Canal Co. were given powers to build their canal, but the original scheme had been modified with a compromise solution and aspects of the rival Birmingham Canal proposal were included in the final approval. The Fazeley line was diverted through Aston and climbed a set of locks to meet the Birmingham Canal at the Newhall Branch. They were then allowed to use the Birmingham Canal main line and the Wednesbury Branch to a place near Ryders Green where a new canal was to be made to Broadwaters with collateral cuts to the collieries. The Birmingham & Fazeley Canal was, therefore, to be built in two sections.

In 1784 the two canal companies merged and they became known as the Birmingham & Birmingham & Fazeley Canal. This long-winded title was fortunately shortened in 1794 to the Birmingham Canal Navigations. It is known by this name to the present day.

John Smeaton was appointed engineer for the Birmingham & Fazeley Canal routes. The contractor John Pinkerton was employed to build the Broadwaters Canal first and then was given the contract to build the Fazeley Canal from Fazeley to Minworth. Thomas Sheasby was contractor for the line from Birmingham to Minworth and the Digbeth Branch. Pinkerton also had the contract to make a section of the Coventry Canal through Hopwas and terminating at the aqueduct over Whittington Brook.

The Birmingham & Fazeley Canal route from Ryders Green to the Broadwaters had enormous potential for industrial development. Coal mining and some iron working already existed. During November 1784 the Castle Iron Works at 'Tole End', Tipton was leased by T. and T. Taylor where they carried on the business of making engine cylinders, pipes, forge hammers, rolls, presses, stamps, bath stove grates, ovens and various other articles in cast iron.

Pinkerton's men were engaged to construct the locks, bridges and aqueducts required to reach the place known as Broadwaters. Eight locks were needed to bring the canal down to the level of the mines at 406ft (od). The waterway was then carried across the River Tame by a brick and stone aqueduct and then on to Great Bridge, Toll End and Leabrook. The area called Broadwaters was literally a collection of pools separated by marshy and boggy pieces of land. A pumping engine was erected here that supplied the canal with water and drained the land for future industrial development.

Several branch canals were also constructed from the Broadwaters Canal at different dates, to serve nearby coalmines and aid the development of mineral property as well as encourage the establishment of new ironworks. They included the Dank's, Gospel Oak, Ocker Hill Tunnel and Toll End Branches. The branch to Toll End included a privately owned section to Horseley, whilst the Ocker Hill Tunnel branch terminated at the entrance to Ocker Hill Tunnel. Unlike conventional canal tunnels, the brick-lined tunnel under Ocker Hill was only 5ft in diameter and conveyed water only to the base of shafts that raised water, by steam pumping engines, to the 473ft (od) for recirculation into the Wolverhampton Level via the (other) Ocker Hill Branch.

The Broadwater's contract seems to have proceeded satisfactorily, but serious problems were encountered once the Fazeley contract was started. Pinkerton had troubles from the beginning. He was not allowed to start work when he wanted and found that labour costs had risen when the men were engaged. There was also a shortage of skilled workers as much of the available workforce had been lost to Sheasby. John Pinkerton finally commenced construction during January 1787 near Mr Norton's mill at Fazeley. For Mr Norton this was a fortunate occurrence, as he was able to sell bread to the workmen.

Local clay, for brick making, began to be worked from March 1787 and a small brickyard was established. Few bricks were made here, but other brickyards were built later at St Martins Field, a field near Hill's Brickyard and at Dunton. Stone was taken from Mr Bretton's stone quarry near Tamworth where Pinkerton put in a rope-worked railway to the quarry face.

Pinkerton employed upward of 300 men on the contract. Most were labourers, but there were also skilled men such as bricklayers. A number were evidently experienced men having worked on other canals before. They included John Walker, a cutter who had started on the Duke of Bridgewater's Canal, and later worked in Yorkshire before coming to Fradley. There was William Dickson, who worked for Pinkerton on the Barnsley Canal and the Dudley Canal Tunnel before going to Fradley in March 1787. Benjamin Simcox was a bricklayer who had spent seven years on the Chesterfield Canal, and worked for Dadford on the Grand Trunk before joining Pinkerton at Fazeley. Together with another bricklayer, Abel Woodwards, this group of contractors built aqueducts, bridges and eight of the locks in the Curdworth flight.

On 8 October 1787 John Houghton, accompanied by John Lee and a Mr Hurst, inspected the work done so far, but were not satisfied with the progress. They were disappointed to find that some jobs had not been done and the standard was poor in certain cases. At Dunton brickyard they found that the bricks in the moulds for burning were made from sandy clay, which would make bricks of poor quality. They also found ill-burnt bricks, soft brick and soft mortar in some of the locks they inspected.

John Pinkerton had completed the level section of the Coventry Canal by December 1788, but had much to do on the Fazeley–Minworth contract. It was the practice to pay contractors in stages and Pinkerton had already drawn money to the extent of his agreed contract and exceeded this amount by £1,000. The proprietors were unwilling to make any further outlay. During February 1789, Pinkerton was told to find his own security and complete the contract within three months. Pinkerton could not agree to this demand and was effectively self-dismissed from the work. It was arranged for canal company workmen to finish the task. The first boat passed along the canal on 11 August 1789, but shoddy workmanship continued to hamper operations through to 1790, when suitable repairs and replacements, had been made.

Boats at this time could only navigate the Coventry Canal northwards through Whittington Brook to Fradley and trader's traffic was generally confined to goods passing between Birmingham and the East Midlands. A pioneer in this trade was the Burton Boat Co., who was quick to establish a wharf, warehouse and depot beside the Digbeth Branch, Love Lane, Aston, in 1790.

Some might view the Birmingham Canal proprietors as autocratic in the various dealings with people, contractors and other canal concerns. This trait was particularly noticeable with the Pinkerton incident and with the contract he completed from Fazeley to Whittington Brook. Ostensibly this length of canal was part of the new section of the Coventry Canal from Atherstone through to Fradley. It was made as part of an agreement between the Birmingham & Fazeley, Coventry, Oxford and the Trent & Mersey Canal Companies, which was put together when representatives of each company met at Coleshill to plan the means of getting access to the Wednesbury mines. As part of that arrangement, the Birmingham & Fazeley Canal Co. would complete the piece from Fazeley to Whittington Brook, but their successors decided to retain possession once the canal was made. This was to provide a very lucrative source of revenue for the Birmingham Canal Navigations as they charged tolls on all traffic on this section.

The Coventry Canal from Fazeley to Atherstone was finally completed in September 1790 with the opening of the aqueduct that spanned the River Tame near Fazeley. The Fradley–Coventry section provided the final link in inland navigation, which joined the Trent & Mersey via the Coventry to the Oxford Canal at Longford. Narrowboats were now able to travel from Manchester and the North West through the Potteries and Midlands through to Oxford where cargoes might be exchanged with River Thames barges for transit to London. By securing the Fazeley & Whittington Brook section, the Birmingham Canal Navigations were able to secure revenue from boats that would have normally avoided their system, passing direct from Fradley to the Oxford Canal.

Sheasby's contracts were less problematical, but still found occasional censure from the canal committee. It was his task to build the locks at Farmer's Bridge, Aston and Ashted, the latter being on the short branch to Digbeth. All of these sections were to become substantially industrialised, although at the time of construction their routes passed through generally undeveloped districts.

Farmer's Bridge locks descended to a level pound at Snow Hill Bridge. The level length of waterway between Snow Hill Bridge and Aston became known as Hospital Pound after the General Hospital founded by Dr John Ash, which was placed near the canal in Summer Lane.

Aston Junction marked the place where the Digbeth Branch diverged. The main line descended through another eleven locks to the aqueduct over the River Tame at Salford Bridge.

This line of canal was to provide an extensive canal frontage for industrial development within the next thirty years, both beside the waterway and nearby. Birmingham's Jewellery Quarter was growing in size on land north of the canal beyond Newhall Street and St Pauls Square, whilst the gun trade came to be a major Birmingham industry around streets placed south of the Hospital Pond, and was concentrated in streets such as Price Street and Weaman Street. Gun making was a skilled occupation that employed many outworkers to fashion and shape the various metal and wooden parts such as locks and stocks. Gun barrels were traditionally bored out at certain water mills, but an increasing number of steam mills provided barrel boring benches to assist with the trade.

Sheasby was involved in building up earthworks for the Aston locks and there was a small aqueduct over Hockley Brook. Industry in this area included Aston Brook Mill, then used for grinding flour, and the Thimble Mill, which as its name implies made thimbles. Sheasby's aqueduct over the Tame was a substantial structure. It carried the canal across the river to follow the valley at the 302ft (od) level as far as Minworth. At Minworth there was another drop of three locks. Between the second and third locks, heading towards Curdworth, was made a substantial embankment, which carried the canal over Plants Brook. Here a wharf was made to serve the Plants Brook Forge, a water mill owned by the Webster family. The Websters were already engaged in making crucible steel and working this steel up into wire at Penns Mill and Plants Brook and the canal came to provide an important service for transport of raw materials and finished goods.

The Digbeth Branch ran level for a few hundred yards and then began a descent through six locks at the hamlet of Ashted. The name Ashted was derived from Dr John Ash, who bequeathed the estate he owned for town development. The land was let, in September 1789, and was divided into parcels and streets laid out 'to secure the benefit of a free and healthful air'. Here the line of the canal followed the boundary between Birmingham and the neighbouring parish of Aston. Parts were in Aston, but the terminus faced Bordesley Street in Birmingham. Bordesley Street ran parallel to High Street, Digbeth, and was linked to this street by roads such as Oxford Street. It was an area that was both residential and industrial.

Each street had its share of courts and alleyways where back-to-back houses were crammed in between brassworks, button workers, 'toy' makers and ironworkers. The demand for coal was paramount and part of the Bordesley Street Wharf was laid out as a coal wharf to supply the immediate area. There was already one canalside mill in existence, known as the Cotton Mill. This mill appears to be the second steam-powered mill in Birmingham. Robinson, Archer & Co. owned the building, which fronted Fazeley Street and was first used for spinning muslin and wick yarn, although it was later adapted for rolling metals by the Phipson family.

Birmingham was not noted for cotton spinning even though Mr Wyatt had perfected a means of spinning cotton in Birmingham long before Arkwright started his process at Cromford Mill. Wyatt did spin cotton at the Upper Priory works for a number of years, but historians usually accept that the climate around Birmingham was not suitable for the establishment of a successful spinning industry. The wetter climate around Manchester proved to be more beneficial. Hence the reasons for the extensive cotton trade that developed around Manchester rather than the Midlands. Transport of cotton was also another factor, and Manchester also benefited through the close location of the port of Liverpool.

Such factors did not deter Gill and Co. from using Robinson, Archers steam mill for making fine yarn. Their brief occupation of the mill, in 1788, utilised two batting frames, two carding machines, two feeding tables, one drawing frame, six roving frames, one spinning frame of forty-eight spindles for course yarn and ten frames of sixty spindles each for making fine yarn, two other incomplete frames, and nineteen reeling machines. The machines were said to spin up to 130 hanks with safety. The experiment failed and Gill offered his plant for sale in December 1788, but Robinson, Archer & Co continued the wick yarn trade for some ten or twelve years more.

Construction of the Digbeth Branch appears to have taken place without serious event during the years 1789 and 1790. By July 1790 boats were bringing spoil down to raise the banks, but this task had to be halted temporarily through a shortage of water. The spoil was probably intended for the section between Ashted Bottom Lock and Bordesley Basin Wharf, which crossed a low-lying section and a stream that fed into the River Rea.

Another canal improvement was made at Smethwick during the years 1788, 1789 and 1790, which opened up additional wharf space and speeded up boat movements over the summit. The greatest hindrance to traffic on the original line of the Birmingham Canal was the locks at Smethwick. Any boat navigating the canal from Wolverhampton to Birmingham had nine to contend with, while those from Wednesbury had twelve to tackle. The writer William Hutton was quite scathing about them when he wrote his History of Birmingham.

This grand work, like other productions of Birmingham birth, was rather hasty; the managers, not being able to find the patience to worm round the hill at Smethwick, or cut through, have wisely travelled over it by the help of twelve locks, which six they mount the summit, and with six more descend to the former level; forgetting the great waste of water, and the small supply from the rivulets, and also the amazing loss of time climbing this curious ladder, consisting of twelve liquid steps. It is worthy of remark, that the level of the earth is nearly the same at Birmingham as at the pits: what benefit would then accrue to commerce, could the boats travel a dead flat fourteen miles without interruption? The use of the canal would increase, the great variety of goods be brought which are now excluded, and these delivered with more expedition, with less expense, and the waste of water never felt; but in the introduction of twelve unnecessary locks, the company may experience five more plagues than fell on Egypt.

The proprietors were certainly aware of the problem, particularly the loss of water. The summit level of the canal was very short and limited to the section between the sixth and seventh locks. Despite the best efforts of the two Boulton & Watt pumping engines, replacing the water to the summit was a slow process. However, it would seem Hutton's advice went unheeded for a number of years.

Some proprietors may have considered the project too costly. For not only were they to incur the expense of lowering the summit, they also stood to lose money from tolls whilst the work was done. Such considerations became less important in 1786, when the new canal from Ryders Green to Broadwaters opened. Traffic increased and an additional burden was placed on the operation of the Smethwick locks. There now was a sudden urgency to reduce the summit level and ease the passage of the boats. Despite the expense, it was decided in 1787 to remove the top six locks. Locks 4–6 and 7–9 were to be taken away completely, while a new set of locks were to be built alongside 1, 2 and 3 to accommodate the extra trade.

Advertisements were placed in *Aris's Gazette* during December 1787 for proposals to cut down the summit of the canal from the western end. These had to be presented to the canal offices in Paradise Street by 4 January 1788. Work began later that year and was conducted in stages.

Excavation work proceeded slowly during 1788 and the early months of 1789. The committee and Beswick, their engineer, visited Smethwick in April and decided to proceed without delay. At the next committee meeting held on 1 May 1789, Mr Beswick was instructed to use every exertion in his power to expedite the work and Mr Bough was told to employ as many additional hands as he may think necessary. On 15 May the committee issued a new instruction. The Smethwick new locks were to be built before the frost set in.

Work now proceeded steadily from the western end on a parallel course to the existing canal. The technique used was to excavate by hand and then boat away the soil. This soil was to be carried northwards to the collieries where it could be used to reinforce the banks damaged by mining subsidence. On 26 June, Mr Bull and Mr Bough announced to the committee that a new section of the canal 12ft below the present course would be made navigable in a few days. In September 1789 Mr Bull received instructions to take down the old Lock House between the sixth and seventh locks. The material was to be used to build two new houses: one at the junction of the Tipton Canal, the other at Smethwick Engine.

By 1789 work on the Birmingham & Fazeley Canal was nearly complete. During April, Thomas Cooper was appointed lock keeper for the locks from Farmer's Bridge to Aston Junction, and in a few months the canal would be open all the way to the Trent and Mersey Canal. The Birmingham Canal now had a second outlet for their traffic and serious work on the Smethwick locks could then start. On Monday 15 March 1790 the canal at Smethwick was shut for three weeks to enable the BCN to draw the water out of the old course through the summit. The canal reopened for navigation again during the first week of April.

It cannot be understated that the reduction of the locks at Smethwick improved traffic. It positively stimulated it! The summit that now stretched from Smethwick to Wolverhampton passed through an area that served some of the richest mines in the district. The potential for new traffic was quite large. Furthermore, with the completion of the Fazeley Canal new markets were opened to local industry. In essence, the backbone of the Birmingham Canal was created when the Fazeley Canal was finished in 1790. Birmingham was now on a canal that could not only reach the ports of Bristol, Liverpool and Hull, but also London. It was only a matter of time before revenue from traffic started to show a marked increase.

With the completion of the Birmingham & Fazeley Canal two canal routes became available to the traders of Birmingham. The older route through Wolverhampton to the Staffordshire & Worcester Canal, Trent & Mersey Canal and the Bridgwater Canal provided the means for canal goods to travel between Birmingham and Liverpool or Manchester. The new canal enabled goods to reach the metropolis. Within a short time other canal links were proposed.

Parliamentary approval for canal construction tended to be a yearly event. Often hidden behind closed doors, clerks, solicitors and bankers would draw up plans, arrange finance, estimate cost and then submit a scheme for Parliament. Public opinion might be consulted, an engineer appointed and even a committee formed to manage the progress of the Bill.

The session for 1789 and 1790 might have included a Bill for a canal from the Essington Coal Mines to Wolverhampton, but those responsible for this idea chose not to proceed at this time, but wait two years. The proprietors of a scheme to unite Birmingham with the River Severn at Worcester were more optimistic. They offered a scheme that went before Parliament in the 1789/1790 session, but suffered defeat in the House of Commons during April 1790. Mr Gilbert's erudite speech gave compelling reasons why the Worcester & Birmingham Canal should not proceed. Considerable investment had been made in building canals such as the Staffordshire & Worcestershire and the Trent & Mersey and he considered that their trade might be threatened by prospective waterways such as the Worcester & Birmingham Canal. Gilbert also considered this new scheme as not needed. In fact he dismissed it with the comment that it was 'not founded in real necessity'.

Church bells were said to have rung out in Wolverhampton once news reached the town of the failure of the Worcester & Birmingham Canal Bill. Yet the Worcester & Birmingham Canal proprietors remained undaunted and presented the Bill again for the 1790/1791 session. In the meantime they honed their argument and developed a wider vision. Their waterway was to be built to barge dimensions to take advantage of the barge traffic that used the River Severn. Had this scheme been completed to the intended proposals, Birmingham traders would have reaped the benefits in future times. Yet, as with other canal ventures, intentions and achievement did not follow the same course.

The Worcester & Birmingham Canal was twenty years in the making. It was commenced near Gas Street and had reached Selly Oak in 1795. It was waterway engineered to follow a direct route rather than the restrictions imposed through following land contours. Consequently, more engineering features were required and extensive embankments and some cuttings were found necessary. These included the barge-wide Edgbaston Tunnel and the long embankment on the approach to Selly Oak. Work continued to make the canal through to Kings Norton and then pass on through West Hill to Hopwood.

Construction of this waterway involved investment in men, materials and plant in amounts and numbers hitherto unprecedented in the region. Negotiations for land began immediately. Sometimes an assessment was required to determine land value. Samuel Garbett, John Kettle, James Watt, Matthew Boulton and Joseph Green were appointed commissioners to determine the value of land belonging to King Edwards School, required for the crucial canal terminus near Broad Street.

Persons were requested to supply tenders for materials by 1 March 1792. Dale (Deal) Baulks and three-inch planks were needed up to 20ft long, also coppice oak, elm and ash timber. Stone for locks and coping bridges, bricks for locks and bridge building as well as wheelbarrows were all required for delivery to land adjoining Mr Walls Lime Wharf. Two thousand tons of coal was also to be sent to Paradise Wharf, enough to burn bricks required for the season.

Work also started on the approach to the West Hill (now Wast Hill) Tunnel. Tenders for the deep cutting were requested in a notice dated 25 February 1792. This contract extended for about half a mile and started from the level at Kings Norton to 40ft in depth at the tunnel mouth. The canal dimensions were 42ft wide at top water and **5 1/2**ft deep. A towing path 9ft wide was also provided for with benching on the opposite bank.

Approval for the Worcester & Birmingham Canal was accompanied by Parliamentary approval for two important linking waterways: the Dudley Canal at Selly Oak and the

Stratford-upon-Avon Canal at Kings Norton. The northern part of the Stratford Canal was to prove particularly useful, when it provided a link with the Warwick & Birmingham Canal near Lapworth, in 1802.

Finance problems continually dogged construction, but finally it was finished to the River Severn at Worcester in 1815. The barge-wide navigation extended as far as Tardebigge near Bromsgrove, but the remaining section to the Severn at Diglis was finished as a narrow-boat canal. It was to be a constant restriction for the boats that navigated this canal between Worcester & Birmingham, as loads were limited to the carrying capacity of the narrow-boat hold (25 tons), whereas 50 or 60 tons would have been possible had the investment been continued and the barge canal finished to Worcester.

The Warwick & Birmingham Canal was more fortunate with its construction deadlines, but this waterway was made as a narrow waterway with no intention of making it wide enough for barge traffic at this time. Work had begun in 1793 on a section that joined the Digbeth Branch of the Birmingham Canal. The first obstacle was the River Rea valley, which lay below the level of the waterway. Contractors had to build up embankments on both sides and provide aqueducts to cross both the course of the main river and the stream, which returned the water from Heath Mill to the Rea. Six locks were needed at Camp Hill to raise this canal to a summit level that extended as far as Knowle. By 1796 the section as far as Henwood had been opened for trading boats and in 1800 the whole line was finished to Saltisford Basin at Warwick.

The Dudley Canal became a competitor to the Birmingham Canal for the Black Country coal and iron trade. It began as a simple extension to the Stourbridge Canal, which connected the Delph, Amblecote and Stourbridge with the Staffordshire & Worcestershire Canal at Stewponey. Both the Dudley and Stourbridge Canals were ready to receive trade by 1779.

It was a link that extended first through a district that produced a number of sand quarries then crossed the River Stour by an aqueduct to reach the glassmaking and fireclay-mining district located to the north and east of Stourbridge. Four locks raised the Stourbridge Canal to a level, which extended through to the terminus basin placed near the Turnpike Road where it crossed the River Stour. Here warehouses were constructed for the storage and despatch of fireclay and merchandise goods. Facing the basin was erected the Stourbridge Canal Co. offices, which still exist today.

Stourbridge Basin was actually at the end of the branch canal, which wound through Amblecote and Coalbournbrook serving existing glassworks and encouraging the construction of others. The main canal diverged from the branch canal near Amblecote and climbed through sixteen locks to the Leys where another level section extended as far as the Delph. The Leys marked another junction where the Fens Branch ran through to the reservoirs and pools, which supplied the canal. The main line turned right and curved round to Brettell Lane before turning again for Dudley. This was an area, which was rich in coal, fireclay and ironstone, and several mines and furnaces came to be established once the canal was built.

Robert Whitworth produced a survey for the intended Stourbridge Canal in 1775. His plan shows Bagues, Dials and Ensell & Hills Glassworks at Oldswinsford and several working fire engines for mines. Belleilsle's, Brettells, Pidcocks, Seagers, Truby's and an unnamed engine at the Level are all located on Whitworth's map in the Brierley Hill area.

The Dudley was then some two miles long. The major engineering features were the original Delph locks, which made an end-on connection with the Stourbridge Canal at the district known as the Delph, with the road bridge being the effective boundary between the two waterways. Delph locks then comprised nine locks, which were placed together in groups. Long-side pounds ran off the waterway between the locks to ensure adequate supplies of water for boats using these locks. The Dudley Canal tapped existing coalmines and like the Stourbridge encouraged many more mining and other iron-smelting ventures. This short waterway terminated at Ox Leasowes, near Peartree Lane, in the midst of an area rich in coal and ironstone. Coal from this district was sent down to Stourport and several destinations along the River Severn.

The Dudley Canal proprietors were keen to extend their waterway and eventually funds were found to construct a link through to the Birmingham Canal at Tipton. Authority to build the link was sanctioned by Act of Parliament in 1785. It was a task not lightly taken as contractors were faced with tunnelling through the hillside and under the centre of Dudley town. Thomas Dadford, engineer to the Dudley Canal Co., had the responsibility of planning the route and designing the tunnel. The chosen contractor was John Pinkerton who was given the work during January 1786. John was heavily committed to the construction of the Birmingham & Fazeley Canal at Fradley Heath and John's nephew, George Pinkerton, was given charge of the tunnel construction. It was a tremendous challenge as the contractors lacked tunnel construction experience and a professional miner was appointed to superintend the works, with miners cutting the way and bricklayers lining the sides, roof and invert with bricks when needed.

Other work included the building of five locks and the open waterway from the Ox Leasowes to the tunnel portal at Parkhead. Tunnel construction proceeded slowly and the proprietors became disappointed with the progress. The relations between proprietors and contractors continued to deteriorate once Thomas Dadford left for a more lucrative post with the Grand Trunk Canal. Pinkerton was released from his contract in July 1787 and it was left to Isaac Pratt and Richmond Aston to finish the work under the supervision of Josiah Clowes, who had replaced Dadford as engineer.

The Dudley Canal tunnel was actually a composite of three separate tunnels. Two short tunnels had previously been constructed as part of the previously mentioned private waterway for Lord Ward, completed by 1778. The new section of tunnel was 2904 yards long and joined the existing branch at Castle Mill Basin. It was built with traditional mining techniques. Some twelve or thirteen shafts were sunk along the line of the tunnel and miners drove the headings between the bases of the shafts to link them up and create the line of the tunnel. These construction techniques created a tunnel, which was neither straight, nor of uniform width. There were places where it opened out into wider places (caverns) and elsewhere it was narrow with a low roof. Construction of the tunnel was finally finished in 1792, when the canal opened to traffic. For some four years (1792–1796) a stop lock was provided within the tunnel at the Castle Mill Basin end to check boats passing between the Birmingham Canal and the Dudley Canal. This lock was replaced by another stop lock at Tipton Green where Lord Ward's private branch joined the Birmingham Canal.

Boats navigating the completed tunnel were thus restricted. Parts of the tunnel were left unlined where the rough and ragged rock greeted boatmen as they worked their craft through this subterranean waterway. No towing path was provided and craft were propelled through the tunnel by poling and legging. Professional leggers were frequently employed to assist the passage but boat crews also took their turn to push the boats through. The completion of the Dudley Tunnel opened up another link through to the Severn from the heart of Black Country industry and Birmingham.

Six years later the Dudley Canal was further extended through the completion of their No.2 Line (Netherton Canal) through Lapal Tunnel to the Worcester & Birmingham from Selly Oak. This proved to be another great venture, for which the engineer deserves great credit. The Netherton Canal was carried along the hillsides and valleys on the same level through to Selly Oak. Three tunnels were needed, one to pass under Gorsty Hill, a short tunnel was made near Halesowen and a third, long tunnel, was cut under the hill at Lapal. At 3795 yards the Lapal Tunnel was the longest canal tunnel to be built in the Midlands. It also was to be a source of maintenance problems throughout its existence. Stoppages and closures were not uncommon. Lapal Tunnel provided the third link through to the Severn at Stourport. But, for craft navigating Lapal Tunnel, the passage was long and time consuming. Some carriers elected to send their goods by other routes in preference.

The Dudley Canal opened to Selly Oak in 1798 and later, under the guise of the Netherton Canal, came to build warehouses beside a canal basin, made by them in Gas Street. It was a little piece of the Dudley Canal situated in the heart of an important wharf area in Birmingham.

Another important canal link was the waterway made to serve existing coalmines at Essington Wood. It was promoted principally by Wolverhampton businessmen who needed the coal for their industry and perhaps saw possibilities in competition with the existing Bilston, Coseley and Tipton coalmasters. The project came into being under the title of the Wyrley and Essington Canal. The route was surveyed by William Pitt, who was perhaps better known for writing histories and studies of agriculture than canal building. He had the advantage of being local, however. The chosen contractor, John Brawn, was also local.

The main line of this waterway stretches from Horseleyfields Junction (BCN) to Huddlesford Junction (Coventry Canal). It follows a curved and winding route through Wednesfield, Bloxwich, Walsall, Pelsall, Brownhills, Ogley Hay and Lichfield. The nickname 'curly-wurly' is often applied because of the lengthy route it takes.

Much of the canal is at the level 473ft. This section includes the part from Wolverhampton through to Ogley and the branches Birchills, Daw End and Lord's Hays, which were completed by the Wyrley & Essington Canal Co.. Private branches were also made at Gilpins Arm, Pelsall Common, Slough Arm and Sandhills. Beyond Ogley the main line drops through thirty locks to reach the Coventry Canal. The only other locks on the main route were the stop lock at Horseleyfields Junction and another stop at Sneyd. The stop at Horseleyfields raised the Wyrley & Essington Canal level a few inches above the BCN and was enough to ensure, in theory, that water was not lost to the BCN. The 6-inch stop at Sneyd was completed during 1798.

The Act of Parliament passed in 1792 gave the company powers to build a canal to Wyrley and also provided for a branch to Birchills, Walsall. The 'main line' diverged from the Birchills Branch at Sneyd, where the canal was raised through five locks to the Wyrley level (503ft od). It served the Essington Wood coal pits, which in those days were surrounded by a heavily wooded area. The mines were worked on behalf of the Vernon family, who lived at Hilton Hall. A new sinking was made on higher ground, which led to the construction of another flight of (five) locks up to the level of the mines (about 533ft od). A pumping engine was utilised to supply mine water to the locks.

Water for the Wyrley & Essington Canal was supplied from Sneyd Reservoir, which was placed at the top of the Sneyd lock flight. Sneyd was a small reservoir. It was designed to fulfil the early needs of the canal, which was first promoted to serve the coalmines at Pool Hayes, Essington and Bloxwich.

John Brawn had been working on another project in Hampshire but gradually transferred men to work on the Wyrley Canal. Construction was underway by October 1792 when Brawn commenced the construction of the Wednesfield embankment. Not everything went according to plan and the work took longer than expected. Between 100 and 120 men were at work on the project at any one time. Construction work dragged on into 1794. The canal was finally opened to the Essington mines in November 1794.

Wyrley & Essington Canal proprietors intended the canal to be extended northwards to reach the mineral estates around Great Wyrley, whose only outlet at that time were roads such as Watling Street. By May 1793 the canal committee revised their plans and decided to extend their branch line beyond Birchills to serve existing mines at Pelsall and Brownhills, the City of Lichfield, and provide an outlet for Essington and Brownhill coals to the Coventry Canal. The new scheme relegated the main line to Wyrley from Sneyd to branch status and elevated the branch to Birchills to form part of the main line to Huddlesford. Only the farthest end (some 3 furlongs in length) was to remain as the 'Birchills' Branch. The 'revised' main route swung away from Walsall near Birchills to pass under Green Lane and then head northwards again for Goscote and Pelsall. The Wyrley & Essington Extension Act was passed in 1794 and new contracts were advertised for this job. John Brawn secured much of the work, but part of the work was let to others. A Mr John Carne was given the task of making the Catshill Deep cutting. Two branch canals were sanctioned at the same time. One was to run from Catshill, near Ogley Hay, through to existing limestone mines at Rushall, Daw End and Hay Head. The second turned northwards towards Lord Hay's with the intention of serving a quarry there.

Construction continued through the years 1795 and 1796. The work included the building of thirty locks from Ogley Hay through to Huddlesford. Water supply was a critical factor and long-side pounds were provided where the locks were placed close together to store water as an additional supply. William Pitt also designed a lock that conserved water in circular chambers. It appears that this idea was tried on Lock 18. Despite Pitt's best efforts, water shortages would present problems for the canal company when the main canal was opened to traffic in May 1797.

The branches took longer to complete. Lord's Hays branch was partially completed in 1799 in a modified form. It was diverted under the Bloxwich Turnpike to terminate at a basin and railway interchange wharf. A single-track canal company tramroad was constructed from this basin to the New Essington Wood Colliery terminating at the pit near the existing canal lock branch. Coal was brought down the tramway and onto boats destined for markets as far away as Coventry. Construction of the Daw End Branch took longer to achieve. The branch from Catshill to the Park Lime pits had been completed by the summer of 1801. An advertisement was then placed for a contractor to complete the remaining part from Park Lime Pits through to Hay Head. This work, it seems, was finished during 1802.

In order to improve water supply, a scheme for a new reservoir near Norton, which became known sometimes as Cannock Wood and otherwise Cannock Chase Reservoirs, was proposed. Work on this scheme was begun as early as 1797, but proceeded slowly through to 1800. Heavy rains led to the bursting of the dam of Sneyd Reservoir during June 1799 that caused considerable flooding. The Brawns were delayed from completing contracts elsewhere as they had to make repairs to the dam and reservoir. The failure of Sneyd Dam may have influenced the canal committee to appoint Thomas Dadford Junior to build the dam for the new reservoir.

Cannock Chase Reservoir was a great asset for the company. It provided an increased amount of water as the dam was altered and raised. By 1823 the area enclosed amounted to 150 acres. The company had enough water spare to sell to the BCN and other canals.

The Wyrley & Essington Canal was the first commercial waterway to serve the town of Walsall, but the closest the route passed to Walsall was the terminus of the Birchills Branch and Bloxwich Wharf beside the turnpike road. Powers for the Birmingham, Birmingham & Fazeley Canal Co. to build a new canal from Broadwaters to Walsall were sought and granted in April 1794. The same Act also gave powers to build a canal from Bloomfield to Deepfields.

The Bloomfield to Deepfield cut, as it was known, would have shortened the BCN main line from Tipton to Coseley by a considerable amount. But work on this section required a tunnel under the hill at Coseley. It proved to be a difficult project to undertake. Construction of this canal began at the Bloomfield end. By 1798 the cutting had proceeded from the old canal into to the land of Mr Beebee. In the process the new line had severed Lord Dudley's private canal from Foxyard to Roundshill, which ran 6ft above the level of the BCN. At the same time, work went ahead with the Walsall Canal and two of the collateral branches sanctioned in the Act.

Jacob Twigg and Joseph Smith made the canal from Broadwaters to Walsall. The work was let in two parts. The first began at the Broadwaters end and proceeded to Darlaston. Land levels have changed since this canal was constructed, chiefly through mining subsidence, and the magnitude of their work is now difficult to appreciate. A deep cutting was made north of Broadwaters. Instructions were given to the contractors to boat the rough 'shift' away, but the sand was to be laid on the adjoining land. By May 1798 the work on this section was complete and the committee instructed Twigg and Smith's work to be measured. Mr Hood, the company engineer, was then left to consider what payment they were entitled to.

Twigg and Smith signed the second contract in April 1798 and were to execute the remainder of the cutting on the Walsall Canal by 1 January 1799. Although the excavation work had been completed in 1799, parts of the canal remained unfinished. In March 1800, it was reported that the work on the wharf at Walsall had not yet begun. During March 1800, Jacob Twigg was given the contract to cut the Toll End Branch at five pence per cubic yard. About this time Twigg was also involved in the Bilston Canal cut. This canal was authorised in the 1794 Act. It was to commence in the land of John Sampson in Darlaston, and pass through the lands of Thomas Loxdale, his undertenants and others to terminate at the Meadows, Bilston.

Meanwhile doubts had been raised about the propriety of completing the Bloomfield to Deepfield Canal. The work included the driving of a heading through and the sinking of necessary shafts upon the line between Bloomfield and Deepfield. Twigg signed a contract for the cutting from Bloomfield to the tunnel mouth. Problems were encountered over the sale of land and in particular that belonging to Lord Dudley, and there were also construction difficulties. Work was suspended and was not to be recommenced for a number of years.

The building of the short Willenhall Canal was then considered. This too had been sanctioned by the 1794 Act. It was to commence at Darlaston, above the footbridge over Bilston Brook, through various lands, including those owned by Thomas Loxdale, to terminate at David Barn's farm. Jacob Twigg was given the contract to make the first 600 yards in June 1803. Twigg was allowed two months to complete the work and was to receive £190 for the job.

It would seem that Jacob Twigg carried out much of the new construction work for the Birmingham Canal at this time. But there were some jobs he did not get. In 1800 a branch canal was proposed across Birmingham Heath towards the Soho Manufactory of Matthew Boulton. This canal left the old line at Winson Green and terminated at a place, which later became known as Soho Pool. Boulton had at one time considered a railway, but had later changed his mind. Twigg brought down his price to four pence three farthings per cubic yard for his quote. His offer was bettered, however, by Thomas Jenkins and James Cope who said they could do the job for three pence farthing. In July 1800, Jenkins and Cope were awarded the job.

By 1800 an important network of waterways had been established throughout England which was to encourage a tremendous increase of industry along its banks. Nature had bestowed on the West Midlands a varied resource of minerals. Hidden beneath the surface were seams of brick clay, coal, fireclay, ironstone and limestone. Their working was initially restricted as the greater part of the West Midlands area was once covered by forest.

Timber from the forest was frequently felled for construction purposes, but also provided a ready source of charcoal. Up to the eighteenth century, charcoal that was used for the smelting of iron, demanded by industry and shipbuilders, rapidly depleted the resources. Iron making proved to have an insatiable appetite for charcoal, which led to restrictions being placed on the amounts of timber used for this purpose.

Attempts to smelt coal with ironstone had mixed success. Dud Dudley of Tipton successfully smelted ironstone with pit coal in 1619 and used this process at furnaces at Cradley, Himley and on Pensnett Chase. Prime evidence for this discovery was documented in D. Dudley's own work, 'Mettallum Martis', published in 1665, some thirteen years after the end of the Civil War. These were difficult times and doubts were raised as to the accuracy of the process. Yet, anything Dudley did at this time was handicaped because he had backed the royalist cause. His work has received better recognition in recent years and it is often accepted that he made a significant contribution to the use of coal to smelt iron. Other contemporary workers equally deserve credit, as do successive generations of ironmasters, which included John Wood and Abraham Darby. It was Darby, working at Coalbrookdale, in the valley of the River Severn, who devised the coke smelting process, which became the basis of the modern iron industry.

The word iron was a very general term, especially when talking about quality. During those early times, as later, the product of the blast furnace, be it from the charcoal or coke smelting processes, was termed pig iron. The composition was a variable make comprising iron with other metallic elements and waste matter. The quality was improved through working the iron in the finery. Charcoal fuel was used in preference to coal, or coke, as a better quality of iron was achieved. Many terms were devised to describe the different brands of iron, which ranged from ordinary tough through to triple best. The measure of iron production was therefore not just confined to the smelting but also the make of bar iron.

The Black Country had all the basic ingredients for iron smelting: coal, ironstone and limestone, and there was a long-established iron industry associated with the several water-powered mills connected with the River Stour and River Tame. In 1737 no less than 9,000 tons of bar iron were worked annually in the Birmingham and Black Country district by the smiths and nail rod workers. The hand-made nail industry was then extensively conducted throughout the Black Country. They required a comparatively soft iron where 'ordinary tough', 'blend' and 'cold short' were produced for the slitting mills, which sliced the iron into nail rods.

Both coal and ironstone had been dug from measures close to the surface since at least medieval times. Court rolls and manorial records for the thirteenth century mention coal extraction in the Halesowen and Kingswinsford district and coal and iron mining around Sedgley and Walsall. Names such as Dudley Wood and Gornal Wood reflect the fact that the area was once wooded, and sources of charcoal would have been made available for smelting local stone at the bloomery and later the blast furnace.

Conversion of coal to coke for smelting purposes came to replace the traditional method of charcoal smelting. The first coke-smelting furnace was erected at Bradley, near Bilston. Some accounts quote this date between 1757 and 1758 and it was certainly there by 1767 as James Brindley includes its location on his survey of the proposed Birmingham Canal. Other smelting furnaces took longer to establish. Tipton had one in the 1780s and then others followed around Bilston and Tipton.

Brass was another metal that was in demand, particularly in Birmingham, where a number of brass foundries were established. There was also a related trade known as stamped brass foundry work where items of brass were fashioned by the press or die stamp. Brass was an alloy of copper and zinc where the greater percentage was metallic copper. The percentage of copper and zinc was varied to suit the purpose of the brass required. Brass was brought to Birmingham by road, but during 1742 Mr Turner established a brass house in Coleshill Street for the making of brass to supplement local demand.

The manufacture of brass was then conducted by the calamine method where metallic copper was heated in pots with ground calamine (a mixture of zinc oxide and carbonate).

Deep Cutting, Birmingham, 1828.
During 1895 The *Birmingham Weekly Mercury* published a number of articles and drawings as part of
a series entitled 'Old Birmingham'. No.13 was entitled 'The Crescent and its Canal Sixty Years Ago'.
The artist copied a work by local painter Frederick Henshaw, produced in 1828. The title caption was
actually wrong as the view depicted was the deep cutting from the Brewery Wharf looking towards
Broad Street. Whilst the accompanying text tried to reconcile the image with the Crescent and was
essentially incorrect, the engraving, however, captures much of Mr Henshaw's attention to detail.
(*Birmingham Weekly Mercury*)

When the Birmingham Canal was opened, copper was brought by inland navigation
from South Wales, where an important copper smelting industry had developed around
Swansea and Neath. Calamine was carried from mines in Derbyshire. Three new brass
houses were established at Broad Street in Birmingham, Smethwick and Spon Lane, and
all were placed on the banks of the old Birmingham Canal, where copper and coal were
delivered by boat. Calamine brass making required a specialist knowledge that required
the skill of mixing calamine and copper in the correct portions and heating for a required
amount of time in a collection of pots. The work was frequently supervised by a person
who could tell by eye when the molten brass was ready to be drawn off and poured into
ingot or plate moulds.

Metal manufacture, be it of either the ferrous or non-ferrous kind, came to be an
integral part of local industry as the district came into the nineteenth century. This was
also an important time for trade on canals. 1801 was not simply the start of a new century,
it signalled the start of the Canal Age!

three

CANAL AGE

Canal transport provided the principal means of moving goods for West Midlands industry through to 1840. Coal was the greatest single commodity carried by West Midlands' waterways. The many mines placed among the coalfields of South Staffordshire and East Worcestershire raised many thousands of tons each year. An important percentage went to the iron smelting and finished iron industry, which had grown up alongside the pits, others came to towns such as Birmingham where there was a considerable industry in making brass, iron and steel goods. These many and different articles, which were known as 'toys', gave Birmingham an international reputation as the 'Toy Shop' of Europe.

Mining of coal increased yearly from these pits and production was aided by the building of steam-driven winding engines to draw the coals from underground. Local people called these engines 'Whimseys' and the flat pit chains, used to raise the coal and ironstone and which clattered noisily over the pulley wheel, became known as 'Rattlechains'.

A miner's lot was the daily routine of walking to the pit shaft, being let down the shaft in a vessel known as a bowk and then walking, or crawling, along the headings to the face of work. Thick coal miners received a higher wage than those who got the coal from the thinner measures. Yet both were subject to the dangers and perils of working in a seam of coal. The roof might give way or the side collapse in. There was danger from suffocation from methane gas, or an explosion and fire. Water was another hidden enemy as underground watercourses or old working might be encountered bringing a rush of water and potential drowning for the miners unlucky enough to be working nearby. Sometimes a mixture of sand and water were encountered and underground workers found this combination just as deadly as the quicksand found on the surface.

Wages for a day's work varied around the 3s mark, with thin-coal miners earning less than 3s and thick-coal miners earning 3s or more. Each miner received a quantity of drink daily, which might amount to two quarts in volume, and there was also a regular allowance of coal for domestic fuel. The wage varied with the state of the trade. Sometimes the coalmine proprietors (coalmasters) were forced to make wage cuts and in these times miners voiced their anger and occasionally rioted.

Many miners were generally employed under a system of contract work, where a chartermaster, or butty, would agree to get the coal for a set rate. He undertook to supply men, boys and their tools. On a large coalfield several butties might be employed. It was a method of work that was open to the iniquitous truck system, where wages might be paid as goods or beer from the butty's shop.

Another use of coal was the production of town gas. The manufacture of town gas was instigated at the Soho Foundry where William Murdoch made experiments with the distillation of coal and retention of the gas formed. Town gas was first produced commercially for street lighting during the second decade of the nineteenth century when various private ventures were formed to manufacture it. Murdoch might have derived inspiration from the coke hearth where coal was burnt in the open. Yet he and other contemporary workers devised the method where coal was heated in a closed system of retorts that enabled the collection of gas.

Gas works might be erected privately or for public use. Where gas was supplied for public consumption an Act of Parliament was required. The first Parliamentary enquiry into the gas industry was conducted during 1808, but investment in the gas making industry was hampered through the war with France and the economic conditions of the period. Thoughts turned to gas making again once the war with France was over. Several schemes were then proposed across the country. The Birmingham (Gas Street) establishment was erected for John Gostling, but was taken over by a private company, the Birmingham Gas Light & Coke Co., following their grant of Act of Parliament in 1819. Gasworks schemes were then approved on a regular basis. Rival supplies were also sometimes established. The Birmingham & Staffordshire Gas Light Co. came into being in 1825. With works at Swan Village it was well placed to serve both parts of Birmingham as well as the heart of the Black Country.

Notices for the 'Intended Birmingham Gas Light Co.' were printed in January 1817. It was proposed to raise by subscription a capital of £100,000 for 'erecting and maintaining Gas Light Works and apparatus for lighting up the public streets of the Town, and the houses, shops and manufactories of such persons as may be desirous of the same, by a company of proprietors, to be called the Birmingham Gas Light Co.'. The Birmingham works was the first to be erected in the West Midlands, but was soon joined by a number of other gas light works. Birmingham Gasworks was built alongside a timber wharf road, which adopted the name 'Gas Street' once the gasworks came into operation. Town gas was made from certain types of coal that were heated in iron, and later fireclay, retorts. Coke and coal tar were produced as by-products. The gas from the retorts was passed through purifiers and stored in gas holders prior to use. Local coals came to be in increasing demand to supply the Birmingham Gasworks, as well as those established at Dudley and Wolverhampton.

There was a close relationship with the iron trade and miners' wages were particularly affected by the price of iron. The coalmasters and the ironmasters were particularly keen to ensure the success of their trade and careless expenditure in time of economic depression would lead to bankruptcy and mine closures. The years that succeeded the victory over the French at Waterloo proved particularly difficult and there were moments of strife amongst the mining community. On 7 May 1822 a group of coal and ironmasters met at the George Inn, Walsall to express their resolve and confirm their beliefs. Thomas

Price was elected chairman for the meeting and afterwards the following statement was published in the local newspapers:

That the sole and entire cause of the disruption has been a refusal of the workmen to work at the rates of wages, which have been offered to them (which exceed those given in other mining districts), and not as industriously propagated, the payment of wages otherwise than in money. That the present low prices of all necessaries of life, reduced prices of coal and iron, render such refusal on the part of the workmen highly injudicious, unreasonable and unwarrantable, tending to prolong the disturbance of public peace and to drive the iron and coal trades to other parts of the kingdom, and eventually to produce the ruin and starvation of the workmen and their families: and therefore that this meeting will neither agree to or to sanction any other rates of wages than those which the workmen now refuse to accept.
(*Aris's Gazette*, 13 May 1822).

Iron goods and ironstone were important cargoes for the canal carrier. The greatest development of the West Midlands iron industry took place during the first half of the nineteenth century. A list compiled of British blast furnaces for 1796 shows that there was a furnace at the level, beside the Dudley Canal, a furnace at Brierley, two furnaces at Bilston, three at Bradley, one at Graveyard (Gornal), one at Dudley Port, two at Tipton and one at Gospel Oak. Their combined output amounted to some 13,000 tons. Between 1800 and 1860 the numbers of blast furnaces increased in number until over 160 were built.

The smelting furnaces were concentrated along specific sections of waterway. West of the range of the Rowley Hills, furnaces lined the Dudley Canal from Windmill End to the level, Brierley Hill and were also located around Brettell Lane on the Stourbridge Canal. East of Rowley the route of the Old Birmingham Canal came to serve a large number of furnaces from Oldbury through to Wolverhampton. The Walsall Canal and its branch connections also possessed several smelting operations. By contrast, the Wyrley & Essington Canal had few furnaces, despite potential sources of ironstone being available.

Ironstone was found throughout many parts of the Black Country, but was concentrated in particular spots. Workable deposits were found around Netherton and Blowers Green and a long curving strip that stretched from Oldbury and West Bromwich round through Tipton, Coseley, Bilston, Wednesfield, Willenhall to Bloxwich, and Walsall. Mines commonly extracted both ironstone and coal. Individuals and partnerships worked minerals either for the supply of the basic elements, or to supply an iron making business. Newspaper columns frequently contained details of sale and these contain information detailing the extents of the workings:

To IRON AND COAL-MASTERS AND OTHERS

TO be LET, or SOLD, by private Treaty, all the Mines of Coal and Ironstone, which remain ungotten in the ETTINGSHALL COLLIERY, and also all the Machinery, Rail-roads, Waggons,

Wharfs, and Erections belonging to same. The Mines are proved, and a pair of shafts have been sunk to and gotten Blue Flat Ironstone, which is found regular and good.

There is now two Pits at work getting Coal and Ironstone, and other pit shafts are sunk down through, the thick coal, and also through the Gubbin and Balls Ironstone, which may be sunk down to the other mines at a small expense, the water being very little.

There are two Winding Engines on this property, one of which is in the deep, and pumps the water out and winds the mines.

Also to be let or sold, the Land, and all the Mines of Coal and Ironstone under the same, called or known by the name of Burrow's Flat and the Oldnalls, situate at Ettingshall, containing 6A.3R, or thereabouts, and nearly adjoins the above Colliery, only a narrow sling of Land dividing the two properties. Part of the Thick Coal has been gotten, and the remaining part is dry, and also the Gubbin Ironstone; all the Mines below the thick Coal are in the whole.

(Birmingham Gazette, 25 January 1836).

Furnaces were erected close to the mines where the ironstone was mined. Most had a canal frontage, but some were located on the coalfield and sent pig iron by tramroad to the nearest canal basin. Furnaces based on the canalside also had the added advantage of receiving limestone by boat. As local ironstone and coal measures were exhausted, iron smelters exploited other mineral properties, often using the canal to bring these minerals to the furnace yard.

The largest concentration of blast furnaces was located around Bilston, Tipton and Wednesbury. The first Tipton furnace was erected on land opposite Lord Ward's private canal during the 1780s. Another was erected on land that belonged to John Bickley at Bilston. When the Dudley Canal Tunnel was opened in 1792, Benjamin Gibbons, who operated Bickley's furnace, sent iron through the tunnel during the first month of operation. Bickley's original furnace was located near Spring Vale on a plot of land south of the turnpike that ran through from Bilston to the Fighting Cocks. It was a site that was to be associated with iron making for about 190 years. Four furnaces were eventually built there and several generations of ironmasters worked the site.

Bilston iron making will always be associated with John Wilkinson, ironmaster of Shropshire and Staffordshire, who established the Bradley Furnaces. John Wilkinson (1728–1808) must be considered one of the greatest eighteenth century ironmasters. He was associated with iron making at Willey, Snedshill and Broseley in addition to the Bradley works. With the dawn of the nineteenth century, a new name came to be connected with iron making in the district. It was that of Samuel Fereday. During the first decade of the nineteenth century Samuel Fereday, Richard Smith, George Stokes, John Jeffrey, William Stevens and John Rhead formed various partnerships for the working of coalmines, ironstone mines and furnaces around Bilston, Coseley, Sedgley and Tipton. Fereday had considerable success, but lost all when the iron trade went into decline in 1815. Trade in iron making was frequently beset with good and bad years and ironmasters frequently faced bankruptcy in the lean years.

Blast furnaces of Wilkinson's and Fereday's day were constructed squat and square, made of brick and lined internally with firebrick. Each was limited to a weekly make of some 30 tons and was frequently associated with the finery and forge, which converted pig iron into bar iron. The basic process of iron smelting involved the breaking down of ironstone and limestone into a size where they could be mixed together according to an agreed proportion with coke, and sometimes coal, at the furnace mouth.

Furnace labourers assisted with the breaking down of the stone and the wheeling of the mineral in barrows. Others worked with long rakes at the coke hearth. Here coal was heated on an open hearth to remove sulphur impurities contained within the local coals, coal gas was allowed to go to waste. Coke-hearth men worked in appalling conditions, being subjected to the sulphurous fumes as they raked the coals over and over.

The temperature in the furnace was raised by blasts of air, which were forced through the body of the fire by the action of a blast engine, or bellows. With water-powered blast furnaces the turning of the wheel through cogs and gearing worked bellows to create a blast. The steam engine was later adapted to provide a blast through the action of a piston within a large diameter cylinder. In both cases, all air that passed into to furnace was drawn from the outside and entered at that temperature. The furnace mouth was also left open for waste gases to escape. Iron compounds within the ironstone were reduced to molten iron metal that collected at the base, where it separated out into two layers. One contained mostly impurities, known as slag, the other was molten iron. Around the base were arranged a group of tuyeres, which were metal conduits that enabled the iron and slag to flow out of the furnace by a process called tapping. Furnaces were tapped at specific times by the furnacemen, whose task it was to channel the molten iron through a large bed of sand. The channel was made to divide into rows and subdivide finally into a set of open, and equally long, moulds. It was the duty of the men to divert the flowing white-hot metal into the first row to fill all the moulds, then close off the supply through making a dam of sand and then send the flow into the second row and repeat the process filling rows until all the available iron was taken from the furnace. Skill was required to know when to tap the furnace as well as segregate the iron from the slag, which was diverted elsewhere.

The arrangement of moulds resembled piglets suckling at the sow, which gave rise to the name 'pig' iron being applied to the iron collected and the sand moulds became known as the pig beds. Once the iron was cooled it was gathered up for storage or despatch. Despite the careful arrangement of the moulds, weights varied, and before sale each piece of pig iron was weighed and frequently branded with the ironmasters mark. Those who worked at the pig beds faced the daily hazard of burns from molten iron. A greater danger existed with the tuyere where defects could result in an explosion spraying molten metal over the workers with disastrous consequences.

One market for the pig iron was the foundry where iron was melted to be recast in moulds of specific shape. Early production of what was known as cast iron was directly performed at the furnace yard where iron from the furnace was run into moulds of the shape required. The iron foundry used both local and other iron. An early canalside foundry was located in Broad Street, Birmingham, called the Eagle Foundry. It was established in 1775, some two years after the completion of the Paradise Street Branch of the Birmingham Canal Navigation.

An extensive trade in Shropshire pig iron had developed on local waterways, where pig and bar iron produced at furnaces and works in East Shropshire were taken down the River Severn to Stourport and along the Staffordshire & Worcestershire Canal and

Shakespeare Foundry, Wolverhampton.
The artist for this engraving found a rare perspective looking down from the railway viaduct across the Birmingham Canal at Horseleyfields. (Great Western Railway Guide, 1860)

Birmingham Canal. This trade lessened when more blast furnaces were established in the Black Country and greater supplies of cheaper pig iron became available. Cast-iron manufacture was assisted through the invention of the cupola by ironmaster John Wilkinson. The cupola provided the means of a more practical means of melting pig iron and foundries came to employ their use. The Eagle Foundry produced a range of cast-iron goods, which first included stove grates, but later extended to encompass steam engine parts, bone mills, malt rollers, pumps, pulley blocks, anvils, hammers, fencing, hurdles, iron windows, water troughs and ranges.

Many other foundries were erected close to the waterway, where boats might deliver coal and sand, and cast-iron goods be despatched in a similar manner. Several iron founders specialised in the production of holloware, iron fencing and gates, oil lamps or stoves and grates for homes and the workplace.

Holloware is the collective name for pots and pans, which was a commodity in regular demand. West Bromwich had a number of founders, but three main families dominated the local holloware industry: the Bullocks, Izons and Kendricks. All had canalside properties where coal, pig iron and sand were brought in by the boatload. Canal carriers also called to pick up the finished article destined for distant markets. William Bullock established the Spon Lane Foundry alongside the top lock at Spon Lane. The foundry, which dates from about 1805, had a basin that joined the Wolverhampton Level of the Birmingham Canal Navigations. At that time the main route of the Birmingham Canal Navigations passed through Spon Lane. Traffic destined for Dudley Canal, Tipton and Wolverhampton all went that way. Spon Lane was also the point where the branch canal to Walsall joined. Bullock's foundry was therefore well situated for canal commerce. Some of this strategic importance was lost after canal improvements were carried out during the 1820s and 1830s, but the old main line still remained busy. Boats continued to serve Bullock's foundry and the host of other works that lined this part of the waterway. The Spon Lane Foundry was taken over by George Salter & Co. in 1885. Salter's were a local firm noted for products that incorporated springs. These included spring balances and the safety valves on boilers. Spon Lane Foundry continued to make castings for Salter's and also to receive coal by boat.

Local smelting of iron also encouraged the production of finished iron goods. The puddling process became the principal process of converting pig iron to malleable, or wrought, iron, which in this form could be worked in to wire, or rolled into sheets, bars or hoops. It is a process for which Henry Cort has received the lion's share of recognition although many other individuals made it a workable process. It is also probably true to say that there was little radically new in Cort's invention. His skill was to adapt the ideas of other ironmasters working independently and crystallise their ideas into what became the basis of making wrought iron in volume.

Improvement to Cort's method finally led to the adoption of puddling furnaces at all ironworks that were engaged in the manufacture of wrought iron. Black Country ironworks had banks and puddling furnaces installed and randomly erected around the site. This industry created a completely new job, the puddler, whose task it was to take iron and work it up into a ball within the furnace, which projected the heat down onto the iron. Another person, the underhand puddler, assisted with working the iron in the furnace. To some extent he was the apprentice learning the trade. The puddler had the skill and judgement to work the ball to the correct composition. They had a range of tools and tongs at their disposal for holding and turning the iron and every time a ball of iron left the furnace the time taken in working the iron was called a heat. Moneys were paid to the puddler for the amount of iron worked and these provided the wages for both him and his assistant.

Although Cort's method provided for iron going straight from the furnace to the rolling mill, it was generally preferred to remove slag residue retained within the puddled iron. Each ball of iron was then taken to the hammer, worked by the shingler, who with repeated blows was able to expel waste matter and remaining slag from the ball. The act of hammering produced a bar shaped piece of iron, which would then go to the rolling mill. It was Henry Cort, who in another patent, had set out grooved rollers as a means of shaping iron and grooved rolls continued to be an important part of the metal rolling process for years to come.

The rolling mill was a colourful place. Pairs of rollers, driven by a steam engine, or a water wheel, were placed in the centre of a designated floor space. Men, whose job was termed a 'roller', would pass the bar of metal through the rolls, back and forth, each time reducing the thickness, but increasing the width. All forms of rolls were used. Smooth breaking down rolls assisted the first process and then grooved rollers shaped the metal into a special form. By this method sheet and strip, and hoops and rails were made. With each pass of the metal the red, or white-hot form would run along the floor to be caught by special tongs held by the roller to be threaded through the rolls again.

Pig Beds, Willingsworth Furnaces.
The tapping of the blast furnace was part of the daily operation of the blast furnace and relied on the skill of the workmen to draw off the molten iron at the correct moment and channel the flow into the network of moulds formed in the sand. (Sandwell Public Libraries)

Casting Pig Iron at Springvale Furnaces.
Sand beds were employed at the base of all blast furnaces to collect the pig iron. This was a hazardous place to work, apart from the problems of dealing with molten metal, the tuyeres through which the blast was directed could explode, showering the men and boys working on the beds with hot iron and slag with dreadful consequences. (Ray Shill collection)

Puddling furnaces came to be installed in ironworks across the Black Country. When John Addenbrook arranged for the construction of the two Moorcroft furnaces beside the Bradley Branch in 1800, puddling furnaces were also included as part of the plant. At least five puddling furnaces and two preparing fineries were recorded in a sales notice for January 1804.

Most Black Country rolling mills and puddling furnaces were also placed alongside the canal or had access to it through tramroads or private railways. The supply of pig iron was delivered by canal boat as was the large amounts of coal needed to fuel the boilers, puddling and reheating furnaces required for operation. The iron produced by these mills all received a brand depending on the quality produced. These might be sent out as finished products or passed onto another works that specialised in a particular type of goods.

The forge was another large user of coal. Forges and smithys have existed since the dawn of the Iron Age. Through the strength of the smith white-hot iron was repeatedly hammered into shape. With every blow of the hammer hot slivers of iron would fly away as bright sparks, and scatter the floor of the forge as scale. It was a process that produced a stronger iron and one that was sought for both military and commercial purposes. Water mills, and later steam engines, provided a suitable hammer power to pound out the hot metal.

Another tide of increased iron production came during the 1820s when several new furnaces were erected. A few were made to a new and radical design, which was to become the standard in later years. These furnaces were made circular and tapered towards the top. The basic fabric of the furnace was brick and firebrick, which was bound together by iron hoops. They were also taller than the early square furnaces and required a method of mechanical haulage to draw materials to the furnace mouth.

Iron production remained a speculative venture for the capitalists who chose to invest in it. Profits could be high but the price of iron often fluctuated and it was just as easy to lose money. London investors J.H. Shears, Robert Small and John Taylor found the iron trade a hard lesson to learn.

They had made investments in mineral property and ironworks at Acrefair, near Ruabon and Monmouthshire. During 1825 they acquired the mineral property belonging to John Attwood, which included furnaces at Dudley Wood and Netherton, leased from Lord Dudley. There were six blast furnaces, two at Netherton and four at Dudley Wood, capable of making 360 tons of pig iron a week. The Corngreaves Iron and Steelworks consisted of forges and rolling mills. The chief produce of these works was nailrods for the local handmade nail trade. These works were capable of making 300 tons of rod and bar iron. The Wolverhampton mines had recently been leased from Lord Darlington. Pits had been sunk and ironstone raised, but some measures were deeper than the existing pumping engine could cope with. A more powerful pumping engine to drain them was needed. Seams of ironstone were also available at Corngreaves complete with a good vein of coal, and these were developed after they took over the estate.

An early acquisition was the Brierley Hill Ironworks, above the nine locks on the Dudley Canal. These works were the result of a combination of two separate undertakings on both sides of Mill Street. The first Nine Locks Ironworks, which stood on the west side of Mill Street, was started about 1801 by George and Thomas Holcroft. Robert Hornblower owned the land. Robert also owned the land opposite upon which Brierley Hill Flour Mill was built. The name 'Mill Street' was derived from the flourmill, which the Hornblower family later converted into the Brierley Hill Ironworks. The Hornblowers then took over the Nine Locks Ironworks and subsequently erected steel cementation furnaces for the production of blister steel. William Hornblower faced bankruptcy in 1824 and the iron and steelworks were put up for sale. They remained unsold until June 1825 when Henry James offered to purchase them for Small, Shears and Taylor. The plant then comprised powerful rolling mills, forges and steel works. The rolling mills were nearly new and it was first intended to remove them to Corngreaves. During July 1825 the future of the Brierley Hill works was reconsidered, they were worth more standing than removed, and a decision was taken to put them back to work. Brierley Hill Iron & Steelworks were conveniently situated for receiving iron from Netherton and Dudley Wood furnaces, which lay on the same canal. It was also decided to put up an additional forge at Corngreaves and take the fineries from Brierley Hill there, prepare the iron and send such parts as may be required to the Brierley Hill Works to be rolled into sheets, plates and hoops.

As early as 15 July 1825, Mr P. Taylor had arranged for construction of a steam engine and blast cylinder at the Neath Abbey Ironworks for the new furnace at Corngreaves. Work on building railroads, sinking pits and building a new steel forge, erecting steam engines and ironworks at Corngreaves were all conducted during 1825. The railroads provided the essential link not only to move coal and ironstone to the furnaces but also to provide the means of transporting goods to the canal at Dudley Wood. A tramroad over a mile long was constructed to link the Corngreaves Steel and Ironworks with Dudley Wood furnaces and the Dudley Canal. The British Iron Co. took possession of the Attwood properties on 9 November 1825. Surviving blast furnace statistics for 1826 quote that combined produce of the British Iron Co. in the Black Country averaged over 14,500 tons a year. It was a figure that exceeded any other local company production.

Small, Shears and Taylor's investment proved to be an excessive amount. The iron and steel trade was again on the down turn and the price of iron was falling. The lawyers were called in an attempt to reclaim some of the moneys spent by Small, Shears and Taylor from Attwood. The legal action went on for years and the only real winners were the lawyers and solicitors who acted for both parties. Small, Shears and Taylor's company, the British Iron Co., was brought to the verge of ruin and receivership in 1843. Out of the ashes of the failure came the New British Iron Co., who had a more successful tenure at the Corngreaves Works.

Other ironmasters fared better than Small, Shears and Taylor's baptism into the iron industry. A new generation of ironmasters was to become pillars of the local iron and coal industry and their families become dynasties of ironmasters. The names included John Bagnall of West Bromwich, who built up an extensive trade based on furnaces and ironworks at Golds Green and Golds Hill. The furnaces at Golds Green were located beside the 'old' Wednesbury Canal, or Balls Hill Branch, and were also near to the Danks Branch and the Walsall Canal. Tramways crossed the intervening land linking coal and ironstone pits with the furnaces and Golds Hill ironworks.

The Sparrow family came to have extensive property around Bilston and operated rolling mills and furnaces (originally Bickley's) by the canal. They constructed a tramway, about a mile in length, that headed north towards Stow Heath where a bank of new blast furnaces was made. George Jones, who began as a miner and charter master, gained an interest in the iron trade with a new furnace at Coseley. He then took over Sparrow's Bilston furnaces, but lacking access to the mines, which continued be used by Sparrow, arranged to develop a new mineral estate to the west at Sedgley Park. Jones had a new railway built that crossed the canal and came to serve not only the mines but also a new ironworks at Spring Vale.

Between the years 1825 and 1830 Black Country iron making saw a surge of new production as another ten sites were established.

New Furnaces 1825–1829

(As per H. Scrivener, History of the Iron Trade, 1854)

Furnace Location	Canal	Number of Furnaces
Barbers Field, Bilston	Birmingham Canal	1 (1826), 1 (1828)
Brettell Lane	Stourbridge Canal	2 (1825)
Chillington, Wolverhampton	Birmingham Canal	2 (1829)
Corbyns Hall	Railroad to Stourbridge Canal	3 (1825), 1 (1829)
Leys	Stourbridge Canal	2 (1828)
Parkfield, Ettingshall	Birmingham Canal	2 (1826), 1 (1827), 1 (1828)
Union, West Bromwich	Union Branch, BCN	2 (1828)
Willingsworth	Gospel Oak Branch, BCN	2 (1827), 1 (1828)
Wolverhampton	Birmingham Canal	1 (1825), 1 (1827)
Windmill End	Dudley Canal	2 (1825)

Steel, which was part of the output of the Corngreaves Works, was another local product that was made throughout the district. Birmingham and Black Country steel making might have been overshadowed by the making of steel at Sheffield, yet a local supply was very relevant for the making of swords, knives, edge tools and goods known as steel toys.

The 'toy' trade included the manufacture of steel jewellery, buckles and buttons. A trade in making steel jewellery developed in Wolverhampton during the seventeenth century, but the Birmingham trade, through the benefits of the fly press, was able to increase production and establish a reputation for the making of these items. Birmingham's Steelhouse Lane was not named in any casual manner but derived its name from Kettle's Steelhouse placed at the bottom of the lane near what is now Lancaster Circus. By 1731 both Kettle and Cartwright (Coleshill Street) had a steel house in Birmingham. Both works used Swedish iron that was heated with charcoal to make steel.

In canal days steel-making plants existed at different places. In addition to the previously mentioned Brierley Hill, Corngreaves and Websters (at Penns, near Minworth) there was an important steelworks at Brades, Oldbury owned by the Hunt family. Paul & Co. also had a steel plant at Aston Junction and the Attwood family were associated with

Brades Steel Works, Oldbury.
One of the most dangerous occupations in the steel edge-tool trade was at the grinding wheel. Here workers are seen at the grindstone putting the edge on steel blades. In view of the differing qualities of grindstones, dust from the stone presented a cumulative health hazard in later life. It was also not unknown for faults in the wheel to cause the stone to be rent apart with severe injury to the worker sat astride the stone. (Ray Shill collection

a steel plant at Corngreaves and the Adelphi Steel Works in Bridge Street, Birmingham. The Brades Steel Works were placed alongside the original route of the Old Birmingham Canal, which was reduced to a basin serving the steelworks when the section of canal was straightened from Whimsey Bridge, Oldbury to the Brades.

They used Swedish iron, which was first treated with charcoal in cementation furnaces. Each furnace was built in the shape of a cone. Layers of iron and charcoal were stacked inside and allowed to burn for about a week. The resulting product was called blister steel and this product was broken up again and mixed with more charcoal in fireclay pots. The long amphora-shaped pots were then heated in another furnace where the ingredients melted and produced good quality steel, known as crucible steel.

Brades specialised in the making of edge tools. Steel from the crucible pots was forged and shaped ready for sharpening. Workers spent long hours astride grind stones putting edges on blades and tools, constantly breathing in the dust, from the stone, which would shorten their lives. Brades steel was also sent into Birmingham by road or boat for sale at their warehouse, in Ann Street.

Canal and road carriers also brought Sheffield steel into Birmingham for sale from a variety of merchants' warehouses. Other edge tool makers like Yates of Rocky Lane, Aston, would have drawn a supply from sources such as these or possibly had direct deliveries to their works beside the Birmingham & Fazeley Canal.

Coneygre Furnaces, Dudley Port.
Richard Smith, agent to Lord Dudley & Ward, made an important contribution to the local iron
trade developing mines, minerals and furnaces on the extensive Dudley estate. This engraving shows
the bank of three blast furnaces and loading incline as seen from the canal side with carriers' boats
engaged in the iron trade passing by. Also visible is the canal wharf, warehouse and stacks of pig iron
ready for despatch. (Great Western Railway Guide, 1860)

The steel pen industry developed in Birmingham, during the 1820s, through the efforts
of people like Joseph Gillott and Josiah Mason. Sheet steel was required for cutting out
the pen nib blanks and Sheffield steel was preferred to other locally made steels. Steel was
rolled at one of the local rolling mills before going on to one of the growing number of
pen making firms. Here the universal hand-worked fly press was used to stamp out the
nib shape for working up to the finished product.

Metal rolling, be it non-ferrous or ferrous, was originally the preserve of the water
mill. Several metal rolling mills were placed along the Hockley Brook, River Rea, and
River Tame. It was common for rolling mill owners to provide rolling facilities to which
the metal owners brought their goods for rolling to shape. James Pickard was the first to
establish a steam-powered rolling mill in Birmingham, and in fact the world. In 1780 his mill
machinery was at the cutting edge of technology. Pickard's mill was the first to use an engine
capable of rotative motion through a simple and effective concept that employed a crank
and flywheel. Such was the ingenuity of the invention that even the great James Watt had to
devise another method, which became popularly known as the sun and planet engine.

Pickard's mill, first leased to Charles Twigg, came to be used principally for rolling non-
ferrous metals such as copper and its alloy, brass. Later, Pickard enlarged the site to include
a flourmill and bakery in his own name. Baileys Directory (1783) lists under Birmingham
that Charles Twigg's was a rollers of metal, grinders and borers of gun barrels at the steam
mill Snow Hill. The entry went on to elaborate with the following advertisement:

This mill is erected for the above purpose, and also for polishing of steel goods, finishing buckles, buckle Chapes, and a Variety of other articles, usually done per Foot Lathes. The whole is worked by a steam engine and saves Manufacturers the Trouble of sending several Miles into the Country, to Water Mills.

Water rolling mills retained a vital role through to the year 1830, but the problems of a lack of continual water supply often restricted production. Some water mills had steam engines installed to provide a back-up supply of power. Other metal rollers decided to erect steam-powered rolling mills beside the canal.

Thomas Phipson converted the Old Cotton Mill in Fazeley Street, Birmingham to roll metals and during 1801. Mr Phipson was advertising for metal rollers to work there. Another rolling mill, the New Steam Mill, had been erected to the north of Fazeley Street Bridge about 1793. Newhall Street Rolling Mill was a steam-driven rolling mill erected about the year 1808 on land leased from Caroline Colmore by James Mills and Josiah Chinn. The buildings were erected alongside a private canal owned Colmore that first extended only as far as Charlotte Street, but was later extended under George Street and through to a sand quarry at Newhall Hill. For some unrecorded reason, this branch waterway became known as Whitmore's Arm.

Thomas Gibson established the nucleus of what was to become a complex of works in Broad Street during 1812 and 1813. Gibson purchased land from what had belonged to the Baskerville family and was the former home of John Baskerville, japanner and printer. The level of the ground was above that of the nearby Newhall Canal Branch. Gibson arranged to build a private branch into his property. This branch passed under Cambridge Street to a lock through which boats were raised some 8 or 9ft to the level of a pair of basins, which became known as Gibson's Arm and Baskerville Basin. A steam engine was installed, to pump water up from the Newhall Branch, which was returned every time a boat descended the lock. Amongst the works laid out around the basins were the Union Rolling Mills and Robert Winfield's Brassworks. Winfield had learnt the brass trade whilst apprenticed to Benjamin Cook and then set up business on his own account. Winfield's first lease with Gibson was made in 1824 for a square plot of land adjacent to the Union Mills.

The brass trade was then undergoing a revolution as brass made traditionally by the calamine method came to be replaced by brass made through direct combination of copper with metal zinc (spelter). As more zinc was brought into the district, the future existence of the calamine brass houses at Birmingham, Smethwick and Spon Lane was short. The Birmingham Brass Works shut down their plant between 1830 and 1831, and sold off the steam-powered calamine-grinding mill. Spon Lane Brassworks closed during 1833 and was converted into an iron foundry during 1834. Smethwick, which retained a horse mill to the end, closed down in 1834.

Winfield built up an important trade in brass foundry for the new gas industry supplying brass fittings that were frequently decorated with artwork. Winfield was also a pioneer in the metallic bedstead trade. Benjamin Cook and Thomas Attwood had patented a method of casing iron tubes with brass, which went a long way to establishing the metallic bedstead trade in Birmingham.

An allied process was the production of wire. Steel wire found increasing use in rope and cable making, but also had a historic role as music wire for pianos. Brass wire was used for the making of pins. The firm of D.F. Tayler patented a method of forming a pin complete with head from the same piece of wire and started to produce these pins at their mills at Lightpool near Stroud. They moved to Birmingham during the late 1840s to take over Bethels Steel Toy Works in George Street, known as the Newhall Works. The Newhall Works were placed at the end of Miss Colmore's private canal, Whitmore's Arm, and occupied a strip of land from the canal back to Newhall Hill. In addition to making pins on site, a steam-powered rolling mill was erected on the Newhall Hill side, worked under the name of Edelstein & Williams.

The first section of the Warwick & Birmingham Canal from Digbeth Junction crossed the River Rea and then passed along an embankment towards Great Barr Street Bridge. The Rea Aqueduct was accompanied by another aqueduct over the mill leat from Heath Mill, which was an old water mill on land owned by Sir Thomas Gooch. Before 1800 the mill was known as Coopers Mill, but afterwards became the Deritend Mill, when a steam-powered mill was constructed on adjacent land. Ownership of the site varied and a number of people were associated with running the mill. This mill was probably the property described in sales notices for 1801 and 1802 as having a steam engine with a 51 inch diameter cylinder that worked pairs of rolls and had eight rough and six fine boring benches with stone holes for grinding barrels, sword blades, bayonets, ramrods and edge tools.

Drawing of metal wire from iron and non-ferrous metals became an important trade, where the wire was used to make mesh, pins and screws. By 1803 Deritend Mill was the property of Joseph Cotterill, Wire Drawer. A few years later Wooley, Deakin and Co. had charge of Deritend Mill. During 1810 Deakin & Co. arranged to make a weir beside their works to draw water from the canal into a new pool opposite their works in Fazeley Street, which may have been used to supply their steam engine, but also possibly provided an additional water supply for the water mill and cater for the times when the Rea was short of water. Deritend Mill continued to specialise in the production of rolled metal and wire thereafter. Deakin & Oughton were made bankrupt in 1819 and other people leased the mill buildings. Sometimes multiple occupations were recorded. Robson's Trade Directory (1839) makes the distinction between Deritend Mill and the original Heath Mill. Deritend Old Mills had five separate occupiers, whilst the water-powered Heath Mill was occupied by a steel pen maker.

Robsons Trade Directory 1839

Deritend Old Mills
J. Singleton, wire drawer
Smith and Croxall, general wire drawer
J. Smith, steel and iron wire drawer
J. Wright, grinder polish and matchet maker
S. Walker Junior, German Silver, fancy and plain wire, copper & brass manufacturer
Heath Mills
Ball & Walker, patent steel pen manufacturer

Nickel refining and rolling was another trade, which the Birmingham firm of Evans and Askins did much to promote. The first nickel works was established in George Street on premises, which lay beside Whitmore's Arm, where a supply of ores and coal could be received. Askin first extracted nickel from the cobalt blue waste from the Potteries, but later reversed the trade when he extracted nickel chemically from its ores and exported cobalt back to the Potteries.

Flint glass manufacture was conducted in the Stourbridge district, where the principal factories were located away from inland navigation. Flint glass was made from a mixture of sand, alkali and red lead that was fused together in refractory clay pots. A special type of sand was required to make flint glass. Local sand was not suitable. Sand was brought from Lynn in Norfolk or Yarmouth (Isle of Wight) to ports such as Gloucester or Gainsborough and then consigned by canal carriers' boats to the glassworks. Later sand from Fontainbleu in France proved to be the preferred supply.

Litharge, or red lead oxide, was manufactured from lead heated in a reverberatory furnace. Blair & Stevenson of Tipton and Atkins & Nock of Smethwick were important suppliers of litharge. Both factories were located beside the canal and usually despatched this material by carriers' boat. Local chemical works also usually supplied the alkali, which was also needed for glass making.

The clay for the pots was a fireclay obtained locally. Fireclay was a solid stone, mined as coal from the depths of the ground. Fireclay measures were found below the heathen, stinking and sulphur coal measures and comprised a band of first 'old mine' clay and then several bands of 'new mine' clay. The principal fireclay district extended northwards from Stourbridge and Wollascote to Shut End and Gornal and eastward beyond Cradley to Dudley Wood and Halesowen.

The old mine fireclay produced the best of these clays and was sought after to make glasshouse pots. Lesser grade clays were employed to make retorts for gasworks. All other grades tended to be used to make firebricks. Fireclay mining was long associated with the Stourbridge glass industry. The many works were located near the glassworks they served and consequently were a considerable distance from the nearest navigable waterway. Yet as the following notice shows, good pot clay was taken into Stourbridge Wharf from where it was despatched to Stourport by canal, or to Bristol by the River Severn Navigation.

Glass pot clay works – to be sold by Private Contract – all that glass pot clay and coal works in Parish of Oldswinsford, near Stourbridge, in county of Worcester, heretofore the property of John Bourne, Clay Merchant, together with Fire Engine, pit Shaft, now ready for work, gins, and warehouses at Bristol, Stourport and Stourbridge and at The Lye. The clay works at the Lye are the only works that supply the whole Kingdom with pot clay, without which glass cannot be made; and unless this work is carried on (which is not intended by the present owner) the whole glass pot works is likely to come into so few hands that the price will be considerably advanced. For further particulars apply to Mr Botfield, of Great Dawley or to Messr Marshall and Lewis, attornies at Law, in Bridgnorth, Shropshire.
(*Aris's Gazette*, 15 December 1783).

Interior of Jones & Smarts' Glassworks 1800.
The making of flint glass involved the mixing of sand, lead oxide and potash in specific proportions.
These ingredients were then heated in fireclay pots to produce a molten mixture known as 'metal'. In
this engraving the metal is extracted from the coal-fired furnace to be blown into various shapes by
the team of glass blowers. (Ray Shill collection)

Toledo Works of Charles Reeves.
This engraving shows the sword manufactory of Charles Reeves in Charlotte Street, Birmingham and
the adjacent private arm of the canal, the Whitmore's Arm. The cone is believed to be the glass cone
of St Pauls glassworks, which closed around 1858. (Great Western Railway Guide 1860)

Coalbourn Flint Glass Works, the Property of Joseph Webb.
Birmingham, Brierley Hill, Dudley and Stourbridge had their share of glassworks, where fine flint glass
was produced for the domestic and foreign market. (Great Western Railway Guide 1860)

Refractory clays also existed around Dudley Port, Tipton and elsewhere. In 1801 a
brickmaker was needed to make firebricks at the firebrick works, Long Acres Colliery,
near Wolverhampton. Wilkinson and Turner made firebricks at the Dudley Port Fireclay
Works during the first years of the nineteenth century. Bricks were produced in various
sizes for furnace lining in iron, copper, brass and steel works. Clay stone raised to the
surface was left to weather over the winter and then ground down to make the bricks.
Some of the clay mined was known as pot clay, which was a dark shiny clay, suitable for
glasshouse pots, melting pots and crucibles. Pot ground clay was sold from the canal side
near Dudley Port Bridge.

Old mine clay measures produced the best clays around Brettell Lane, Delph, Lye and
the nearby Cradley. Colour varied from near white, through grey to black. New mine
fireclays might approach the quality of the old mine clays, but frequently was not as good.
Those mines and fireclay works located around Brettell Lane and the Delph had access
to the Stourbridge Canal and were able to despatch both clay and finished fireclay goods
by boat.

The most prized clays were the pot clays, which were moulded into the glasshouse pots
used in the glassworks around Stourbridge, Brierley Hill, Dudley and Birmingham. Once
the clay had been brought to the surface, it began to break up into a powder, a process
that was assisted through weathering. It was ground up by hand and the pug mill into a
powder and mixed with water to make a malleable plastic material capable of moulding
into shape.

Canal construction enabled the development of the flint glass industry in Birmingham and Birmingham Heath. No glass appears to have been made there until 1785 when Isaac Hawker set up a small glassworks behind his shop in Edgbaston Street. The first canalside works in Birmingham were constructed for Johnson & Shakespeare in 1798, in Bagot Street, beside the Birmingham & Fazeley Canal. Brueton Gibbins was proprietor for some twenty or more years through to 1835 when Charles Thompson and George Shaw took over the Aston Glassworks. They remained in charge until the glassworks closed in 1843. On 29 May 1843 the presses, moulds and effects at the Bagot Street Glassworks, were offered for sale along with a quanity of glassware, cullet, borax and 20 tons of Isle of Wight and Lynn sand.

Bacchus and Green were responsible for the setting up of the Union Glass Works in Dartmouth Street in 1817. Their premises were originally placed opposite the Union Flour Mill and had basin access to the Digbeth Branch of the Birmingham & Fazeley Canal. Surviving invoices show that they obtained coal from local merchants, fireclay (for the pots) from Francis Rufford of Stourbridge and Lyman sand from Joseph Smith carriers at Horninglow who had brought the load from Gainsborough. George Bacchus, and George and Joseph Green formed the original partnership, but Joseph Green later left to manage the Aetna Glassworks in Broad Street. Union glassworks later transferred to a new location, in Dartmouth Street, and was carried on by George Bacchus & Sons until 1860 when George Bacchus retired from the trade. Stone, Fawdry & Stone then had charge of the business until the late 1890s.

The Belmont Glassworks were located above Ashted Tunnel and had a wharf beside the southern end of the tunnel on the Digbeth Branch. The glass cone was directly above the tunnel and must have been a significant landmark for boatmen navigating the canal. Belmont Glassworks was built and capable of making glass by September 1811 when the premises were sold to Thomas and Rice Harris. The Harris family at this time had charge of a glassworks in Fazeley Street. They sold the Fazeley Street site and concentrated on making glass at the Belmont Glassworks. William Gammon & Son owned these glassworks by 1835.

Thomas Harris began as a glasscutter before going into the glass making trade. Harris's Fazeley Street glassworks were probably located on the north side of the New Steam Mill with wharf space beside the Digbeth Canal. Early newspaper advertisements mention a cast steel furnace for sale in Fazeley Street during 1801 and it is likely that these premises were adapted as the glassworks. When Thomas and Rice Harris vacated the Fazeley Street works, the premises were adapted again for other purposes. Hicklings Chemical Works later occupied the wharf land north of New Steam Mills.

John Gold, a Birmingham glasscutter, leased property from Caroline Colmore to set up a cut glass works on the west side of Whitmore's Arm between George Street and Caroline Street. Gold's works became known as the St Paul's Glassworks. Thomson and Wilson later acquired this business. They continued to make glass there through to about 1858. During February 1858 the eight-pot furnace, cone, mixing and moulding pots were advertised for sale and the premises were converted for other purposes. Gold was also involved with the Aetna Glass Works in Broad Street where the Hyatt Hotel now stands. Aetna received supplies of sand by canal that was delivered to the basin that faces Broad Street. Joseph Green and then Alfred Arculus were later proprietors of the Aetna Glassworks.

Rice Harris established another glassworks in Broad Street after moving from the Belmont Glassworks. These premises, although not placed beside the waterway, were situated close to both the Islington and Oozells wharves. They were first known as the Islington Glassworks and were noted for big ugly cones, which belched out continuous clouds of black smoke. F.C. Osler owned a third glassworks in Broad Street. He made fine cut glass and chandeliers on the premises and made glass on a separate site in Freeth Street. Here was located Oslers glass cone and a wharf beside Icknield Port Loop. The Osler family built up an important reputation for making fine glass and chandeliers, but they may not have been involved in this business at all were it not for Thomas Osler, who founded the family glass making business. Thomas was educated at Bristol and first entered the medical profession as a general practitioner. He practised in the Bristol and Bridgewater area. In those days medical men visited their patients on horseback, but an accident to his knee made riding painful. Thomas Osler chose to come to Birmingham and eventually went into the glass trade.

Another two glassworks were established at canalside locations on Birmingham Heath. John Hawker had the works beside the turnpike at Springhill, and alongside the main Birmingham Canal, whilst Shakespeare & Son set up another in Lodge Road beside the Birmingham Heath Canal Branch.

Canal improvement continued to provide greater benefits for the canal user after 1800. Within the Birmingham area improvements were carried out to straighten some of the kinks in the line of the canal during the period 1795–1805. They included colourfully named locations such as Botany Bay and Sandy Turn. Botany Bay was better known as Birmingham Heath. But for those who went there this was a wild and barren district. To some it must have been like travelling to the penal colony in Australia. When the canal was first made there was a particularly tight turn at Winson Green. Late in the eighteenth century a deviation was made to shorten the route and at the same time create two small reservoirs along the former course. It is perhaps ironic that the name Botany Bay was chosen for this particular area because later both a workhouse and prison were built close to the canal at Winson Green.

Sandy Turn was near Sheepcote Street. The line of the canal from Birmingham first turned westward in a loop near a farm called the Oozells and passed under Sheepcote Street. It then curved back on itself at Sandy Turn to meet Sheepcote Street for the second time before again swinging northwards towards Ladywood. About 1800 work was done to improve the canal at this point. Rock was cut away to make the curve at the Oozells wider so that boats could pass with ease. A new course was also cut to eliminate the tight loop called Sandy Turn. The part, which ran towards Sheepcote Street, was filled in, but the name Sandy Turn was retained by the company and came to apply to that stretch of canal near Sheepcote Street.

During April 1808, John Rennie's plan for a new canal link between the Walsall Canal at Toll End and the summit level at Tipton was placed before the Birmingham Canal Committee. It was a scheme that used existing pieces of waterway with sections of new waterway. The 1783 Birmingham & Fazeley Act had provided for a branch from Toll End towards Horseley. A private canal link with locks had joined the end of the Toll End Branch to reach the Horseley collieries that belonged to Dixon, Amphlett and Bedford, and which had been built during the years 1793 and 1794. Proposed branches from the summit level down to mines in the Puppy Green district of Tipton also came to be considered from time to time. Committee minutes refer to an application in March 1801 by Hateley & Jesson to serve their new colliery near Puppy Green, which involved the making of a branch with two descending locks. Agreement for tolls and tonnage could not be made. During 1802 a more extensive waterway through the lands of Hateley & Jesson to the lands of Foley & Whitby was considered, again without apparent resolve. Rennie's link proved to be more successful.

During May and June 1808 land was purchased from Botfield & Co., Fereday & Co. and the representatives of the late Richmond Aston. In September minutes record that an agreement had been made with a Mr Nock and others to build the locks, bridges and other works on the Toll End Communication. Joseph Smith was contracted for the cutting at five pence per yard. Mr Fereday supplied lime and Mr Armishaw provided the timber. Rennie's plan included the purchase of the private canal through Dixon's Horseley Estate, which was finalised during 1809. Meanwhile construction proceeded quickly on the new section from Horseley through to Tipton Green. By 30 June 1809 the communication between Toll End and Tipton Green was reported nearly complete when open boats had to negotiate twelve locks down from Tipton Green to the Walsall Canal.

There was another kink in the canal between Sandy Turn and Ladywood Bridge. This piece was straightened between 1810 and 1820 and the former bit of the canal became a dock and wharf. Sandy Turn continued to be a trouble spot, boats frequently grounded there. By 1816 a scheme was formulated to build a canal from Sandy Turn to the Old Turn. In July, Jacob Twigg was instructed to inspect the embankment proposed for the deep cutting to Ladywood Bridge. Arrangements were made to purchase the necessary land from the Birmingham Grammar School. But, work on this project began slowly and took a number of years to complete. A plan of the intended canal drawn in 1821 shows the line passing through a short cutting. The single towpath ran alongside the eastern bank. As construction of this canal neared completion, the work was delayed in February 1824 because of an objection made by Miss Colmore. The cutting had crossed her land. The committee minutes note that work was suspended until a proper understanding was obtained. It was a matter soon resolved, for later in 1824 John Freeth Junior, clerk to the BCN, was able to report that the deviation had opened.

When the Napoleonic Wars ended, Britain was in the clutches of economic crisis. The papers often carried long lists of people facing bankruptcy and partnerships dissolved. However, within a few years trade flourished. New mines and ironworks were established and there was an increase in demand for branch canals to serve them. The main line was again clogged with traffic. In some places it had become shallow and boats became stranded on the shoals. The proprietors again faced the danger of losing trade if they did not improve their canal.

After John Wilkinson's death, his ironworks and furnaces at Bradley had passed into the control of John Turton Fereday. In February 1817, Fereday was noted as using the towpath near the works as an iron wharf. During April 1817 the BCN contacted Mr Adams, executor to Mr Wilkinson, about the towpath and it was decided to build a new line of canal to avoid the Bradley ironworks. A short cut was sanctioned which became known as the Bradley deviation. The new line simply cut across the curve as it passed by the Bradley furnaces. The work was accomplished in only a few months and finished in January 1818.

Rennie had also suggested a shortening of the line of the canal through Oldbury in 1807. It was proposed that a deviation or new line be made from the aqueduct at Oldbury to Rounds Green. Nothing was done at the time, but in June 1818 the plan was reconsidered. Two years later tenders were invited to cut a canal along a similar route to that suggested by Rennie. It was to run from Aqueduct Bridge to the Brades Hall Estate. The work was let as two lots. Lot one was a cut from Oldbury to the Brades, which joined up the neck of the wide loop through the centre of Oldbury. Lot two was a straightening of the canal through the Brades Estate, the old line went through the Brades Steelworks, the new one bypassed it. Six contractors tendered. The cheapest quote was clearly that tendered by Joseph Smith and he was awarded both contracts. However, the system of letting by tender has its faults, the cheapest quotes may not be the best. Joseph Smith's quote was far too low. He himself had to admit that he could not complete the job in the time allotted.

BCN Proprietors Minutes
(PRO RAIL 810)

	Contract 1 (£-s-d)	Contract 2 (£-s-d)	Total (£-s-d)
Tredwell & Wood	£1,844 0s 11d	£816 0s 1d	£2,660 1s 0d
Samuel Hyde	£1,660 0s 0d	£850 0s 0d	£2,510 0s 0d
Thomas Jackson	£1,668 5s 10d	£780 6s 8d	£2,448 12s 6d
Jacob Twigg	£1,724 0s 0d	£685 0s 0d	£2,409 0s 0d
Thos & Benjamin Bayliss	£1,619 0s 0d	£720 0s 0d	£2,339 0s 0d
Joseph Smith	£989 0s 0d	£458 15s 6d	£1,447 15s 6d

It was agreed that Smith should sign for contract no.2 and that the other contractors be contacted again as to what they could offer. Thomas Jackson in partnership with Samuel Hyde came down to £1,450 and the contract was given to them. Both contracts were sealed and completed by the end of May 1820. By November 1820, Smith's cutting at the Brades was proceeding well. 17,000 cubic yards of earth had been excavated and 4,738 yards remained to be cut. Jackson and Hyde's works were not so easy. In February 1821, it was reported that rock had been encountered in the deep cutting at Oldbury. Jackson asked for a further £1,121 7s 6d to complete the job. The improved line at Oldbury was opened May 1821 and evidently led to an increase in boat movements.

Thomas Jackson and his partner were also anxious for other work. At the time the BCN needed various repairs done to the puddles and banks along the line of the canal. Jackson and Hyde offered to repair the section from Spon Lane to Tipton. In March, when they found the rock cutting was not as serious as previously thought they offered to do the repairs for a £100 on top of the £2,571 7s 6d. The committee agreed.

By 1820 the Birmingham Canal proprietors were faced with two serious problems. The first was that despite recent alterations to remove some of the curves and turns the main line was still too long. The second was the water supply. The recent working of mines near

Capponfield had drained a company-owned reservoir. Even though water was pouring into the canal from the different mine engines, there still was not enough water to maintain the traffic from available sources. A new and bigger reservoir had to be built.

Between 1822 and 1824, the canal company contemplated several improvements. A shorter course for the canal across Rotten Park Valley and Birmingham Heath was considered in 1823. The next year a revised plan for the Bloomfield to Deepfield Cut was examined. But perhaps the biggest scheme was a new canal from West Bromwich to Tipton to serve the business interest of local coal and ironmasters. Land was purchased for a large reservoir at Rotten Park and a site for a further reservoir was investigated at Rushall. However, to carry these schemes into being and to suggest practical solutions required a talented engineer.

On 19 March 1824 the BCN committee decided to engage Thomas Telford to examine their canal. Telford came to Birmingham on 28 June and immediately after meeting the proprietors set out to examine the works. He spent four days examining the system then returned with his report. Meanwhile tenders had been placed for a branch canal from the old line near Swan Village to mines at West Bromwich. It was known as the Ridgeacre Cutting. Tenders were received:

Jacob Twigg, Darlaston	£3,309 18s 8d
Hyde and Jackson	£4,372 0s 0d
William Treadwell, Droitwich	£4,687 10s 9d
John and James Frost	£4,909 17s 5d

The contract was awarded to Twigg, but then the matter of extra payment was discussed as to whether Jacob Twigg should provide boats. Twigg was later allowed to increase his tender by £150 to allow for the hire of boats. Jacob Twigg was slow to embark on his contract and by December 1824 little progress had been made. Up to this time the favoured practice of excavating a cutting was by the boatload. But Thomas Telford was used to more practical methods. When building the Caledonian Canal, Telford had employed railways to assist with the moving of heavy materials. Now he recommended that Twigg be furnished with a set of iron rails to make a road. Telford presented his report before the BCN committee on 24 December. He had spent five months looking at the problems in between his other projects. He was to write, later, in his autobiography, his initial thoughts on the matter:

Upon inspection I found adjacent to this great flourishing town a canal little better than a crooked ditch, with scarcely the appearance of a haling path, the horses frequently sliding and staggering in the water, the haling lines sweeping the gravel into the canal, and the entanglement at the meeting of the boats incessant; while at the locks at each end of the short summit crowds of boatmen were always quarrelling, or offering premiums for a preference of passage, and the mine owners injured by the delay were loud in their just complaints.

Telford examined the problems set before him and found a solution. He decided that the many bends should be eliminated and a direct canal be cut from Birmingham to

Smethwick. At Smethwick a 70ft deep cutting through the summit was proposed and then the straight line of the canal was to be continued through to Tipton and the ridge at Bloomfield to Deepfields, north of Coseley. In one stroke the main line to Wolverhampton was to be reduced from 22 miles to a mere 14 miles and the part from Birmingham to Tipton was for the first time to be at the same level. Telford also proposed a 40ft wide waterway with perpendicular banks properly walled to ensure a good haling path on both sides.

In January 1825 Telford prepared the plans and sections for the contractors. These plans were given to a committee that comprised John Cargill, John Wilson and Thomas Townshend for examination. Meanwhile Jacob Twigg was urged to complete the Ridgeacre Branch. Estimates were also prepared for the Bentley Branch. This branch was to run from the Walsall Canal to furnaces then being erected at Bentley for the Earl of Lichfield. This canal project was later to be known as the Ansons Canal.

At the start of March 1825, Jacob Twigg reported quicksand in the ground at Ridgeacre. But, the railroad was now laid and he now promised to increase his exertions. Mr Mare reported that Twigg had actually done little work on his contract. The BCN decided that Twigg had been negligent and therefore had broken his contract with them. He was removed and the contract given to Jackson and Hyde.

During the BCN committee meeting of 18 March 1825, it was reported that Jackson had engaged in the construction of the Ridgeacre Branch. A week later, the BCN authorised Telford to complete a contract with Mr Townshend, or other persons he may think proper, to excavate the earthworks mentioned in his report. The work involved was to make a new canal across Birmingham Heath. It was a project that was to isolate the old main line through Icknield Port and Winson Green to two separate loops and forge a straight canal between them. Work on the excavation was under way on 24 June. By this date Mr Townshend had laid down a railway to convey the earth across the valley near the soap works.

Telford produced in August 1825 a detailed set of specifications for sundry improvement for the BCN. They specifically related to the line of the canal from Birmingham to Boulton & Watt's works at French Walls and the construction of the reservoir at Rotten Park. They show that Telford was responsible for effective replacement of the old canal with a new one of greater width and substantial build. His plan was laid out in five parts. The first alteration was referred to as 'across Sandy Turn, Birmingham'. It was to commence at the point where the three branches of the canal separate near to Hodnot and Everitt's and terminate at Ladywood Bridge. Much of the alteration was on an embankment. Telford suggested that the material be obtained by lowering the fields the canal passed through near Ladywood Bridge. The material thus obtained was to be boated to the site.

Thomas Telford was adamant that these fields were not to be cut down lower than 1ft above the canal top water. He also insisted that the topsoil be removed, laid aside, and carefully replaced in an even manner afterwards. Telford was equally specific about the dimensions of the waterway. The bottom breadth of the canal was to be 20ft and the depth of water 5ft. There was to be a towing path 10ft wide on either side of the canal and at a height of 1ft above top water. All tranverse slopes both in the waterway and on the banks were to be at the rate of two horizontal to one perpendicular. The puddle was to be 3ft thick and extend under the whole breath of the canal. And that same 3ft thick puddle was to be extended into the middle of each bank. The puddle within the canal was to be covered with a 2ft thick layer of earth, sand or gravel. The body of the embankment was to be consolidated as the work progressed under the direction of a superintendent, while the slopes were to be regularly and neatly dressed.

The towing path was to be made of crushed Rowley rag laid to a depth of 4in upon another 4in of furnace cinders. The Rowley ragstone was to be properly broken so that no stone should exceed 4oz in weight. The waterside of each towing path had to be protected by standard wooden piles. Each was to be driven into the ground at the edge of the top water line. These piles were to be covered by a wood capping 8in wide and 6in thick, which was to be secured at 5ft intervals with a mortice and tenon and spiked through. Behind the capping a row of close sheet, 3in thick, piling was to be driven to a depth of 3ft from the top of the cap and nailed thereto. The whole of the piling was to be of sound oak and the top of the cap 12in above top water. A new bridge was also to be built at Ladywood Road to Telford's specifications.

Sections 2–4 concerned the new line of canal across Rotten Park Valley, Birmingham Heath to the French Walls. This improvement commenced at Ladywood Bridge and proceeded in a gentle curve for a short distance before becoming a straight line across Rotten Park Valley. The course of the old canal was crossed on three occasions. The earth for the embankment at Rotten Park was to be obtained from the cutting of the canal across Birmingham Heath. That for the valley between Winson Green and the soap works was to be procured from the cut from the soap works to French Walls Works.

Telford realised that the cut across Birmingham Heath would generate more earth than was required for the Rotten Park Valley embankment. He suggested that the vegetable soil should be first stripped off and left in the fields beside the canal for the farmers to use. Some of the remaining spoil was also to be used to fill the small reservoir near Winson Green Bridge. The rest was to be used to strengthen the embankments and create a uniform slope down to the fields no greater than 1.5:1. The residual soil for the Winson Green embankment was also to be used to strengthen the sides. A straightening of the old line between Winson Green Reservoir and the Windmill was also carried out. Land was acquired from Miss Colmore in 1825 for the purpose.

This part of Telford's grand plan crossed the old canal at three points. The first junction was at right angles as the old canal passed from Icknield Port to Winson Green. The old canal was re-crossed for the second time after Winson Green Bridge and for a third time at the soap works. To assist with the construction Telford recommended that iron rails and sleepers be purchased by the canal company and lent to the contractors. The dimensions of the canal, rules of construction, etc. were to be the same as for the Sandy Turn section. Three bridges to Telford's specifications were to be constructed by the BCN on this part.

Telford's final specification referred to Rotten Park Reservoir. It was a scheme that tested the great engineer. The dam was the difficult part and Thomas spent a considerable time trying to sort out a suitable pitch for the slope. His final plan proved to be a model for many future schemes. William Mackenzie was appointed inspector of works and proved to be a very able engineer. In September 1825 Jacob Twigg was dismissed from his post as engineer to the BCN and replaced by Mackenzie. Jacob Twigg's luck now changed. His business failed and by 1833 he was bankrupt. On Christmas Eve 1833 his property at Darlaston was sold by auction.

At the start of 1826 new interest was generated in the canal from West Bromwich to Tipton across what was popularly known as the Island. This area of land was so named because it was bounded by canals on all sides, hence an island! Brindley's old canal, the Tipton Green to Toll End Communication and the Walsall Canal completely surrounded a mineral-rich area, but it was difficult to reach without expensive construction. Several schemes had been proposed. One favoured by Thomas Price, ironmaster, suggested a canal from the pound between the fourth and fifth locks at Ryders Green to the pound between the fifth and sixth locks at Tipton Green. Two locks would be needed on this line, each of 6ft 6in fall.

In January 1826 two ironmasters, Mr Dixon and J.T. Fereday attended a meeting of the canal proprietors. They were there to urge them to proceed with a communication between the Old Wednesbury Level and the Tipton Green fourth lock pond. Later that month Telford inspected the works then in hand, viz. the Sandy Turn Embankment, the reservoir and feeders, Rotten Park Valley embankment and the line across Birmingham Heath and was satisfied with the progress. He also put forward his scheme for reducing the summit at Smethwick to the Old Wednesbury level and to communicate it with the mines lying in the district known as the Island. Thomas Telford was again left to draw up his plans in writing.

The line across Birmingham Heath to the Soho Foundry was to create problems for the BCN. During 1826, Miss Colmore was again to involve herself in canal company affairs. One of Miss Colmore's tenants, a Mr Norton, had given the contractors permission to excavate on the corner of his land. The contractors were to give him the topsoil, and in return had to fence off his property from the diggings. This was duly done, but Miss Colmore came to hear of it and presented both Telford and Townshend with court orders to refrain from the excavation. The matter was taken to the Court of Chancery. Telford did not have to attend, but Townshend the contractor, McKenzie the resident engineer and Williams the navigator responsible for the work all had to give statements. Eventually the matter was resolved.

Telford's line followed a straight course across Birmingham Heath to French Walls. Several sections of Brindley's canal became loops off the main line. The largest remain today as the Oozells, Icknield Port and Soho Loops. Others were closed in part and became just arms or basins. The work was continued beyond French Walls. The old canal was widened and carried through Smethwick in a deep cutting. Vast amounts of earth were extracted and taken away by boat. McKenzie's notebook, which still survives in the library of the Institute of Civil Engineers, has a coloured plan depicting the progress of the excavations.

Telford's improvements created some spectacular engineering features. The great cutting at Smethwick must rank amongst one of his greatest achievements, but all along the route from Birmingham were features of note. The Dudley Turnpike crossed on a skew single-span brick bridge, which is remarkable by even the standards of modern engineering. There is Galton Bridge where the single-span cast-iron bridge made by the Horseley Co. has become a landmark feature. Another landmark is the listed Engine Aqueduct, made from iron, which conveys the Engine Branch over the new main at Smethwick, whilst further north is the Steward's Aqueduct, made from brick and stone, which conveys the old main line over the new main line near Spon Lane.

The new main line continued on to the bottom of Spon Lane locks, where the old Wednesbury Canal was straightened and widened as far as Pudding Green. Here was formed the new junction with the Walsall Canal. The new main line was continued a little further to cross the Union Branch and head towards the Albion where a branch was made at right angles to coal mines on the Gower Estate. Here construction work ceased. The Gower Branch included a tall embankment to pass over a branch of the River Tame, but any further construction towards Tipton involved a tall embankment across the Sheepwash Valley. Work on this section did not commence until 1836 and by then Thomas Telford was dead. Meanwhile the work already done was making vast improvements for the carrying of goods and favouring the carriage of merchandise.

four

MERCHANDISE TRAFFIC

The building of a network of canals through the West Midlands brought considerable benefits to local business and enabled the development of industry not only located on the canal side but at a distance from the waterway. Benefits were immediately apparent to those who chose to exploit mineral resources such as coal and ironstone mines, but there was also a growing merchandise trade, which supplied a far greater market.

Telford's new main line provided a significant improvement for boats travelling between Birmingham and Wolverhampton, but the work was only half complete by 1829 when construction terminated at the Albion and Gower Branch. Contractors had, during 1829 and 1830, built two branches north and south from the Tipton and Toll End Communication along a level section that followed the course of Telford's intended route from Birmingham through to Coseley. Tipton Green furnaces were served by the northern branch, which joined the pound below the third lock on the Toll End Communication. Thomas Townshend was given the task of building this link, which headed north and then turned east to the furnace yard and formed what was later to become the Three Furnaces Branch.

The southern branch also turned off below the third lock on the Communication Canal and ran south and then east along the perimeter of the Horseley Estate. The eastern section formed what became known as Dixon's Branch, whilst the main line was continued for a short length further south and included an aqueduct over Park Lane. The land then fell rapidly away at Park Lane and the intervening section between this aqueduct and the Albion became the next target for the canal builders. The massive embankment across Sheepwash Valley was achieved through engineering techniques perfected for the railway age. Plans for the Sheepwash Embankment were presented during 1834. The contract was given to Thomas Jackson who completed the job between 1836 and 1837, when the new main line canal was joined up with the Toll End Communication.

J. Walker was now engineer to the Birmingham Canal and it was his task to survey and supervise the work on several important projects. The Sheepwash Embankment was one of two challenges set before him. The other was the completion of the Bloomfield to Deepfields Cut that had been left unfinished. Mr Townshend had been awarded the contract to make Coseley Tunnel in September 1835. Work proceeded through 1836 and

1837 and in addition to the tunnel deep cuttings were required at either end. Work on the tunnel began in January 1837 after shafts were sunk from the surface. Cutting through the rock was made with difficulty. Walker noted in a report to the BCN Committee, for June 1837, that the tunnel makers had encountered loose strata where coal had been mined.

Tipton (Factory) Locks and Coseley Tunnel were finished in 1838 when Telford's main line was completed through to Deepfields. A long section of the old main line through Bradley, Wednesbury Oak and Bloomfield was now relegated to branch status, whilst the main line was directed under the hill at Coseley. Another long section of the old main line from Smethwick through Oldbury to Tipton was similarly bypassed.

Coal mining in the Titford district encouraged the construction of another canal link to mines, such as those belonging to Haines & Spittle. Not far from these mines was a Birmingham Canal Reservoir. Titford Reservoir had been constructed between 1773 and 1774 to provide a source of water for the old Birmingham Canal Navigation. A feeder from this reservoir was directed to the short summit level at Spon Lane, and continued to supply the summit after the alterations of 1788–1790. Thomas Telford changed this arrangement when he revised the method of water supply during the years 1825–1830. A new feeder was constructed through from Titford to Edgbaston Reservoir during this period and the old feeder course to the summit was abandoned. William Fowler devised a scheme to build a navigable canal from the old main line at Oldbury through six locks to Telford's feeder from Titford Reservoir. This feeder was then widened for navigation as far as the reservoir and across the face of the dam to mines near Whiteheath Gate, which could hitherto be only reached by a long tramway. Construction of this branch was conducted during 1836 and 1837 and boats commenced using this canal from 4 October 1837. The level at Titford was 511ft (od), the highest navigable section then, and the highest navigable section now on the Birmingham Canal Navigations.

Such were the extensive alterations of 1825–1838 that much of the old line became a branch waterway, whilst a fast route was created for boats to bypass the congestion that built up around the ironworks, foundries and furnaces that lined the old waterway.

Not all canal schemes were promoted successfully, however. Thomas Telford's last venture for a new waterway that joined the Regents Canal, in London, with the Warwick & Birmingham and Stratford Upon Avon Canal was one that failed. The plan was first proposed during 1829 and received considerable interest amongst Black Country coal and ironmasters. Despite various attempts to proceed with the scheme opposition from railway promoters finally saw an end to the venture. Despite the powerful railway contingent, many important iron and coalmasters came together to discuss the London Canal Bill in 1836. The list of names present was a fair representation of the existing Black Country industry:

12 February 1836
London Canal Meeting, Ironmasters and Coalmasters Present
Michael Grazebrook in the Chair

W.H. Sparrow & Co.	Bilston Ironworks
Philip Williams & Sons	Wednesbury Oak Ironworks
G. & E. Thorneycroft	Shrubbery & Bradley Ironworks
M. & W. Grazebrook	Netherton Ironworks and Dudley
John Barker	Chillington Ironworks
James Foster	Stourbridge Ironworks
George Jones	Coseley Ironworks
William Ward	Priestfield Ironworks
James Batson	Great Bridge Ironworks
Edward Dixon	Horseley Colliery
Samuel Dawes	Bush Farm Colliery
Richard Bradley (for Sir Horace St Paul)	Willingsworth Ironworks
Bradley, Barrows & Hall	Bloomfield Ironworks
Walter Williams	Albion Ironworks, West Bromwich
Edward Amphlett	Horseley Colliery
W. & G. Firmstone	Leys Ironworks, Dudley
John Round	Hange Colliery, Brades, Tividale
James Spittle	Wednesbury Colliery
Tipton Furnace Co.	Tipton Furnaces
Charles Birch	Bilston Furnaces
Chavasse & Co.	Cutlers End Colliery
John Dudley	Corbyns Hall Ironworks
Elizabeth & Samuel Holloway	Squarefield Colliery
Banister, Banks & Co.	Tividale Colliery
Richard Haines	Cophall Colliery
John Turton Fereday	Brades Colliery and Monmore Green Colliery
Ryding & Hunt	Swan Colliery
John Ryding	Balls Hill Colliery
B. Best (for R. Small, J. Shears and J. Taylor)	Corngreaves Ironworks
Thomas and Isaac Badger	Old Hill
Philip Williams & Co.	Union Furnaces, West Bromwich
John Bagnall & Sons	Goldshill Ironworks
George Parker	Coneygree Furnaces, Tipton
Houghton & Foley	Furnace Colliery
John Houghton	Whimsey Colliery, Oldbury

The interest of the ironmasters present clearly showed a lack of confidence in the existing arrangements. Boats venturing along the canal network to London had to negotiate many locks and several summit levels. Telford's scheme had promised to ease the journey, but contractors were already at work building the railway from London to Birmingham. Canal schemes like this had little prospect of success and regrettably our canal system was the poorer for it.

Banker, ironmaster and MP, Richard Fryer was one of the chief voices behind another proposal that would link the Birmingham & Fazeley Canal through Pelsall to the Staffordshire & Worcestershire Canal, near Calf Heath, as well as providing a new link from the Staffordshire & Worcestershire Canal to the Trent & Mersey Canal near Stone. One of the prime beneficiaries was the Pelsall Ironworks, which belonged to Fryer and happened to be on the line of the intended route. This scheme also failed and was quickly forgotten.

Merchandise carriers became quite numerous from 1800. They came from a variety of backgrounds. Some were road hauliers, who added the canal trade to their supply trade. Others specifically set up to carry on the waterways. They owned or hired a fleet of boats, which would ply a certain section of waterway. Common routes included the trade to the North West uniting the towns of Manchester, Chester and Liverpool with the Potteries and the Midlands. Another group tackled the route to London and the South serving places like Coventry, Leamington, Oxford, Reading, Rugby, Northampton and Watford. A third group served the Severn ports such as Stourport, Worcester and Gloucester, whilst a fourth looked to the East Midlands and the towns and cities of Derby, Gainsborough, Leicester, Newark and Nottingham. By these means carriers used inland navigation by canals and navigable rivers to reach many English manufacturing centres and supply many places with Midlands manufactured goods. These routes provided the means of import and export to other countries and lands.

Timber consignments were important canal traffic, but details of which were often hidden under the word merchandise. Timber had important uses for building purposes and for making carriages and furniture. British timbers included oak, ash and elm and these were frequently advertised for sale on estates around the country during the early part of the nineteenth century. Carriers would collect logs and trunks from the nearest wharf. Felled trees would be carried by road to these spots to be loaded into boats. This timber might reach the yard by canal or canal and river navigation.

Foreign timbers were imported via Hull, Liverpool or London. Thus it was that timber might be brought from America, India and Scandinavia to supplement British homegrown woods and supply the canalside timber yards, which grew up in Birmingham, Wolverhampton and elsewhere in the Black Country. Imported timber frequently included deals, battens, flooring boards and ceiling laths. The Port of Gloucester became an important receiving point for foreign timber once it had been established in 1827. Merchandise carriers vied with each other to bring the timber along the Severn to Worcester or Stourport, before transfer into a narrow boat hold and the final leg to a local timber yard, where it would spend time lying in the open for seasoning before use.

The Birmingham Timber Co., in Broad Street, had a wharf in Broad Street from 1793. They regularly advertised timber for sale. In 1802 sales included Riga, Danzig and Memel fir timber; Riga oak logs; Petersburgh, Norway and Archangel red and wood deal, hemp, ruffia, Swedish iron, tallow, tar and potash. Several yards were located alongside the Birmingham & Fazeley canal. Joseph Shipton, John Shelton and John Medes were in partnership at the Water Street timber yard until 31 December 1807, when Joseph Shipton left to set up another yard in Charlotte Street. Shelton's yard was carried on as Jones Shelton & Co.. Attorney Joseph Shipton decided to hand over control of his yard to son James Shipton and his cousin Maurice Shipton. J. & M. Shipton were trading from Charlotte Street by 1818 when they had baywood, deals, American pine and Norway timber for sale. W. Smallwood had a wharf at the bottom of Snow Hill that was known as the Honduras Wharf. Honduras provided an important supply of mahogany and Smallwood regularly had in yard supplies of mahogany in logs, boards and veneers. Smallwood also obtained mahogany from Spain. He also sold oak deals and boards as well Baltic and American timber. Mahogany was a favoured material for making furniture and local manufacturers no doubt benefited from the ease of supply. Several timber yards stocked this wood. In 1820 Jones, Shelton and Co. had stocks of both Spanish and Honduras mahogany.

Michael and James Shipton expanded their trade through taking yards at Wolverhampton and London. They also established a warehouse at Gloucester once the Gloucester and Berkeley canal opened for traffic. The Shiptons retained Charlotte Street through to the early 1830s, when James Shipton became involved in other business ventures.

Veneers were thin strips of certain woods that were cut and shaped to be inlaid into the surface of another wood. These veneers, were frequently made from expensive woods and when applied new were quite colourful. Different types of furniture, including boxes, chairs, desks and tables made of cheaper woods, had veneers included as decoration for an otherwise plain surface.

Timber merchants also dealt in slates and tiles for roofing purposes. Roof tiles were made in various local brickyards and especially around Yardley on the Warwick and Birmingham Canal, where the tile makers had a ready market for their wares. Slates were supplied principally from North Wales, but there were some that were also obtained from Westmorland. Slates were brought by coastal vessel from quays and ports near the quarries to the nearest inland navigation port. Liverpool initially had an important role, but with the development of Gloucester trading vessels frequently made the journey along the Welsh coast to the Severn Estuary at Sharpness, where they proceeded along the canal to Gloucester Docks. Bangor, Festiniog and Villenhelly became well known for slate supply. Slates were sold according to size and lots of 1,200. The largest were known as queens, which was a semi-official size that ranged from 30in by 18in up to 36in by 26in. More common sizes, in diminishing size order, were empresses, princesses, duchesses, countesses, ladies, doubles and singles.

James McTurk had slates and roof tiles on sale at their Lionel Street slate wharf in 1826. During 1829 M. & J. Shipton had on sale best Festiniog slates that included queens, duchesses, countesses and ladies. The completion of the Worcester and Birmingham Canal had opened up a new route for timber traffic into Birmingham. Several timber depots were opened on Worcester Wharf to take advantage of the River Severn timber trade.

Timber yards provided bark for the tannery trade. Few tanneries were placed at canalside locations. Birmingham had one beside the Warwick & Birmingham Canal near Heath Mill. This tannery was established about 1800 and remained in use for some thirty-five years before the premises were adapted for other industrial purposes.

Urban growth led to a bigger demand for slate and timber. By 1854 timber yards were common canalside features. In Birmingham yards existed beside all navigable waterways, but the largest concentration was at Worcester Wharf on the Worcester & Birmingham Canal. In October 1854 the Birmingham Journal carried several advertisements for timber merchants. Grant Brothers had established a yard at 60 Cambridge Street, the previous August. Messr Grant described themselves as timber deal and slate merchants and wholesale importers from America and the Baltic.

Wooden surfaces were protected by layers of varnish, which were applied over a period of time, each covering being allowed to dry before another was laid down. Varnish making was essentially a secret process, where the ingredients were mixed together according a recipe of the varnish maker's own design. Components included certain gums and resins that were principally imported from Asia. Linseed oil was another important ingredient, which was produced from crushed seeds from the flax plant. Flax fibres were also in demand for weaving into linen. Linseed oil was imported, like the gums and resins, into Britain and brought by carriers' boat, or wagon, to the varnish works. Samuel Thornley established a canalside varnish works in Lionel Street beside the Birmingham & Fazeley Canal and opposite the Water Street Rolling Mills. Meredith Brothers also had a canalside works in Lionel Street.

A similar product was lacquer, which incorporated a specific resin, lac, which was applied to a surface and heated in an oven. Lacquers were of particular use to brass fitting and ornament makers. When lacquers were applied to the surface of a brass casting or stamping, the dull brass surface was enhanced to a bright colour that ranged from yellow through to gold.

Canal carriers brought the essential ingredients for the making of a host of chemical compounds.

The demand for acid for metal treatment encouraged the establishment of several local chemical works. Birmingham town had a number of works that had been established for the treatment of ferrous, non-ferrous and precious metals. It was an industry that had begun with Samuel Garbett (1716–1803). Garbett had formed a partnership with Dr Roebuck for a laboratory for the assay and refining of gold and silver and manufacture of sulphuric acid. Another manufacturing chemist, contemporary to Garbett, was Robert Turner.

Some Chemical Terms

Aqua Fortis – Weak Nitric Acid

Borax – Sodium Borate

Copperas – Hydrated Ferrous Sulphate

Muriatic Acid – Hydrochloric Acid

Oil of Vitriol – Sulphuric Acid

Pearl Ash – Potassium Carbonate (or Copper Acetate)

Potash – Potassium Carbonate

Roman Vitriol – Copper Sulphate

Salt of Tartar – Potassium Carbonate

Soda Ash – Sodium Carbonate

Verdigris – Copper Carbonate

White Vitriol – Zinc Sulphate

Turner had a chemical works in the Jewellery Quarter facing Great Hampton Street. Turner produced oil of vitriol, aquafortis, roman vitriol and brilla there using lead vats, retorts and kilns. A horse mill was employed to grind down the basic ingredients. Turner's works were capable of turning out between sixty and seventy bottles of vitriol weekly. Both Garbett's and Turner's works were located a considerable distance from the nearest waterway, but chemical works established after 1800 were frequently built alongside the canal.

William Shorthouse, varnish and chemical maker, of New Market Street, transferred his acid making vats to a canalside site in Shadwell Street. Here Shorthouse established a works next to Heaton's Rolling Mills and alongside the Birmingham & Fazeley Canal. The Digbeth Branch, noted for the several glassworks established along its banks also had four chemical works. Armitage and Clarke who inherited Garbett's business moved acid making to a new site in Love Lane. Abel Peyton set up a new works in Oxygen Street and John Badhams established an acid and colour works in Dartmouth Street. Hicklings took over a site in Andover Street, near Fazeley Street Bridge, which they converted into a works to make artificial manure. All four works had access to the canal. By 1806, the business of Gregory Whyley & Co. of Bordesley aqua fortis and blacking makers was established beside the Warwick & Birmingham Canal. Whilst on the Worcester & Birmingham Canal chemical works were set up at Lifford, Selly Oak and Wheeleys Lane, in Birmingham.

Dobbs' Lifford chemical works was by far the earliest of this latter group. It was in operation on the same site from about 1793 through to 1847. Dobbs had moved his acid factory to the canalside location before the Worcester & Birmingham Canal had been completed there, but clearly benefited from trade when the waterway opened. The Lifford Chemical Works are not to be confused with the present Lifford Works, which were established by Sturge Brothers. Dobbs' works existed on the off side of the canal near Lifford. The plant was quite extensive, and included lead houses encased by bricks and covered by slated roves. There were stills, receiving jars, retort houses, bleaching chambers, vats and boilers, and a manganese mill. Lifford Chemical Works' site fell into disuse, but later was occupied by the West Suburban Railway Co., which used the land for their railway.

John Sturge began in the chemical trade making dyes at a small chemical works alongside the River Severn at Bewdley. He moved to Wheeleys Lane, Birmingham during 1823 where a similar plant was set up. Brother Edmund Sturge then joined the business and the firm began trading as Sturge Brothers. An important product of their works was citric acid, which was used in dying and calico printing.

Sturge acquired another works at Selly Oak during 1833, which was adapted for the making of oil of vitriol. The Selly Oak Works were located beside the towpath side of the Worcester & Birmingham Canal and had a basin that crossed under the towpath to serve the premises. Sturge's works were not the only chemical plant in Selly Oak. Mr Crooke had a soap and candle works there. Crooke's works were supplied with iron pans and boilers to process tallow to make stearine wicks, nightlights and candles.

At Tipton, there was a place known as Factory. Early census details and local parish records show that Factory was an industrial area inhabited by working families. It gave its name to the junction and locks on the canal and is forever remembered for that reason. The origin of the name is chiefly down to one man, James Keir, friend and one-time associate of Matthew Boulton and James Watt. In 1780 Keir and Blair established a chemical factory beside the canal on the site of the Old Bloom smithy. They purchased lead ore from Derbyshire and commenced manufacture of litharge and red lead, which was used in the manufacture of flint glass. Canal transport was anticipated almost from the start. In March 1781 Keir applied to the Birmingham Canal Navigations to make a cut across the towpath into his works.

From 1782 Keir also began to make alkali from salt, which was then used to manufacture soap. Yellow and mottled soap was produced. James also made a yellow metal, known as Keir's metal, which was an alloy of copper, zinc and iron. Keir's metal was used to make window sashes, but Keir had developed it to sheave the bottom of Navy vessels. Unfortunately the Admiralty decided not to use this product and the alloy found few practical uses. The Muntz family were more successful with their alloy combination, known as Muntz's metal. Their alloy proved popular for sheathing wooden ships' bottoms particularly to combat the destructive activities of certain marine worms.

Commercial carriers were used to carry the soap and also, no doubt, the lead ore and lead oxides. By 1795 James Keir also possessed a canal boat, which may have been used to collect coal from his colliery at Tividale, established in 1794. In later years Tipton soap

White Lead Works, Birmingham Heath.
William Herbert Architect produced a large engraving of the white lead works, Birmingham Heath. In this enlargement of a section of the engraving the detail of the offices belonging to the lead works is seen as well as the nearby boatyard (Benjamin Brettell) where number of new boats are shown on the bank ready for launching. (Local Studies Department, Birmingham Reference Library)

works were carried on by John Stephenson and Son who continued to produce both lead oxides and soap until the mid-1830s. The land was subsequently acquired by the Oxford, Worcester & Wolverhampton Railway who converted the site into a railway and canal interchange basin.

Adkins, Boyle and Nock established another soap works during 1818. Their chosen site was beside the line of the old Birmingham Canal at Soho, Smethwick where soap and red lead came to be manufactured. Boyle had previously been the manager at the Tipton Soap Factory, but had joined Thomas Adkins and John Nock in this new venture in 1817. The Atkins family eventually gained control of the Soho soap factory and carried the business on for a number of years (as Thomas Adkins & Sons). By 1866 it was one of three works manufacturing alkalis in the district. Soho Soap Works was initially placed alongside the route of the old Birmingham Canal. When the BCN straightened the main line through Smethwick to Telford's directions, the Soho Soap Works were served by a truncated half-loop of the old canal, which joined the new main line.

Other soap works included the Cold Water Soap Co., who had the Victoria Works alongside the private Dowler's Arm in Plume Street, Aston. Soap manufacturing plant was advertised for sale here in September 1881.

Lead had an important use in the local flint glass trade and as white lead as a paint ingredient. The British White Lead Co. and later George Atkins were associated with the Heath Lead Works, at Birmingham Heath on the Icknield Port Loop during the 1840s and 1850s. White lead, lead sheets and lead piping were made here during this period. The plant as described in 1850 included oil reservoirs, vats lined with lead, two grinding mills, mixers, washing mills, smelting and other furnaces and two ranges of carbonating troughs fitted with slate bottoms. A 30hp steam engine provided the power for the works.

Chance & Hartley were responsible for the building of an alkali works at Oldbury, when land was leased from John Houghton, the BCN clerk. Houghton owned a considerable amount of land at Oldbury and Spon Lane and Chance's Chemical works were built beside a private canal branch, which connected with the old main line, known as the Houghton Arm. In later years this branch also became known as the Chemical Arm, perhaps for obvious reasons.

During 1835, Chance built an extensive chemical manufacturing plant on the northern bank of the canal branch. In 1846 the manufacture of sulphuric acid was commenced there. Sulphuric acid was found to have many uses, which, in addition to the treatment of metals, included the manufacture of sulphates for fertilizer. Sulphuric acid, a corrosive acid by nature, was used at ironworks and galvanising works to clean metal. The acid was carried in large glass containers called carboys, and canal boats were commonly used as the means to take the acid from chemical works to ironworks. The concentrated acid often contained impurities and was usually brown in colour. It was often referred to as 'vitriol' or 'brown oil of vitriol'.

Chance Brothers built up a large fleet of boats. By 1846 Chance was sending cabin boats to Liverpool with ash and soda, and returning with stone from Nantwich. Their boats also made relatively short journeys. The Coventry Canal letter books have correspondence concerning trade in iron pyrites from the Glascote and Baddeseley collieries that commenced in 1849. It was anticipated that the traffic would be a boat a week. The Coventry Canal Co. desired to know the reason for the transport in order to charge a correct toll. Chance Brothers explained that they required the pyrites to extract sulphur and iron. By 1850 they were paying tonnage to this canal.

Trade in cotton and wool is generally considered to be a Northern speciality with the vast numbers of Lancashire cotton mills and Yorkshire woollen mills turning out a large quantity of goods. Yet the local waterways did have a few mills, which at one time or another had dealings in this market. Birmingham's steam-powered cotton mill in Fazeley Street has already been discussed. There were also cotton mills at Fazeley, near Tamworth with carding and spinning machines owned by Peel, Hardy & Co. Wolverhampton had an early worsted mill at Horseleyfields, which was in full work by 1801 and owned by Henry Penn, a Kidderminster carpet maker.

Worsted yarn was produced from medium or long fibred wools, which were first carded and then spun. Penns Mill had one carding engine and four spinning engines driven by a steam engine. Carding was a process for preparing fibres for spinning. Cylinders covered with wire teeth (cards) received matted fibres, which were separated through combing out and straightening by the action of the revolving drum. The straightened fibres were then sent to the spinning engines where the spindles spun the fibres into yarn. Henry Penn also had three scribbling engines that blended two or more fibres together. In another part of the premises were millstones, lathes and boring benches for grinding and boring gun barrels.

Penn was made bankrupt in 1801, but the factory continued to be used for other purposes thereafter. Canal carriers' cargoes included cotton goods, frequently known as 'Manchester packs', which were brought to the Midlands from wharves in the North West such as Castlefields on the Bridgewater Canal, in Manchester.

Weaving of belts and braces was conducted at the Brace Factory, Erdington, owned by the Carpenter family. The Brace Factory was placed beside the Birmingham & Fazeley Canal near the bridge that carried Holly Lane over the waterway. A steam engine provided the mechanical power for belt and brace making and the canal brought the coal for the engine. Brace making ceased when Samuel Alfred Carpenter died in 1870 and the factory was then briefly used for button making, before being taken by Alexander Parkes and Josiah Mason and converted for a refinery for nickel ores.

Traffic in corn was another important trade, which was handled chiefly by the carrier. A number of canalside steam-powered corn mills received grain traffic by canal to grind down to make flour and bread. Water- and wind-powered mills had long been employed to work grain into flour, but that same technology, which assisted the rolling of metals, provided the power for the carding and spinning of cotton and wool as well as the winding engines to raise minerals; it also produced an engine capable of turning mill stones. Another factor was the quality of the flour. People were concerned about flour being adulterated by some bakers to produce poor quality bread. A new idea was formulated, which involved the milling and baking on the same site. Joint stock companies were formed by public subscription to run a selection of mills and gave the shareholders the right to a regular amount of flour or bread.

The banks of the BCN had a number of flourmills, where the canal provided the means of transport for grain and coal. Sufficient finance was required to build a steam-driven mill. Joint stock companies established several mills where funds were provided by shareholders. These mills were more than simple places to grind wheat and corn into flour. They were also bakeries that produced bread in quantity. All were tall buildings comprising four or five stories. Canalside flourmills and bakeries provided an essential service to the growing local population. The merchandise canal carriers transported imported grain from ports such as Gloucester and Liverpool to the mills, whilst locally grown cereals often came to the mill by road.

Birmingham had the greatest concentration of combined steam-powered mills and bakeries. The Birmingham Union Mill, in Holt Street, was built alongside the banks of the Digbeth Branch Canal. It was established by the Birmingham Flour & Bread Co. that was formed in June 1796. This mill ground wheat into flour and also baked the flour to make bread. These were troubled times where wheat grain was expensive and bread was often adulterated with cheaper grains and other substances. Union Mill came into existence to supply a growing need for wholesome bread. Pickard's Flour Mill in Snow Hill had been the first, in Birmingham, to use a steam engine to grind wheat to make flour, and bread was also baked on site. However, the quality and price of his bread was called into question and Snow Hill Mill was attacked by rioters on at least two occasions.

Union Mill was the first of the joint stock company mills to be built in Birmingham. It was also the first of the many flourmills, in the district, to be erected at canalside locations constructed with the specific purpose of drawing on the advantages of canal transport.

Old Union Mill, Digbeth Branch *c*.1900.
The Old Union Mill had a long life. The original buildings commenced milling during 1797 and milling continued through to the 1880s when a serious fire substantially damaged the premises. The mill was completely rebuilt and it is the rebuilt mill that is shown in the photograph. (Birmingham Arts & Industry Magazine)

The subscription for Union Mill was limited to £20,000 in £1 shares. Each shareholder was entitled to buy a weekly amount of bread and/or flour. Union Mill, Birmingham, commenced work on 18 August 1797 grinding wheat bought from the Birmingham market and other sources within a 20-mile radius of the mill. In addition to catering for shareholder needs, the mill supplied loaves of bread to the asylum, hospital, soup shop and barracks. The buildings comprised the mill, complete with millstones and dressing machines, the bakery, engine house and a canal wharf beside the Digbeth Branch of the BCN. Four stones were provided for the mill, although only three were generally in use at any one time. The bakery comprised five ovens and generally four ovens were used for baking at a time. The annual consumption of coal was about 400 tons, which was equal to a boatload every three weeks.

Steam-powered mill construction increased during the nineteenth century. Birmingham had the largest concentration. Albion Mill was established beside the Newhall Branch in about 1803 and then the New Union Mill, on the old main line, was opened during 1813. There were three mills below the locks at Farmer's Bridge. Two were in Snow Hill, one was known as Old Steam Mill and the other as Eagle Flour Mill. A third in Princip Street was called the Britannia Mill. One of the Snow Hill mills, perhaps the Old Steam Mill, was also known as the Salutation Mill. The Salutation Flour Mill, described in 1822 included a steam engine and comprised a storeroom, retail shop and ten-quarter malt house. Three hundred sacks of flour were produced per week. There were also a small mill, known as Central, on the Digbeth Branch near Belmont Row, Town Mill in Summer Row close to Friday Bridge, a mill in Icknield Port Road on the route of the Icknield Port Loop; the Midland Flour Mill, on the new main line near St Vincent Street and also Lucy's Mill alongside the Worcester & Birmingham Canal. Once the New Union Mill was opened the original Union Mill became known as the Old Union Mill. The Union Mills brought about a stabilisation of prices and brought the business of milling and baking together as a large-scale operation. The success of the Birmingham ventures and others in London encouraged other joint stock ventures, such as the Union Mill that was owned by the Wolverhampton Flour & Bread Co..

Wolverhampton had a concentration of flourmills in the Horseleyfield district. Horseleyfield was a name of a street that joined the Walsall Turnpike and extended across the canal towards the centre of the town. It ran along a parallel course to the canal and between this road and the waterway was enclosed a considerable canal frontage. Here was built Penn's factory and worsted mill and Wolverhampton's first gasworks. The canal carriers Crowley, Hickling & Co., Thomas Best and Heath, and Tyler Danks all had wharves and warehouses in this area. The first steam flourmill was constructed near to the alms houses and occupied 2,418 square yards of land beside the canal. By May 1801 Mr Norton was the tenant of this mill.

Finance for the construction of Wolverhampton's first flourmill was found privately, but in 1812 another joint stock company was formed to build a rival venture on vacant land north of Crowley's Union Wharf. The Union Mill was financed through a subscription of 14,000 shares at £1 each. The first bread was baked the following year. Other canalside mills included the Horseley Mill, owned by Edward Harrold, and Albion Mill, owned by James Bradshaw.

Albion Mill came into Bradshaw's ownership during the early 1830s, although this mill might have been built a few years earlier. The land and basin that served Albion Mill was leased to Henry Pratt in 1828. The Pratt family were, at one time, associated with mills at Bloxwich, Ettingshall and Stoke on Trent. They also established a merchandise canal carrying business. Henry Pratt went into partnership with James Shipton, timber merchant of Wolverhampton, Birmingham and Gloucester and laid the foundations of an important carrying concern for grain and timber. They were also public carriers and conveyed all manner of goods in direct competition with the neighbours Crowley, Hicklin & Co. Henry Pratt built the first merchandise warehouse on Albion Wharf during 1828 (a second was built about 1832). James Shipton gained control of the Shipton & Pratt's carrying trade during 1831, when John Shipton joined the partnership in the place of Henry Pratt. They then traded as Shipton's.

Their warehouses at Albion Wharf had one of the longest connections with the canal trade in the Midlands and these buildings were still in use for this purpose during the late 1950s. They survived until the summer of 2003 when developers pulled them down for new housing. Until the end the name Shipton's painted in black paint was visible from the canal towpath.

Pratt's Mill, Bloxwich was erected beside the Wyrley & Essington Canal. The Ettingshall Mill (commonly called the Bilston & Sedgley Mill) was a large building with its own basin that ran under the mill and connected with the main line of the BCN. This mill was constructed about the year 1809 on land leased from Lord Dudley and Ward and had a number of owners including Pratt. The first owners were probably William Smith Bickley, Edward Hickman and George Deakin, who traded as Bickley, Hickman & Co. at the Bilston Steam Mill until 1814. Bilston Mill canal basin was used for both loading and unloading purposes. The mill was supplied with five pairs of French stones and one pair of Derby stones, which were driven by a steam engine with a 36in diameter cylinder. There was a dressing machine, a smutting machine and a set of elevators. 1,200 bags of flour were produced per week. Outbuildings included dwellings, a two-stall stable, a gighouse and open shed for twelve or fourteen horses. In 1834 the power of the mill engine was quoted to be 45hp. There were four dressing machines that maintained output to 1,200 sacks per week. Several ovens were erected on the premises to bake on a large scale.

A second mill was placed near Pothouse Bridge, Bradley. Tipton had two flourmills. One was placed beside the old main line near Owen Street and was sometimes referred to as the Tipton Green Mill and also the Dudley & Tipton Mill. Tipton Steam Mill was in use by 1803 when the owners advertised for a journeyman baker to assist baker and miller at Tipton Mill. The second mill, another Union Mill, was located beside the Tipton Green locks.

There was a mill beside the old BCN at Canalside, Oldbury, whilst Nock's Mill at Great Bridge stood close to the Walsall Canal. Rowley had a steam mill alongside the Dudley No.2 Canal. Here a 20hp engine was employed to turn two pairs of French stones. Machines on site were capable of getting up 200 sacks of grain per week. Walsall had several flourmills, but not all were canal served. The most notable of the canalside mills was Albion Mill, alongside the Walsall Locks Branch. This mill, erected in 1849, continued to be associated with the flour trade throughout the twentieth century and has only recently ceased milling. Trade directories also record a Birchills Steam Mill, which may have been near the canal. Some mills had a relatively short existence. Those at French Walls, Smethwick had a brief existence as a flourmill during the early years of the nineteenth century. This steam mill had four pairs of French burrstones, a dock for loading and unloading boats and stabling for eight horses. James Watt purchased the mill and later arranged for its conversion into an iron and steelworks.

Milling was not just confined to wheat. The corn trade actually covered a variety of items, which were both home and foreign grown. Ireland supplied large amounts of corn, which was shipped into ports such as Gloucester and taken further by river barge and canal craft. Barley, beans, flour, Indian corn, linseed, oats, oatmeal, peas and wheat were all classified as corn. One of the biggest importers was J. & C. Sturge.

Joseph and Charles Sturge were corn factors. Joseph Sturge had first started as a corn factor in Bewdley in 1814, and was later joined, in partnership, by Charles during 1822. The corn factors' business was precarious, and fortunes were easily won or lost. The Sturges had warehouses in Gloucester Docks where corn was imported. Sturge also had offices at 266 Broad Street, which were on the corner of Gas Street next to Griggs' corn warehouse, and a canalside warehouse in Cambridge Street. The main traffic to Birmingham was wheat, barley and some oats, and wheat for bread making comprised the bulk of this traffic. Corn was generally measured in quarters, which was equivalent to eight corn bushells. Weights varied, however, and Sturge's corn circulars mention at least two variations on the quarter and two on the bushel. Flour was measured in hundredweights.

Corn circulars mentioned current prices for a number of different produces that were dealt with at the Corn Exchange. Prices were set regularly for wheat, fine wheat, rye, barley, fine barley, malt, fine malt, white peas, 'boilers', hog peas, beans, tick beans, oats, fine flour and second's flour. All might end up in sacks to be carried in the hold of a narrowboat. On 6 March 1828, there was a meeting in Birmingham of farmers, mealmen, maltsters and corn dealers at the Public Office. Their purpose was to establish a corn exchange in Birmingham. John Greaves chaired the meeting, which decided to elect a committee to petition the Birmingham Street Commissioners with a view to setting up an exchange.

Certain canal carriers continued to specialise in the carriage of corn. W. & S. Foster were carriers who conveyed grain. They had their own mills at Tipton, which no doubt was an inducement. The local corn exchange dealt. William Foster started the business and operated a fleet of canal boats from his wharf near Factory Junction. Later the firm became William and Samuel Foster. General goods were carried and their fleet operated between London and Ellesmere Port. Boats owned by them included *Chatsworth*, *Dover Eliza*, *Florence*, *Harold*, *Leeds*, *Paris*, *Ranger*, *Rose*, *Rugby* and *Wye*. Iron ore and phosphates were amongst the goods carried from Ellemere Port.

The increasing iron trade continued to provide additional revenue for the canal carrier and local iron making received an additional bonus when Henry Hall, working at the Bloomfield Ironworks, Tipton, patented an improvement to the puddling process that reduced wastage and correspondingly increased production. Smelting furnaces continued to increase in number and outstrip local resource. More and more ironmasters developed mines away from their furnaces and brought ironstone by the boat for smelting. Canal carriers were also employed to bring ironstone from mines outside the district. By 1840, chalky ironstone came to be brought by boat from mines in North Staffordshire, whilst mines near Bedworth, Warwickshire also came to provide a ready supply.

Steam engine technology had created a demand for engineering works. Pioneers in this trade were Boulton & Watt who established the Soho Foundry alongside the Birmingham Canal at Smethwick during 1796, where castings for their various engines were produced. Another important engineering works was opened at Horseley, Tipton beside the Toll End Communication. The Horseley Works built up a well-deserved reputation for a variety of products. Their cast-iron bridges are still to be found at various canal locations. In addition to structural ironwork, the Horseley company also made a number of steam engines.

Non-ferrous metals were of considerable importance to industry in Birmingham and the Black Country. Brass, in particular, was widely used. There were many brass founders in Birmingham who fashioned the metal to a variety of uses. Bedsteads, gas tubing and ornaments are some examples to which it was put. Brass was first obtained from Bristol or from Cheadle in Staffordshire.

The price fluctuated and/or increased at the whim of the brass manufacturers. Birmingham businessmen believed that they could make cheaper brass themselves. The Birmingham Metal Co. established in 1780 was a syndicate of local businessmen whose aim was to buy brass and pass on the corporate benefits of group buying to their members. A transcript of the October 1785 meeting confirms that membership was restricted to users. Proprietors of the Birmingham Metal Co. included Peter Capper, John Darby, John Izon, Matthew Boulton, John and Samuel Pemberton, William and Thomas Price, and Thomas Underhill, who were all connected with the iron trade at the time. They also set out to manufacture brass themselves. Matthew Boulton and Peter Capper preferred to establish a brass manufactory at Swansea because coal was cheap in that district. Other members of the syndicate who wanted to set up a brassworks in Birmingham overruled them. Boulton resigned, but work went ahead to build the Brasshouse.

The Brasshouse was erected beside the Birmingham Canal and faced Islington (later Broad Street). According to the historian, Hutton, the cost of brass was reduced from £84 to £64 a ton after the Brasshouse opened. Brass comprises an alloy of copper and zinc. In the eighteenth century copper ore was brought up from Cornwall to be smelted into copper in the Bristol area. Zinc was brought from Somerset as calamine (zinc oxide) and both the copper and calamine were heated together in a furnace to produce brass in works such as existed at Bitton, St Philips and Siston. Brass was also made at Cheadle using copper smelted in Warrington and calamine from Derbyshire. As far as the Birmingham Brasshouse was concerned it seems that the copper was brought up from Bristol and South Wales, while the zinc may have come from both Somerset and Derbyshire. Commercial carriers would have been used for the transport; there is no evidence to show that the metal company possessed boats or paid canal tolls.

Copper was found in Cornwall, Devon, Ireland, North Wales and the Isle of Man. Once the ore was extracted, metallic copper was separated from the ore through heating in a furnace. It was a process that used a large amount of coal. Copper works were noted for their many chimneys belching out black smoke. Cornwall provided a rich supply of copper and several Birmingham businessmen, including Boulton and Watt, were involved with a syndicate to get the ore. People who mined in Cornwall were called 'adventurers', but it seems that this adventure was one too many and by 1800 the syndicate had been wound up. Cornish copper ore was transported across the Bristol Channel to South Wales where coal was in ready supply. Smelting of copper ores to produce copper metal in South Wales had commenced towards the end of the eighteenth century. Works had been established at Llanelli, Neath and Swansea. Swansea was particularly fortunate with good supplies of coal nearby.

Several smelting works were established near Swansea along the banks of the River Tawe, mostly with the aid of money from outside interests. Fenton & Co., also known as the Chacewater Co., established a copper smelter called the 'Rose'. Chacewater operated mines in Cornwall and used Swansea coal, both at Rose and in Cornwall. John Morris, a Swansea coalmaster, wrote to Boulton & Watt and mentioned this subject. His letter dated 11 April 1781 shows that a party of Birmingham businessmen were keen to establish a brassworks in the Swansea valley and a copper works had already been established by the Chacewater Co.

I have further to add that I have been informed that a set of gentlemen in Birmingham intend to set a brassworks in this country; as a coal proprietor I shou'd be happy to supply them with that article as I am satisfied the coal I have is of superior quality and you would be able to observe from the situation of my works, that I cou'd supply it cheaper than any other person in this neighborhood, which you well know is of the first consequence to a manufacturer of this kind. Last year I engaged with the Chacewater Comp/y to supply them with coal, & let them have a spot to build a Copper Works upon the Swansea River which is just now completed and I think that I could also let you have a very eligible piece of ground for the same purpose.

The Rose was actually controlled by Birmingham interests from 1793 until 1820. Their flyer for 1796 stated that they produced both copper and brass. Another syndicate of Birmingham businessmen set up a second works in about 1792. It was built next to Rose, presumably on the piece of ground alluded to by John Morris. The Birmingham Works was run by the Birmingham Mining and Copper Co. Copper ore was shipped from Cornwall and Devon to Swansea often in vessels that carried 125 tons at a time. The ore was off loaded into barges and taken up the River Tawe to the works.

It seems that copper was principally made for Birmingham interests, but sales were made to other customers. Proprietors of the company included Thomas Pemberton (Birmingham Brasshouse) and F. & S. Smith (Eagle Foundry). Copper ore was purchased by their agents or taken from their own mines until 1832, when the decision was taken to dissolve the partnership and close the copper works. The shutdown process began after Christmas and workmen began to be laid off. Copper production continued as long as the ore was delivered. The last shipment arrived in March 1833 and tough cake copper production then ceased.

Some copper was recovered from the bottoms of the furnaces and irregular shipments were made to Birmingham throughout 1833 and part of 1834. In 1834 the plant was offered for sale and disposed of. The firm was continued until 1838 in order to wind up their affairs. In addition to these two works, there were others set up by London and Bristol businessmen. A network of local agents was set up in large towns such as Birmingham and arranged for the carriage of the copper to their customers. The demand for copper in towns such as Birmingham increased during the first two decades of the nineteenth century. New copper works were set up as the Britannia Works on the Birmingham & Fazeley Canal at Aston. P.H. Muntz also operated a rolling mill in Water Street beside the Fazeley Canal that had been Birmingham's first steam-powered mill.

Copper was usually transported as tiles or tough cake (bar copper), but was sometimes was also carried as sheet. It was sent by coastal vessel to Bristol or Gloucester and then transferred into a Severn trow for Stourport (and later Worcester). The carriage by canal boat completed the journey to the West Midlands. Matthew Boulton required copper to manufacture coins and tokens at the Birmingham Mint, in Hockley. Good quality metal was required and at first it was sent in the form of sheets. The Rose Copper Co. appears to have been an early supplier. Matthew Boulton was a large shareholder in that company.

In 1805 Boulton entered into a new agreement with Pasco Grenfell to supply him with 600 tons. A price of £84 per ton was agreed, which was based on the price of copper (£68), rolling (£14) and carriage (£2). So large was the order that Pasco Grenfell actually supplied the copper from three sources. One portion came from his rolling mill at Temple Mill on the River Thames. Mr Sherratt's barge was to call for the first consignment at the end of January 1805, but a flood delayed the despatch. Sheet was also sent from the Greenfield Mills in North Wales via Liverpool. It arrived in Birmingham in boats belonging to Bradley or Henshall & Co. A third source of copper was Freeman and Co. who had a long-standing arrangement with Pasco Grenfell to supply copper.

The John Freeman Copper and Brass Co. had works both in Bristol and Swansea, but it was the Bristol plant that supplied the Mint with copper. On 13 January 1805 Boulton wrote to Grenfell with the rates of carriage from Bristol to Birmingham. It was stated that it would cost 10s per ton from Bristol to Stourport and about the same from Stourport to Birmingham.

By 1829 Boulton & Watt were buying tough cake copper for the Birmingham Mint from South Wales. The Hafod Works, which belonged to John Vivian & Sons, sent tough cake regularly to Birmingham. They used Gloucester traders to collect the copper. The *Belinda* and the *Sarah* were regulars on the run that picked up the cake from the Hafod Works at Landore on the River Tawe. They brought it down the river and across the Severn estuary to the Port of Gloucester, where it was handed over to Southan and Co. carriers. Southan brought it up the Severn and the Worcester & Birmingham to Worcester Wharf from where Boulton usually collected it.

The Port of Gloucester shipping imports were regularly published in local newspapers at this time. The Birmingham Journal often carried this information, which no doubt helped Birmingham metal merchants to keep track of the traffic. They show that in addition to Southan, William Partridge and Humphrey Brown also carried copper in their boats. The was a regular traffic from Neath, where the Crown Copper Works were located. The *Fame* often arrived at Gloucester Docks with a cargo of copper and spelter, and sometimes brass, to hand over its cargo to the carrier William Partridge & Co.

Another supplier of cake copper was James Harwood who was agent to the Birmingham Mining and Copper Co. until the works shut down in 1833. Harwood set up in business as

Harwood and Hodgkins at Sherborne Wharf and dealt in coal, cokes, brick and lime. He also continued to handle copper there. Williams, Foster & Co., Pasco Grenfell, Freeman & Co. and Crown Copper all sent loads of tough cake to the Birmingham Mint between 1834 and 1839. John Freeman Copper and Brass Co. had a wharf frontage in Broad Street from an early date. Clearly copper and brass was brought by canal to their warehouse opposite the Brasshouse and no doubt they were a large supplier of copper to the Brasshouse. The Birmingham Brasshouse was taken over by Thomas Pemberton in 1831 for use as a metal warehouse. Brass continued to be made there until about 1850. Rate books for this later period show that Pemberton owned an extensive property, which included warehouses, shops, a steam engine and machinery. There were also several houses on the site.

Brass was made at Spon Lane and Smethwick. Two brassworks were located beside the Birmingham Canal from an early date. That at Smethwick apparently was extant before 1780 and remained as a brassworks until about 1834, when it was converted into an ironworks. Their location on the canal would suggest that copper was brought in by canal to be converted into brass. On 12 December 1832, the Smethwick Brass Co. wrote to the Birmingham Mining and Copper Co. for 20 or 30 tons of shot copper. The request was declined as stocks were being run down. Little is known about the Spon Lane brassworks except its location. It stood between Kendrick's Works and Spon Lane and had wharf frontage beside the old line of the Birmingham Canal.

Muntz metal was another alloy of copper and zinc, but which had a higher percentage of zinc. It was patented by the Muntz brothers, George and Peter, in 1832 and quickly replaced copper as the metal used to sheave the bottom of wooden ships. George Muntz took over the French Walls Steelworks, Smethwick in 1842 and converted it to make the yellow metal. His bother Peter established a separate concern at Ryders Green to make Muntz's metal. Both works relied heavily on canal transport to provide them with copper, zinc and coal.

A new process, which made brass from copper and zinc (spelter), superseded the older calamine method. By the mid-1830s there was traffic in spelter along the waterways. Gloucester shipping returns mention spelter as early as 1830. Spelter was regularly consigned by canal and there was traffic in this product to several local brass works. Elliot's Metals received spelter by canal soon after they set up their Selly Oak works in 1863. Elliot's works fronted the Worcester & Birmingham Canal, but received coal from the BCN. During the first years of their operation, Elliot's engaged in negotiations with the BCN for the most favourable tolls for coal. The proprietors refused their request, however, because the amount carried to their works did not justify the reduction. The Selly Oak works was gradually enlarged and eventually had two basins, which joined the Worcester & Birmingham Canal and most traffic was received by canal boat. Ekington and Mason (later Elkington's) established copper works at Pembrey and used electrolytic means to extract copper and other metals such as silver and gold. Elkington's also set up an electroplating works in Birmingham during 1841. These premises were located on either side of the Birmingham & Fazeley Canal in Newhall Street where they produced silver-plated wares. A wharf was established beside the canal so that coal and chemicals could be delivered to their premises. By 1850 business had improved and additional wharf space was sought from the BCN.

Elkington's works also bounded the Whitmore Arm, which came off the Fazeley Line between the seventh and eighth locks. This was a lengthy branch canal that passed under Charlotte Street and George Street and terminated not far from the Parade. The Whitmore Arm served various works including coal merchants wharves and a timber yard. At the terminus was a copper and brass works once owned by H.H. Vivian & Sons. During the latter half of the nineteenth century copper began to be manufactured in the West Midlands. The first was the Tharsis Copper Works. It was built beside the old BCN at Oldbury and processed the waste copper ores produced by Chance's chemical works. During the First World War another copper works was established near Walsall. The James Bridge Copper Works was erected beside the Walsall Canal in 1917. The old basin that previously served the ironstone mines had a new lease of life to receive coal brought to the works by canal.

With the increasing general availability of zinc metal a new process for coating iron with zinc for general protection against corrosion and rust first came to be used in Britain during the 1830s. J. Crawford's patent of April 1837 opened the way for commercial manufacture. By 1843 two firms were trading from Birmingham making galvanised goods. These were Morewood & Rodgers of Broad Street, and Tupper and Co. of Berkeley Street. Morewood's business also became associated with the firm of John and Edmund Walker of Gospel Oak Ironworks from 1847. Walker's had an important trade in making cannon balls, but this form of ordnance was rapidly becoming outdated and Walker's looked to other forms of revenue; a new galvanising plant at Gospel Oak provided a new business opportunity for the firm.

There soon developed a structural demand for sheet iron for roofing purposes. Several iron rolling factories in the Black Country, located around Bilston and Gospel Oak, were adapted to make galvanised sheeting. Such sheets were provided either flat or corrugated. The machines that corrugated the iron gave additional structural strength for the roof. Not all ventures proved successful, the Galvanised Iron Co., with works in West Bromwich, Darlaston and Corbyns Hall failed in 1849. Morewood's also had difficult times and the name Morewood was featured in several company titles thereafter.

Items to be galvanised were cleaned in an acid bath before being dipped in a bath of molten zinc. It was a technique that had been long practised in the trade of tin plating. The West Midlands are rarely associated with the tin plate trade, although there were firms in the district engaged in this trade. The best-known area for tin plate was South Wales, where many firms came to be established. Wolverhampton had a group of tin plate works in the Horseleyfields area located near the junction with the Wyrley & Essington and Birmingham Canals. W. Henderson owned the Horseleyfields Tinplate Works that made rolled sheet iron as other ironworks. There was also a tin house building where tin pots were used to heat up tin to a molten state and cast iron and lead pickling vats employed to clean the iron before coating with tin. These works were sold to William Hanbury Sparrow, who renamed these works Osier Bed and supplied them with iron made at the Osier Bed Furnaces, Bilston and his other furnaces near Stoke on Trent. Baldwin & Sons, who already had works at Wilden and Stourport, established another Tin Plate Works at Horseleyfields. These works were built on a strip of land placed between the Osier Bed Works and the Crane Foundry.

Hay was common traffic from agricultural areas, and boats returned with loads of coal. Hay was used as provender to feed horses, etc. in municipal and industrial undertakings.

Canal carriers often carried ale, beer and spirits. Crowley, Hicklin and Co. were included amongst a group of carriers, which provided lock-up boats for wines and spirits. Brewing was usually conducted on a small scale by retail brewers supplying the needs of their customers through brewing on their premises. Some breweries produced bottled ales intended for a wider market.

Barley was used to make malt for brewing and vinegar making. The malthouse was a common canalside feature, where barley was brought by boat to be steeped with water and allowed to partly germinate. The skill of the maltster relied on the knowledge of when to stop germination and grind the barley grains to extract the malt. Canalside breweries were less common at this time. Wholesale brewing had yet to gain favour and only certain firms chose to brew for the trade. Retail brewing where a beer shop, or public house, owner brewed to serve those that frequented their establishment was far more common. Malsters did well by this arrangement and despite a tax on malt, had a lucrative market amongst the retail brewing trade.

Another element in brewing was the hops used to flavour the beer. Hops were principally grown in Kent, Sussex and Worcestershire and were picked during August and September. Each season hops were sold to the brewers, often in pockets that bore the name of the grower and year. Pockets of hops were regularly sent with merchandise carriers to merchants' warehouses for distribution.

Beer and ale brewing generated a certain carriers trade particularly with the barley used for malting. One of Birmingham's earliest breweries was located beside the Birmingham & Fazeley Canal in Blews Street. It was known as the Britannia Brewery and functioned as such until about 1812 or 1813. Few breweries then existed in the district and the number around Birmingham, at this time, was limited to two or three who undertook the wholesale brewing trade. Most brewers were associated with the retail brewing trade, brewing on their premises to suit the needs of inn or beerhouse customers. Those who owned the Britannia Brewery seemed keen to compete for the bottled beer trade, for which the Burton Brewers had a ready market, or the stout or porter produced by the Guiness Brewery at Dublin, and looked to the canal to distribute its beers to a wide market.

It was a business not given to the greatest success and eventually the Britannia Brewery closed down and the premises were subsequently used as a nail factory and later a bedstead factory. The Birmingham Brewery, near Broad Street, was served by a canal basin from about 1815. The brewery and maltings were built beside the Paradise Street branch rising gradually to the higher level at St Peters Place. Like many ventures of the time the brewery was financed by a group of people who all had shares in the concern. After the brewery closed the malting continued to be worked by Henry Mitchell to c.1880. Brewing required a good supply of water and many local breweries were established in areas where water could be pumped to the surface. Most Birmingham and Black Country breweries were placed away from the waterway. Yet there was one individual, Walter Showell, who embraced canal transport. Showell established his brewery at the Crosswells, near Langley Green, to tap a good supply of water. He maintained a fleet of at least seven cabin boats between the Crosswells Brewery at Langley Green and distribution depot Crescent Wharf in Birmingham. They also worked to destinations such as London and Stoke. The maltings (although modified and enlarged) still remain a canalside feature on the Titford Branch Canal. Their present owners are the

Wolverhampton & Dudley Breweries who still make malt by traditional methods. Other local brewers who had canal traffic included the Holt Brewery at Holt Street that was established by Fulford, and although not directly on the canal was close enough to receive traffic sent to the Digbeth Branch. Davenports Brewery, Bath Row, was directly on the Worcester & Birmingham Canal and received coal by boat until the early 1960s.

Several Burton brewers had ale stores in Birmingham and there was traffic in beer and empties from the larger breweries in Burton on Trent. Carriers appear to have been the principal means that beer and ale reached the West Midlands, but in later years some of the breweries owned boats. There was the *Stockport*, for example, which was a boat owned by Samuel Allsopp & Sons and was registered in Birmingham in 1914.

Coventry Canal letter books mention trade in ale along the canal from Fradley to Whittington Brook or Huddlesford by Pickfords and later Bridgewater Trustees. No doubt an important part of these goods was carried to Lichfield, and perhaps Wolverhampton (Huddlesford) or Birmingham (Whittington Brook). Details of this trade can often be gleaned from overcharges.

Ale Traffic Carried by Duke of Bridgewater's Trustees Coventry Canal Letter Books

Date	Steerer	Route
1 December 1850	Mayfield	Fradley–Whittington
5 January 1851	Mayfield	Fradley–Whittington
17 January 1851	Hodgson	Fradley–Huddlesford
22 January 1851	Mayfield	Fradley–Whittington
2 February 1851	Jno Hill	Fradley–Huddlesford
21 February 1851	Hodgson	Fradley–Whittington
28 February 1851	Hodgson	Fradley–Whittington
16 March 1851	Harland	Fradley–Huddlesford
1 April 1851	Rice	Fradley–Whittington
4 April 1851	Mayfield	Fradley–Whittington
9 April 1851	Hodgson	Fradley–Whittington
17 April 1851	Hodgson	Fradley–Whittington
22 April 1851	Mayfield	Fradley–Whittington
6 May 1851	Hodgson	Fradley–Whittington

Bass, Ratcliffe and Gretton had an ale store in Cambridge Street, and there is mention of this store in the 1845 trade directory. Later this store was moved to 74 Newhall Street. Ind Coope also had a store in Broad Street, Birmingham, which dates from the time they established a brewery in Burton in 1863. A year later, 1864, Ind Coope had moved to 158 Great Charles Street that had wharf premises beside the Newhall Branch. Ind Coope called this wharf the India Wharf after the India Pale Ale produced by their brewery. The large Burton Breweries were Bass, Allsopp, Ind Coope and Worthington. All were connected by a complex railway system, which had developed from the 1860s. However, despite the large volume of traffic sent by rail there remained significant canal traffic from Horninglow and Shobnall Wharves.

One of the earliest carriers of Burton ale would have been the Burton Boat Co.. By 1800 they already possessed a large fleet of vessels. They had narrow boats for working canals such as the Trent and Mersey and wide boats for the navigation of the Trent. They also had three boats built specifically for the Bond End Canal, in Burton, which they had they leased.

Burton's first navigation was the Upper Trent, which relied on two locks at Burton Forge and Kings Mill to maintain a proper navigation through to the natural limit for boats at Wilden Ferry. Burton's main breweries developed on the Trent side of the town lining the banks of this river. Ownership of the Upper Trent Navigation was in the hands of the Paget family who also owned considerable property in Burton. The Burton Boat Co. came to lease the Upper Trent Navigation and made improvements to the river wharves that were situated in the Bond End district of the town. They were also instrumental in the building of a private canal chiefly through the lands of the Paget family from Bond End through to Shobnall during the years 1770 and 1771. It was their intention to capture the trade from the Trent & Mersey Canal, which was also then under construction from Great Hayward through to the Trent. The proprietors of the Trent & Mersey Canal decided to oppose the Burton Boat Co. scheme and continued construction of their canal through to the Trent further down stream. The first connection was made above Kings Mill Lock, but eventually the line of the canal was made through Shardlow to meet the Trent at the mouth of the River Derwent.

Even though the Bond End Canal was completed to Shobnall, all goods passing onto the Trent & Mersey had to be transhipped across a strip of land to the Trent & Mersey Canal. Here the Burton Boat Co. retained a warehouse and also operated a fleet of narrow boats that travelled to the West Midlands or further north. A separate collection of warehouses was established beside Horninglow Road Bridge for the use of the Trent & Mersey Canal Co. and both Horninglow and Shobnall competed for the canal trade of malt, hops, barley and beer.

Every attempt to breach the land at Shobnall was resisted by the Trent & Mersey Co., until the Burton Boat Co. threatened to continue the navigation of the Trent beyond Wichnor thereby providing a new competitive route. The price to stop this new development was to allow the Burton Boat Co. to build a lock at Shobnall.

Burton brewers preferred to send their trade via the Horninglow Wharves, which included the principal brewer Bass, Ratcliffe & Gretton. Some trade was retained by the Bond End Canal and continued through to the 1860s. Timber traffic for Perk's Timber Yard as well as traffic for Allsopp's Ale Store, Hill's Brewery and Meakin's Brewery continued to pass from Shobnall to Bond End and the river warehouses near Fleetstones Bridge. This trade effectively ceased when the railway branches were constructed to the Hay and the brewery extensions made by the major brewing concerns effectively placed much of the traffic in the hands of the railway companies. Midlands' railway contractors then moved in to convert the bed of the disused waterway into a railway. Work commenced on the reconstruction during 1874 and the finished Bond End Railway Branch became a useful addition to the network of tracks that served the breweries, cooperages and other work. Interchange facilities between railway and canal were retained at Shobnall for the canal trade.

five

RAILWAY AGE

Competition from new railway companies became a reality during the 1830s when the first public railways were constructed. Canals in some areas were closed through the loss of trade and some, such as the Leominster and Oakham Canals, even had their routes taken over and converted for railway use. Local canal building continued unabated during the 1840s, 1850s and 1860s and by 1860 some 157 miles of waterway were controlled by the Birmingham Canal Navigation proprietors.

Various factors had led to this final expansion. Traffic increase, new industries and the development of a new coalfield all played a part in influencing the building of new waterways. Birmingham Canal proprietors first became concerned about the amount of traffic using Farmer's Bridge Locks. These were lighted by gas and worked by day and night and to ease this problem. One proposal considered was to double the flight of locks using the large side pounds as the second set of locks, but this idea was dismissed in favour of a totally new waterway. The final scheme that was adopted became the Tame Valley Canal.

It was built over a four-year period with the engineering help and skills of William Fowler and James Walker. A young John Robinson McClean also assisted in this venture. Construction involved extensive engineering features with a long deep cutting through the sandstone at Perry Barr and extensive embankments beyond. The Tame Valley was a very straight canal and remains a credit to the engineering skills of the day. First plans had the canal following a curved route from Great Barr through to Wednesbury, but the route was revised to divert northwards and make a junction with another proposed canal, which was to link with both the Tame Valley Canal and Daw End Canal, when the possibilities of new mines being opened on Cannock Chase became evident.

Whilst plans for the Tame Valley Canal were finalised another important set of negotiations led to the merger of the Birmingham Canal and Wyrley & Essington Canal. The Wyrley & Essington Canal remained independent through to 1839, when arrangements were finally made for the merger with the Birmingham Canal Navigations. Events then overtook planned work. The Curly-Wurly, as it was sometimes known, was in some ways a neglected waterway. The potential for new industry along the banks was great, but industry was in decline. Mines and ironworks were closing or had closed. Essington Wood Collieries had ceased operation and few of the coal pits on the Brownhills

Colliery were in work. The mines in North Walsall with their reserves of ironstone had not been worked to their full potential and local businessmen were concerned for the declining traffic. Walsall businessmen petitioned both the Birmingham Canal Navigations and the Wyrley & Essington Co. for more links. The northern outlet for their traffic along the Wyrley & Essington Canal was then restricted to Huddlesford and Wolverhampton. Walsall businessmen went as far as employing an engineer and contemplating a short junction canal from Birchills to the Walsall Canal. Their action was only forestalled by the agreement of 1839. It was the Birmingham Canal Navigations that earned the right to finish off what became known as the Walsall Junction Canal.

Parliament sanctioned the merger of the Wyrley & Essington Canal and the Birmingham Canal Navigations in 1840, but the Birmingham Canal engineers had already spent time improving fences, towpaths and bridges. The Walsall Junction Canal was first completed during 1841 and was essentially a flight of eight locks that climbed up from the Walsall level to the Wolverhampton level, a rise of 65ft. Thomas Townshend was appointed contractor for the Walsall Locks in July 1840. He quickly set to work on excavation then commenced building the locks and bridges. It was the contractor's task to purchase bricks, stone, timber and ironwork. Bridge building had its share of ironwork. Local foundries provided castings for the bridges, such as the supporting beams. Walsall Locks appears to have been Townshend's last contract for the Birmingham Canal Navigations. He went on to make various railways before suffering bankruptcy.

Several new contracting partnerships came to do work for the Birmingham Canal on the Tame Valley and other connecting waterways. The Birmingham Canal Navigations had already contemplated various schemes to link with the Tame Valley and reach the mines around Willenhall, Wednesfield and Bloxwich. One scheme was a railway from the Ansons Branch that headed north into the middle of the Bloxwich Colliery district and land owned by Lord Hatherton. Contracts were let in 1839 for the making of this railway that was to be known as the Hatherton Railway.

Hatherton Railway was a single-line narrow-gauge tramway that ran alongside a wharf at the end of the Ansons Branch. It passed close to the Earl of Lichfield's Bentley furnaces and brought both coal and ironstone onto the canal from Lord Hatherton's mines. Hatherton was one of the first BCN-owned tramways, another was the Bunkers Hill Tramway constructed during 1845 by James Frost, surveyor and contractor to link the short Willenhall Branch with mines in the Bunkers Hill district on the boundary between Bilston and Willenhall.

Coal and ironstone mining around Willenhall and Darlaston developed during the 1830s and 1840s. Several of the large iron making firms had long tramways that were gradually extended towards Portobello, Willenhall and Wednesfield. Following the merger with the Wyrley & Essington Canal, the line through Willenhall was revised as the Bentley Canal. This waterway left the Anson Canal and passed through Sandbeds near Willenhall to join the Wyrley & Essington Canal near Willenhall. Flights of four and six locks were required to convey boats between the Wednesfield and Walsall levels. The Wyrley & Essington Canal at Wednesfield was made some 6in higher than the Birmingham Canal at Wolverhampton, but this was changed during the 1840s and the same level at Wolverhampton was maintained through to Ogley Hay and Daw End.

The first contract for the Bentley Canal was let to John Woodward from Brighouse in January 1841, whilst the remainder for the Bentley Branch Extension was given to local contractors Matthew Frost and John Bate during July 1841. The contract for the Tame Valley was also let in January 1841 to William Radford of London. Radford decided to decline the job and was replaced by a group of contractors, Tredwell, Jackson, Bean and Gerrard, who agreed to share the work.

Severe frost hampered construction during November 1841. Masonry work on both the Bentley and Tame Valley Canals was stopped although digging was allowed to continue, no doubt, to the complaints of the navvies who had to cut through the frozen ground! The Bentley Canal, the second new link with the Wyrley & Essington Canal, was completed during 1843. James Shipton was amongst the first to send a boatload of merchandise along the canal in June 1843.

The Tame Valley was finally completed in 1844 and formed a new double towpath waterway that connected the Birmingham & Fazeley Canal at Salford Bridge with the Walsall Canal at Ocker Hill. Thirteen locks were needed to raise the waterway from the Erdington Pound and the Walsall level at Perry Barr. At the same time the Birmingham and Warwick Junction Canal was completed to join Salford Bridge with the bottom of Camp Hill Locks on the Warwick & Birmingham Canal. The combined route provided a diversion for traffic to avoid the congestion of central Birmingham and head directly to the heart of the Black Country. It must rank as one of the first, and one of the few, canal bypass scheme in the country.

Managers for a greatly enlarged Birmingham Canal Navigation found it necessary to revise staff levels and organisation. During 1842 a decision was made to increase the number of inspectors looking after the day-to-day operation. Five people were appointed to look after the four districts into which the BCN was divided:

BCN Districts
(PRO RAIL 810)

District	Name	Salary
1	John Bourne	£163 16s
2	Joseph Smith	£130
3	William Collins	£130
4	Richard Stephens	£180
4	James Thomas	£130

The engineer at Ocker Hill was Edward Nock at salary £248

Birmingham Canal workers were actively engaged in various projects at the same time. Perhaps their most important task at this time was the repair and replacement of the locks between Ogley Hay and Huddlesford. Many of the thirty locks required extensive repairs. The Wyrley & Essington Canal also had some wooden swing bridges that the BCN replaced.

The Rushall Canal was the third, and last, link with the Wyrley & Essington to be finished. It was completed in 1847 and needed nine locks to join the Tame Valley Canal with the

Daw End Canal near Hay Head. Construction of the Rushall Canal had been delayed whilst contractors worked to complete the Bentley and Tame Valley Canals. Meanwhile Dugdale Houghton set about contacting landowners and preparing costs. His letter to John Freeth, clerk to BCN, shows some of the basic problems that beset any new project:

Birmingham 28 July 1842

Immediately after the last meeting of the committee I waited upon Mr Maclean with the plan of the Rushall line of canal and with him examined the lands through which it is intended to be made in order to ascertain the state of the crops. We found that by far the greater number of fields had either mowing grass or wheat or oats growing upon them and that any interference there would be a serious charge for damages. I therefore with the approbation of Mr Freeth delayed taking any proceedings to ascertain the quantity of land that would be required for the canal from each field. I however seen the agents for most of the landowners and explained to them the nature of the proposed agreement and have as yet found no objection. The meadows are now free from grass and I am in hopes of being able to lay some agreement before the committee at the next meeting.

I am, dear sir
Yours truly
Dugdale Houghton

Houghton did not find the fields clear until the end of September, when he set out a centre line and determined the quantity of land required. Another two years would pass before work would start. During October 1844 Houghton wrote again to Freeth informing him that the whole of the line for the canal was set out and the men were marking out on the land. Many agreements for the land had been signed and he was about to progress the outstanding land purchase from Miss Goodall, Captain Dilk, Sir George Scott and Lord Hatherton. The contract for cutting and making the canal was given to Frost and Bate, who were later to go onto build a section of the Birmingham & Wolverhampton Railway.

In 1846 a second major merger brought the Dudley Canal into the Birmingham Canal Navigations network and extended the limits of the navigation to Delph and Selly Oak. They already had Aldersley, Huddlesford, Whittington Brook, Fazeley, Salford Bridge, Digbeth and Worcester Bar where junctions were made with other waterways. The Dudley Canal Co. had made a number of improvements during the 1830s. Brewin, their engineer, had been employed to shorten various short sections on the Dudley No.2 canal. Slight realignments were made around Primrose Hill and a more determined alteration was made near Netherton Church. The canal at this point followed the contours of the land around the hillside. Brewin determined to cut through the hill with a short tunnel and divert the canal along the direct route, whilst converting the bed of the old waterway into a new reservoir. Brewin also speeded up the passage through Lapal Tunnel through a novel water wheel arrangement.

The passing of the London and Birmingham Railway & Birmingham Canal Navigations Arrangement Act (1846) was to have a significant influence on future canal affairs. This act permitted the building of the Birmingham, Wolverhampton & Stour Valley Railway alongside the banks of the canal between Birmingham and Wolverhampton. Promoters of this scheme had been an independent group, who comprised the Birmingham, Wolverhampton and Stour Valley Railway Co.. They belonged to a select group of similar companies, which elected to find the finance for construction, but chose for an established railway operator to operate the line. The agreement was not without conditions or provisions to benefit both the Birmingham Canal Navigations and the London & Birmingham Railway. Birmingham Canal shareholders received a guarantee for dividends should their income fall, whilst the arrangement also gave the railway company rights to appoint committee members to the BCN Board and involvement in canal policy. Some historians, who see the BCN as being 'railway owned', have misquoted this relationship. A more accurate description would be 'railway controlled'.

From 1847 the London & Birmingham Railway became part of the London & Western Railway Co. and it fell to this railway company to complete the main line of the Stour Valley Railway to Wolverhampton. Construction of this railway was chiefly carried out during the years 1848–1850 and included some canal diversion and re-routing. The Stour Valley Railway crossed and re-crossed the canal main line. The railway ran close to the New Main Line to cross the Winson Green Loop near Eyre Street Junction. It then followed Telford's route as far as the Soho Foundry before crossing over to the Smethwick side. At Smethwick and Spon Lane the railway ran alongside the deep cutting following the west side canal embankment. It re-crossed at the Albion and followed the east side towpath of the Sheepwash Embankment, hiding forever the sheer scale of the canal company's achievement when they first crossed the Sheepwash Valley some ten years earlier. At Bloomfield the Old Main Line through to Wednesbury Oak was diverted onto a parallel course using part of the subsided Roundshill Canal, whilst the original line was adapted as the Bloomfield Railway Interchange Basin. The Stour Valley Railway then passed to the east of Coseley Tunnel and retuned to the canalside near Spring Vale, crossing the canal for the third time between Spring Vale Ironworks and George Jones' Bilston Furnaces. It crossed the canal again at Catchem's Corner and continued on to Wolverhampton Joint Central Station.

The building of Wolverhampton Central was conducted for the joint committee of the Shrewsbury & Birmingham Railway and the London & North Western Railway and involved the diversion of the Birmingham Canal main line to the south. The original route, which included Shipton's timber yard and packet boat terminal, was requisitioned for the station foundations and railway use, although both ends of the original BCN route were retained as arms of the canal. One served Norton's Flour Mill and annexe buildings. Shipton's moved their timber business to Old Factory Wharf beside the Albion Wharf carrier's depot. Stour Valley Railway construction continued beyond Central Station to Bushbury and included a long brick viaduct across the Wolverhampton Locks.

Another railway construction project was in progress at the same time that passed through the heart of the iron manufacturing district from northeast to southwest. This railway became known as the South Staffordshire Railway and had connections with the Midland Railway at Wichnor and the London & North Western Railway at Bescot. It crossed the Walsall Canal at Great Bridge, passed under the Stour Valley Railway and Birmingham Canal new main line at Dudley Port and crossed the old main line canal near Coneygree. This railway terminated at Dudley where a junction with the Oxford,

Worcester and Wolverhampton Railway was planned. The whole railway, complete with junctions, was sufficiently complete to enable the running of trains from Walsall through to Dudley in May 1850 and became the first railway to serve the iron district. The South Staffordshire Railway was an independent venture possessing its own locomotive fleet, and wagon and carriage stock provided and maintained by John Wright of Saltley. The Midland Railway also had running rights and was able to reach the heart of the Black Country through canal interchange facilities built at Great Bridge.

Construction of railways such as the South Staffordshire and Stour Valley marked the start of a new era for local canals. Traffic on the Birmingham Canal had continued to increase through the 1840s and 1850s following the merger of the Dudley and Wyrley & Essington Canals. But there were other factors, as new industry was established along the canal banks added to the trade. More traffic was also done at the public wharves, which reached factories and firms placed away from the waterway through road cartage. Another new traffic was that generated by and for railways.

Railways in one sense competed with inland waterways, drawing trade onto their metals and away from existing transport routes. In another sense they provided traffic for canals and river navigation. Railway construction generated a demand for materials. Early railways required stone bocks, cast or wrought iron rails and wooden spikes, known as trenails. These were often brought by boat to the nearest wharf. As the railway system was enlarged more and more material was required. Stone blocks gave way to wooden sleepers laid on ballast, longer wrought iron rails, chairs and wooden blocks. Engineering skills increased and more ambitious projects were undertaken. Embankments, bridges, cuttings and tunnels all created a greater demand for stone, bricks and timber.

Railway construction created a particular demand for timber in station buildings, goods sheds and platforms. It was the preferred material for many railway concerns. Each railway was financed by public subscription and finance was consequently limited. The engineer's specification was crucial for costings. Timber structures proved easier to erect and were sometimes provided as temporary buildings before more permanent buildings were made of brick. Bricks were also in particular demand, but every brick made was subject to tax, which was a significant factor at this time.

Brick making was then a seasonal occupation. Both railways and canals drew on the skills of the handmade brick maker, whose knowledge of local clays was essential for the making of bricks. Surface clay was dug during the winter months and left for the frosts and cold to weather and break down. Brick making began in the spring when the clay was ground down by the pug mill and moulded into shape before drying and baking in the kiln. It was process that had been used to make bricks for canals and was now adopted for railway construction. Bricks were used for bridge building, lining tunnels, viaducts and lining cuttings as well as important railway buildings.

The brickyard produced a range of products that included tiles, facing, and common bricks and quarries. The largest commodity was the common brick that was made by the thousand. A tax was paid on all of the brickyard products and this duty to some extent limited production. When the tax was removed brick making saw an increase in demand. Technology also came to the brickyard. Some brickyards already employed steam engines to drive the pug mill, but after 1850 steam power became more common. Machinery was invented to assist the duty of the pug mill. In ordinary handmade bricks the clay had to be prepared to make it sufficiently ductile for pressing into moulds. This method required the mixing of water with the clay and consequently led to the drying of the bricks before placing them in the kilns. Several engineers devised brick making machines that delivered clay to the mould or fashioned complete brick and tile shapes. Bradley & Craven of Westgate Foundry, Wakefield, established a reputation for the production of brick making machines. But there were many others and amongst their numbers was a Mr Oates, of Erdington, who designed a machine that was adopted by the Oldbury Brickworks during 1857. Oates' machines were capable of making twenty bricks per minute. Brick clay was available in many parts of the Black Country and yards made both red and blue bricks. The blue was a particularly had brick used for engineering purposes and was popular for railway and canal bridges, railway viaducts and walling, and many buildings.

New manufacturing methods added to the waterways trade from 1840. More furnaces, more foundries, more metal working all added to an extra demand for coal. Traffic figures reveal a greater demand for coal, but the amount of ironstone, limestone, sand, roadstone and general merchandise all increased. Merchandise carrying companies included many long-forgotten names and some with a familiar connection. Firms like George Ryder Bird, Crowley, Hicklin & Co., John Danks and Shipton's are names that have disappeared, whilst James and Joshua Fellows and Pickfords are perhaps better known. Even though each firm remained in business to profit by the trade their presence assisted the continued increase in trade.

BCN Traffic
Extract of Monthly Figures, in Tons Carried
(From Proprietors' Minutes PRO RAIL 810)

Coal Traffic to	October 1851	February 1853
Birmingham	42,604t 10cwt	52,863t 02cwt
Worcester Canal	17,733t 05cwt	22,171t 10cwt
Warwick Canal	6,774t 05cwt	7,179t 16cwt
Coventry Canal	663t 10cwt	586t 00cwt
Staffordshire & Worcestershire Canal	1,879t 00cwt	872t 10cwt
Whittington Brook & Fazeley	184 05cwt	442t 00cwt
Mining districts	141,584t 10cwt	186,291t 03cwt
Total coal traffic	211,423t 05cwt	270,406t 04cwt

Other Traffic		
Ironstone	48,889t 14cwt	55,783t 17cwt
Lime and limestone	30,115t 05cwt	31,950t 10cwt
Sand	6,771t 05cwt	9,364t 10cwt
Bricks	16,919t 15cwt	15,705t 15cwt
Merchandise and building stone	114,441t 04cwt	136,601t 02cwt
Road materials	11,931t 10cwt	16,081t 02cwt
Grand total	440,541t 12cwt	535,892t 17cwt

Public railways provided a new and speedier means for moving goods. The first railway reached Birmingham during 1837, when the Grand Junction Railway was opened between Warrington and Vauxhall Station. This railway was extended to Curzon Street during 1838 where the Grand Junction passenger station was erected alongside the London and Birmingham Railway station. The railway from London had also opened in 1838 and provided the opportunity for the transport of goods between Birmingham and the North West and Birmingham and London. Other lines were made from Birmingham to Derby and Gloucester. Many canal merchandise carriers stood to loose traffic to the new railways.

Canal carriage had come to encompass a myriad of different merchandise that was destined for the Midlands or was passing through the district between London and the Potteries and the North West. The Birmingham Canal ownership of the Fradley to Whittington Brook continued to provide useful toll revenue. During 1840 two carriers, Kenworthy and Morris, and Herbert and Co. requested a reduction on the tonnage payable on wool travelling from London to Lancashire and Yorkshire. The Birmingham Canal Navigations Co. agreed to the reduction, no doubt fearing potential loss of trade to the railways. The early 1840s were critical times for the canal carrier. Some carriers chose to give up the canal trade, selling on the goodwill and boats to other canal users. Other carriers decided to work with the railways and send items by rail as well as by canal.

A host of different railway operators came into existence between 1843 and 1845 in a similar fashion that canal schemes had been suggested in 1792. Parliamentary committees sifted through the glut of new railway applications weeding out some schemes and allowing only a selection to go through for House of Commons approval. A network of railways was constructed across the country during the years 1845 to 1855. During this period there was also a rationalisation where certain railway companies pooled their assets and merged together. As the larger companies were formed, promoters of new railway schemes frequently elected to have their lines worked by an existing company, thereby saving on the cost of staff, rolling stock and locomotive power. As far as goods conveyance was concerned, carriage, cartage and delivery was a matter to be handled in house, and only a select number of independent carriers were allowed to carry on their behalf.

As far as Birmingham and the Black Country were concerned, three railway companies served the district. These were the Great Western Railway, Midland Railway and the London & North Western Railway. A considerable amount of industry had been established on the banks of the local canals. Despite a growing number of railways in the district, the most effective solution for serving local trade proved to be the railway interchange basin. These basins were established at strategic places for the interchange of goods between railway wagons and canal boats. The boat traffic functioned as a simple extension to the railway system. They collected and delivered to works or specified wharves and worked to a timetable, which ensured goods would be at the interchange wharf for loading.

Canal and Railway Interchange Basins in the West Midlands

Key

BCN	Birmingham Canal Navigations
BDJT	Birmingham & Derby Junction and Birmingham & Gloucester Railway Joint Committee
BR	British Railways
GJR	Grand Junction Railway
GWR	Great Western Railway
LBR	London & Birmingham Railway
LMS	London Midland & Scottish Railway
LNWR	London & North Western Railway
MR	Midland Railway
OWWR	Oxford, Worcester & Wolverhampton Railway
SBR	Shrewsbury & Birmingham Railway
SSR	South Staffordshire Railway
SUC	Shropshire Union Canal Carrying Co.
SVR	Stour Valley Railway
WMR	West Midlands Railway

Basin	*Railway*	*Canal*
Albion, West Bromwich	LNWR, LMS	BCN, Walsall Canal
Bilston	GWR	BCN, old main line
Bloomfield, Tipton	SVR, LNWR, LMS, BR	BCN, old main line
Brettell Lane	OWWR, GWR	Stourbridge Canal
Bromley	OWWR, GWR, BR	Stourbridge Extension Canal
Brownhills	SSR, LNWR, LMS	BCN, Wyrley & Essington Canal
Churchbridge	SSR, LNWR, LMS	Staffordshire & Worcestershire Canal
Curzon Street, Birmingham	LBR	BCN, Digbeth Branch
Curzon Street, Birmingham	GJR, LNWR	BCN, Digbeth Branch
Darlaston	GJR, LNWR, LMS	BCN, Walsall Canal
Ettingshall, Wolverhampton	LNWR, LMS	BCN, main line
Factory, Tipton	OWWR, WMR, GWR, BR	BCN, main line
Great Bridge	SSR, MR, LMS	BCN, Walsall Canal
Great Bridge	SSR, LNWR, LMS, BR	BCN, Walsall Canal
Hawn	GWR	BCN, Dudley Canal No.2
Hay, Wolverhampton	SBR	BCN, main line
Hockley, Birmingham	GWR, BR	BCN, Birmingham Heath Branch
Lifford, Kings Norton	MR, LMS	Worcester & Birmingham Canal

Midland, Wolverhampton	MR, LMS	BCN, Wyrley & Essington Canal
Mill Street, Wolverhampton	LNWR, LMS, BR	BCN, main line
Monmore Green, Wolverhampton	LNWR, LMS, BR	BCN, main line
Monument Lane, Birmingham	LNWR, LMS, BR	BCN, main line
Netherton	GWR	BCN, Dudley Canal No.2
Oldbury	GWR	BCN, Oldbury Loop
Saltley	BDJT, MR, LMS	Warwick & Birmingham Canal
Shropshire Union, Wolverhampton	SUC	BCN, main line
Shrubbery	GWR	BCN, main line
Spon Lane	LNWR, LMS, BR	BCN, old main line
Stourbridge	OWWR, WMR, GWR, BR	Stourbridge Canal
Swan Village	GWR	BCN, Ridgacre Branch
Swan Village	GWR, BR	BCN, Balls Hill Branch
Tipton, Watery Lane	LNWR, LMS, BR	BCN, new main line
Victoria, Wolverhampton	SBR, GWR	BCN, main line
Wednesbury, Leabrook	GWR, BR	BCN, Walsall Canal
Withymoor	GWR, BR	BCN, Dudley No.2 Canal

The building of the interchange depots also encouraged the establishment of boatage depots where rival railway companies might reach parts of the iron making district not directly served by their railway lines. This state of affairs was particularly true of the Brierley Hill and Netherton districts, which were served by the Great Western Railway. Operating a boat service provide a much cheaper alternative than building railway branches and both the London & North Western and Midland Railway companies' boats served this district. Their depots were usually manned by railway staff, and functioned essentially as extensions of the railway that owned the site. The only basic difference was that boats instead of railway wagons conveyed the goods.

Boatage Depots

Depot	Railway	Location
Bishton's Bridge	LNWR & SUC	BCN, Dudley No.2 Canal
Nine Locks	LNWR & SUC, LMS	BCN, Dudley No.1 Canal
Primrose Basin	LNWR & SUC, LMS, BR	BCN, Dudley No.2 Canal
Primrose Basin	MR	BCN, Dudley No.2 Canal
Tipton	BDJT, MR	BCN, old main line
Turners Wharf, Spon Lane	LNWR & SUC	BCN, old main line

Wallows, Brierley Hill	LNWR & SUC	Pensnett Canal
Waterfall Lane	MR, LMS	BCN, Dudley No.2 Canal
Withymoor	LNWR & SUC	BCN, Dudley No.2 Canal

There was also a demand for haulage contractors. The name of William Bishton is closely associated with the Shropshire Union Railway & Canal Co. in the 1850s and 1860s. His father, also William, was a boatman, then innkeeper at the Crown at Dudley Wood Wharf, owned by Lord Dudley and Ward. His sons John, William and later Noah assisted William senior. By 1841, when the census was taken, William (junior) had the job of agent. William Bishton Junior, after his marriage to Priscilla in 1836, had various business ventures first as agent at Dudley Wood and then contractor at Wolverhampton. It cannot be a coincidence that a new canal house was erected at Dudley Wood wharf in the same year as his marriage to Priscilla Hancox.

Benjamin Hancox, chain maker, was an executor of William Bishton's (senior) will, and there was a connection with the chain trade and the Bishton family. The Bishtons had a proof house on Crown Inn land and no doubt were involved with carriage of chain by canal. For William (junior) his business affairs went from strength to strength. It is he, rather than the father, who was involved with the contract to supply horsepower to the Shropshire Union Railway & Canal Co. We find him moving to Cannock Road Wharf, which became the first Shropshire Union Co. Wharf in Wolverhampton. The 1851 census also states that he is a farmer with 300 acres. By the mid-1850s, William (junior) has a new role, that of timber merchant. He developed a timber yard at Cannock Road and remained there for a number of years. He was also involved with other projects including a packet boat through the Netherton Tunnel (1858–c.1863). The Shropshire Union Railway & Carrying Co. utilised both Bishton's wharves at Wolverhampton and Dudley Wood as depots for their carrying trade.

Cannock Chase yielded up vast supplies of coal hidden below. Once noted for early iron working and one of the country's earliest blast furnaces, mine agents now explored the Chase in search of workable seams. The mines that were developed involved considerably more investment than had hitherto been expended in the Black Country. These new mines needed months and years to sink the shafts and open up the work. But the returns eventually came in with a steady supply of coal. The Cannock Chase coalfield might have been restricted to access by the railway companies, but the Birmingham Canal Navigations were determined to have a share.

Canal expansion continued throughout the 1850s. In 1850 and 1851 the feeder from Cannock Chase Reservoir was altered and widened for boat navigation to reach the Hammerwich Colliery and the new sinking, Uxbridge Colliery, that were better known respectively as Cannock Chase No.1 and No.2 pits.

Colliery development around Brownhills and Norton Canes encouraged the making of a new waterway to Cannock. Railway interests also played a part in improvements to the Dudley Canal. The most significant of these was Netherton Tunnel Branch that connected the Birmingham level at Tipton with the Dudley Canal at Windmill End. But other planned work included the Two-Lock Line, a realignment at Primrose Hill and the deviation of the locks at Delph. Parliamentary approval was sought and granted in 1855 (18th and 19th Vict Cap 121). The estimated cost for the tunnel and approaches was £170,000, the Two-Lock Line (£22,000), for improvement at Primrose Hill (£16,000) and new locks at the Delph (£18,000), which made a total of £226,000. In addition, estimates for land purchase and expenses (£12,250) increased the estimate to £238,250.

Construction work was completed during the years 1856 to 1858 and involved a quarter of a mile of embankment, half a mile of open cutting and a mile and three quarters of tunnel, which made a total of some two and a half miles of new waterway. The contractor for the work was George Meakin, who became better known for building railways and railway tunnels. In addition to the tunnel a three-arch aqueduct was built to carry the old main line over the Netherton Branch at Groveland. Mining subsidence subsequently damaged the original aqueduct and the present structure is a rebuild. Meakin's contract also included the building of the Two-Lock Line, which was a short canal that cut across from the Dudley No.2 Canal and through the Hurst Colliery to the Dudley No.1 Canal avoiding the long deviation via Parkhead.

The task of building a new flight at Delph was given to BCN workers. Delph Locks had been completed as part of the original Dudley Canal, but had suffered seriously through subsidence. Their use provided a constant maintenance problem. There were nine locks in the flight, which followed a curved route up the hillside from the Delph to Mill Street Bridge. Engineers decided to straighten the line of locks, retaining and rebuilding the top and bottom locks, and building six new locks in a straight line with square side pounds and overflow weirs. During September 1856 tenders were received for making about 200,000 bricks and stacking them on the ground at the Delph. James Hughes' tender was accepted at 13s 6d per 1,000.

The clear aim of the work was to speed up boat movements from Stourbridge and Brierley Hill through to the railway interchange wharves located around Tipton. Only one obstacle remained to a smooth flow of traffic and this was Brewin's Tunnel. During 1857 plans were drawn up for the BCN chairman, Sir George Nicholls KCB, to convert Brewin's Tunnel into an open cutting.

There are times in Birmingham Canal Co. history where capable people had influence on shaping the destiny of the canal. George Nicholls (1781–1865) was a man whose assistance and expertise was invaluable at this time. Born at St Kevern, Cornwall and educated at Helston Grammar School and Newton Abbot, George Nicholls grew up to enter service aboard the East India Co. ship, the *Abergavenny*. He rose through the ranks to be mate and then Captain. He later worked as a banker and an overseer to the poor. From 1823, he assisted with the fund gathering for the Gloucester & Berkeley Canal and provided vital assistance at a crucial time. During this period he worked closely with Thomas Telford, the engineer, and built up a warm friendship with him. Nicholls was appointed superintendent to the new-founded Birmingham branch of the Bank of England, in 1826, where he quickly became associated with local affairs apart from his official duties. He also became a director of the Birmingham Canal Navigations. From 1834 George Nicholls talents were directed towards the Poor Law, when he was appointed as one of the three commissioners. On reorganisation of the Poor Law Board, Nicholls became its permanent Secretary. He retired from this post in 1851, with ill health, and was rewarded for his long years of public service with the order of Knight of the Bath. Sir George Nicholls then found himself with more free time and part of this was devoted to the affairs of the Birmingham Canal Navigations and the difficult task of finding finance for the many new ventures contemplated.

The job of cutting through Brewin's Tunnel was given to George Meakin, who finally agreed to do this contract for £3,500. Meakin's contract, although extensive, was paid in the time-honoured tradition of members of the committee checking progress and paying off amounts under the certificate system. For the contractor the expense of men and equipment sometimes left him short of money. George Meakin had borrowed money and by 1857 interest payments had become a matter of concern to him. He wrote to the canal committee to secure an additional payment.

Tipton 28 May 1857

To the committee of the Birmingham Canal Navigations

Gent^m

Having received large advances from my bankers to enable me to carry on the above work, the present high rate of interest on so large a sum puts me to a great expense. I therefore beg to take the liberty of asking you to advance me five thousand pounds today in addition to the amounts of my certificates – the said five thousand pounds so advanced to be paid by deducting 10 per cent from amount of your engineers' monthly certificate.

I have yrs
George Meakin

Mr Meakin attended the next committee meeting to explain the obstacles in the way of completing the work and the advantage the advance would be to him. The chairman (Sir George Nicholls) agreed, realising that the advances might be made with perfect safety, and recommended the payment.

Robert Thomas, clerk to the BCN, reported the progress of work in September 1857. He noted that all works were in hand with the exception of Primrose Hill. Those at Primrose Hill were not considered immediately essential and had not been started. Two-thirds of Netherton Tunnel was complete and it was hoped to be open midsummer next or shortly afterwards. Delay had been caused through extra building work, slips and sinkings that added to expense. The cost of completing was now estimated to be nearly £200,000, which was some £30,000 more than budgeted for. Costs on the work had risen elsewhere. Solicitors and agents bills, land and mine purchase (at Tividale and Windmill End), as well as opposition from Lord Ward that had added to the costs in getting the Act were all factors that added a total of nearly £90,000 the bills. Such a large amount led to considerable concern as to how the additional finance might be raised.

George Meakin continued with the work and on several occasions asked for additional advances, all of which were politely, but firmly, refused. Netherton Tunnel was finally completed and opened for traffic during August 1858.

The other major works were the Cannock Chase Extension, Churchbridge Branch and the Wyrley Branch Canal. Extensions were made in the Titford area, where a canal was completed from Titford Reservoir to Causeway Green (1857) and a short section of the Titford Feeder was widened for some 200 yards towards Tat Bank. A third canal-owned tramway was also set out during 1860 to link Short Heath Basin on the Wyrley & Essington Canal with nearby mines alongside the hamlet of Short Heath.

Chambers and Hilton were awarded the contract to build the Cannock Extension as far as Leacroft, which was completed as two lots by the end of 1857, a few months before the South Staffordshire branch railways were completed to Cannock and Norton Canes. In 1856 Chambers and Hilton were also awarded the contract for Wyrley Bank, which was also finished by the end of 1857. The Wyrley Bank Canal was an extension of the Sneyd Locks branch to Essington Wood and came to serve mines at Great Wyrley.

The Churchbridge Branch was commenced in 1859 as an extension of the Staffordshire & Worcestershire Canal Co. Hatherton Branch and had the authorisation of both the BCN and Staffordshire & Worcestershire Co. The task of completing thirteen locks was achieved during 1860 under the direct control of the Staffordshire and Worcestershire Canal Co.. During 1860 the Birmingham Canal Navigations were keen to finish the Cannock Extension to Hednesford to serve coalmines established by Francis Piggott. George Nicholls wrote to Lord Hatherton, chairman for the Staffordshire & Worcestershire Canal, in the hope he might receive financial help to complete the Cannock Extension. He received a reply that left him in no doubt that the Birmingham Canal Navigations had little hope of further help unless control was handed over to the other company:

Sir George Nicholls

My dear Sir George,

My attendance at the Churchbridge locks meeting was impossible, as I was under the influence of medicine at the time, and the day was very bad. It is useless to propound to the Staff and Wor *Canal Co any proposal for contributing to the extension of your canal to Hednesford, unless you can accompany it by some feasible and secure plan for admitting them to a control of trade – I mean to a participation in the control of that part of the trade that is to come down it. Your equal participation in the control of the junction locks was the price of your extension to Rumour Hill, which we should otherwise have objected to. As we had made our extension of what is called the Hatherton Branch up to Church Bridge with the design at some future day carrying the line towards Hednesford Pool, which we considered to be more legitimately our Country than yours. I cannot feel that you can have any claim on us cooperating without offering us some security for equal participation of benefit. Nothing that has passed in our committee could lead me to suppose there would be any indisposition to entertain a proposition founded on that principle. At the same time I shall be glad if any further proposals be made, that you could let it be addressed to Mr Rutter or Mr Markham, as I have found it necessary on account of my frequent absence in Town and elsewhere, (which leaves me little opportunity of attending our Committee) to dictate correspondence in the affairs of the company. I shall be happy at any time to communicate with you personally – I only desire that our clerks should be made the medium of communication with the committee in all matters requiring an answer from that body.*

Yours faithfully
Hatherton

The offer of Mr Piggot to place 500 tons a week of coal onto the canal was sufficient inducement to finish the canal to Hednesford. Authority was given in June 1860 to proceed with the works and the committee later inspected the route, taking their committee boat back from Leacroft to Wolverhampton. Birmingham Canal Navigation minutes do not record the letting of any contract and BCN staff apparently conducted the work. Wet weather hampered progress during the winters of 1861 and 1862 resulting in embankment slips and delaying completion of the waterway until 1863.

Meanwhile railway expansion continued. The Oxford, Worcester & Wolverhampton Railway reached Wolverhampton in 1854, which was about the same time as the Broad Gauge Railway from Birmingham to Wolverhampton (Birmingham & Wolverhampton & Dudley Railway). The new railway from Birmingham to Wolverhampton was owned by the Great Western Railway and was actually provided with both standard gauge and broad gauge tracks so that trains might pass with standard or broad gauge stock.

The South Staffordshire Railway had decided to let the operation of their railway to the engineer John Robinson McClean and McClean was also a partner of the Cannock Chase Colliery Co., which took over the existing Cannock Chase collieries from the Marquis of Anglesey. McClean and Chawner made improvements to the Cannock Chase operation, sinking new collieries and laying an extensive mineral railway to connect them with the Anglesey Branch Canal and the South Staffordshire Railway. John McClean handed over the lease of the South Staffordshire Railway to the London & North Western Railway in 1861 and then actively pursued the making of a new railway from his mines to Wolverhampton. His mineral railway became known as the Cannock Chase & Wolverhampton Railway. This railway never reached Wolverhampton and barely got beyond the Norton Canes Branch Railway, but did extend further north until it joined with the London & North Western Railway branch from Hednesford, known as the Cannock Chase Railway. The Cannock Mineral Railway had been opened from Rugeley to Cannock in 1859 forming a continuous line of LNWR metals from Walsall through their Trent Valley main line. The Cannock Chase Railway was a branch from the Cannock Mineral and came to not just provide another outlet for Cannock Chase Colliery coals, but serve a new mining venture, the Cannock Wood Colliery, which was in the process of being sunk when the Cannock Chase Railway was opened in 1863. The Cannock Chase Railway also made an end on junction with the tramway from Hednesford Basin to Littleworth.

Littleworth Tramway was authorised as part of the same Act of Parliament that promoted the Cannock Extension Canal. It was the only standard gauge tramway owned by the Birmingham Canal. Completed in 1863, in the same year as Hednesford Basin, the Littleworth Tramway provided the means for moving coal from Piggot's mines to the canal as well as the railway sidings at Hednesford. It also enabled coals to be brought from the Cannock Wood Colliery to Hednesford Basin. Cannock & Rugeley Colliery used locomotives to work this traffic.

Cannock Wood Colliery was one of three mines that belonged to the Cannock & Rugeley Colliery Co.. The others were the Valley and Wimblebury pits. Cannock Wood Colliery, as described in 1893, comprised three shafts. Coal was worked by the longwall method and shafts were driven to the deep, shallow and bass seams with gateways usually 40 yards apart. A considerable part of the coal was conveyed by pit tubs placed as they came to the bank on open trucks and taken to the canal where they were screened and sized. The bulk was taken away by the London & Western Railway.

There was an unprecedented demand for iron in the years leading up to the making of the country's railways and it not surprising that demand encouraged changes in blast furnace design. In fact there was considerable improvement during this period. Furnace design changed from the basic square furnace to the circular tapered design during the 1820s. The widest part was known as the bosh, which was near the base, and tuyeres where the iron and slag were run out. The ruling height of furnaces in South Staffordshire was 45ft with a diameter of 12 or 13ft at the bosh. By 1842 the working blast furnaces provided an extensive list, with each furnace capable of producing 60–90 tons of pig iron weekly (see Appendix 1).

Pig iron was produced in different quantities from a mixture of modern and older furnaces, some of which had been in production for forty years or more. Production continued to increase at new furnace locations. Elsewhere the old square-style furnaces were replaced as required. The 1840s represented a time of new furnaces as the ironstone fields around Birchills, Darlaston and Willenhall were exploited. During 1842 Edward Addenbrooke had commenced working the Rough Hay Colliery near Darlaston where both coal and ironstone were available. Pits were sunk and a blast furnace was put into operation during 1843. Addenbrooke looked to the Birmingham Canal Navigations to complete the Tame Valley Canal as soon as possible in order to benefit from the improved communications to this area. Construction of a second furnace was commenced during 1844 once the Tame Valley Canal had opened to traffic.

Increased demand for iron encouraged John Hartland to purchase the Eagle Furnaces at Great Bridge and put them back into use during 1844. Their operation was brief as the land was requisitioned by the South Staffordshire Railway to build a railway goods depot and canal interchange facility. Supply of ironstone was taken throughout the area with each ironmaster working mines at a distance from their mines. For example, John Parsons was working ball and gubbin ironstone near Monmore Green in 1842 and sending the stone by boat to furnaces at Bilston Brook.

Another development was the use of the hot blast process. Blast furnaces had traditionally used cold blast technology where cold air was forced into the furnace through the action of the blast engine. Methods changed during the 1850s where blast furnace owners adopted the hot blast extracted from the furnace mouth and returned it to the boilers to heat the cold air passing into the furnace. The chief advantages included a saving of fuel, which also led to increased iron production.

Littleworth Railway Ticket.
The Birmingham Canal Navigation owned and operated a number of narrow-gauge tramways that were an essential part of their network. They were also responsible for a standard-gauge railway that connected Hednesford Basin with collieries owned by the Cannock Chase Colliery Co., Cannock & Rugeley Colliery Co. and the Cannock & Wimblebury Colliery Co., known as the 'Littleworth Tramway'. Traffic along this railway was regulated, in part, through the issue of railway tickets, such as the example shown. Colliery trains would be issued with these tickets as authority to proceed along a particular length of railway. (Walsall Archives)

This Ticket is to be given up by the Engineman immediately on arrival at the Station to which he is authorised to proceed, to the Chief Officer on duty there, who will be held responsible for this and all such Tickets being at once cancelled and forwarded to the Officer appointed to receive them, so as to prevent the possibility of their being used a second time.

BIRMINGHAM CANAL NAVIGATIONS.
5003 TRAIN STAFF TICKET.
LITTLEWORTH RAILWAY.
TRAIN No. _____ (UP.)
TO GUARD AND ENGINEMAN.
You are authorised to proceed from
Wimblebury Junction to Cooper's Lodge Junction,
and the Train Staff will follow.

Time _____   Signature _____
Date _____   188
[OVER.

The four furnaces at Chillington were completed between 1828 and 1829. Each was 45ft high and 12–13ft in the bosh. During 1848 another two furnaces were erected on the coalfield at place known as Moseley Hole. They also later acquired the Bentley furnaces and operated two modern furnaces there. One of the Bentley furnaces was capable of making 170 tons a week. The Chillington furnaces made iron by hot blast and the gases from the furnaces were used to heat stoves and boilers.

When described in 1869, two furnaces were in use with a make of between 120–140 tons a week. The ores used were the gubbin, ball and blue flats, mixed with Frampton ore, half coal and half coke was used as a fuel, and about 2 tons of coal was needed to make 1 ton of pig iron. The native coal was coked in heaps or hearths. From 20–30 tons of coke were placed around a chimney 7ft high having several openings at the lower part. The larger pieces of coal were placed next to the chimney so as to form channels to it. As the coking proceeded, the heap was covered with ashes. Three days were required to complete the process. The native ironstone was calcined in a kiln, which was iron plated outside and about 40ft high. Calcining kilns were commonly used at blast furnaces where iron ore was heated with coal to improve the iron content. The materials were then raised to the top of the blast furnace by two lifts. One lift served a pair of furnaces and a similar lift was used to raise ironstone to the top of the calcining kilns.

In front of the blast furnace seven double puddling furnaces were built and the iron from the blast furnace was run direct every two hours as required, thus saving on coal at the puddling stage. Two-thirds of make went to the puddling furnaces and one-third went to be cast as pigs at the sand beds. There were three forge trains and three mills for rolling sheet iron, two mills for nail rods, one for merchant iron, and two mills for rolling hoop iron. Thus the Chillington Co. belonged to the most productive group of Black Country iron manufacturers.

Iron making had reached another peak during the 1850s. Profits and success had encouraged wine merchants Howard Fletcher and Benjamin Urwick to enter the iron trade as a business investment. They had Simon Holden Blackwell as partner, whose practical knowledge of the trade was quite extensive. With Blackwell's help a new mineral property was developed at Willenhall that drew on ironstone mines at Portobello and Little London that had been acquired during the years 1853 and 1854. Furnaces were erected beside the Bentley Canal at Sandbeds. Blackwell withdrew from the venture to concentrate on developing the New Bilston Furnaces leaving Fletcher and Urwick in a difficult situation. They took a new partner, Nathaniel Neal Solly, who had gathered experience from a variety of sources. He and his brothers had been associated with several Black Country ironworks, and he himself had previously managed a slate quarry at Portmadoc. N.N. Solly concentrated his efforts at Willenhall and with the help of Benjamin Urwick built up the blast furnace operation there. Their blast furnaces had been working some two years when the greatest failure in the local trade happened. The winter months of 1857 marked a serious decline in demand. Furnaces shut down, banks and shareholders strove to reclaim investments and several iron making firms suspended payments and filed bankruptcy petitions. Fletcher, Solly and Urwick were able to survive the difficult trading time and went on to keep the furnaces at Willenhall going.

Their former partner, S.H. Blackwell was less fortunate. Bad trading caused him to offer the New Bilston site for sale in 1861 and continued poor trading finally forced Blackwell to file his bankruptcy petition in 1863. His failure was enough to bring down the Birmingham Banking Co., who had supported him. Mr Blackwell's works had been highly remunerative, but the five furnaces at Bilston were principally supplied with materials obtained from a distance, about three-quarters of their entire consumption. The water from springs and canal provided a serious hindrance to the mining property and pumping water out of the mines proved expensive. When Mr Blackwell took the estate there were two furnaces erected. He completely remodelled them and built another three. Russells Hall had five furnaces that made pig iron that always produced a good price on the market. Thick coal was used in the make with ironstone brought from Churnett Valley where Mr Blackwell was part owner and some of the produce of his working mine in the Forest of Dean. The ten-furnace combine turned out about 1,400 tons of pigs a week and at the Corbyns Hall and Atlas Works nearly 500 tons of malleable iron was made weekly.

The more profitable firms were able to weather the storm. Many belonged to established ironmasters such as the Bagnall, Baldwin, Barker and Jones families. Perhaps the greatest industrial concern in South Staffordshire belonged to the Bagnall family. John and Edward Bagnall had come to the district from Shropshire as working butty miners. John Bagnall became a colliery owner and with his sons blast furnace and ironworks owners. By 1860 their works consisted of thirteen collieries, six blast furnaces and three malleable ironworks, and staff on a weekly wage bill of about £3,400. Their principal works were then Goldshill Ironworks, on the Danks Branch, Goldsgreen Furnaces, on the Balls Hills Branch, and Capponfield Funaces, alongside the old main line near Bilston.

The Bagnalls had a good record for promoting religious and general education to further the lot of their workers and their families. Goldshill Furnaces had a chaplain, a schoolmaster, a schoolmistress, an infant schoolmistress, a night schoolmaster and an assistant to the night schoolmaster. At Caponfield they had a chaplain, schoolmaster and three pupil teachers. Goldshill had large schoolrooms where 800 people could be seated in divine worship, and at Caponfield there was a church and schoolrooms. Prayers were read every morning at both the works by the respective chaplains, who also conducted full services twice each Sunday, and were supposed to have the spiritual oversight of the men and their families.

By 1860, based on figures compiled for 1859, South Staffordshire had sixty-four pig-iron making establishments comprising 186 blast furnaces, of which 147 were in blast. The pig iron produced amounted to 597,809 tons. The mills and forges comprised 102 separate works that owned a total number of 1,943 puddling furnaces. Ore and ironstone were obtained from a variety of sources. In North Staffordshire there was raised some 349,947 tons of hydrated oxide and 959,000 tons of argillaceous carbonate yearly, and this amount was despatched by rail or canal. The Froghall mines sent 79,327 tons of uncalcined and 13,861 tons of calcined ore by boat to the West Midlands. A brown hematite ore was sent from mines in the Forest of Dean. The bulk, 13,422 tons, was brought into Staffordshire by rail and another 2,866 tons by water. From Lancashire, a red hematite ore shipped on the Ulverstone Canal for Staffordshire, amounted to 6,722 tons, but sent the bulk, of 69,028 tons, via the Ulverstone & Lancaster Railway principally for Staffordshire. From Cumberland, the Whitehaven district continued to send the bulk of their ore, 27,207 tons, by ship principally for Staffordshire, whilst only 3,777 tons went by rail. From Northamptonshire and Buckinghamshire, as near as could be ascertained, 110,000 tons of ore were sent into Staffordshire. Limestone, comprising about 200,000 tons, was converted into lime and about 350,000 tons were used as fluxing stone at the ironworks.

Working conditions for the average ironworker remained harsh and there were moments where lives might be put in danger. During July 1860 there was an explosion at the Brook blast furnaces belonging to G. & A. Hickman, caused through molten metal coming into contact with water from the tuyere. The tuyere was a large iron nozzle of the blast pipe that was prevented from melting by a stream of water being made to revolve in a secured chamber between its inner and outer surface. When, however, by accident the molten metal was allowed to rise up to the level of the tuyeres, they burned and melted. The water from the jacket began to escape and an explosion was the inevitable result. The keeper of the furnace had delayed tapping the furnace until it boiled up to level with the tuyeres, when the water flowing out amongst the metal led to a rapid generation of steam and a large quantity of molten iron was driven out at the tapping place. Three blast furnace workers were caught by the hot metal and two were burnt from head to foot. They died from their injuries. John Anderson, furnace keeper was more fortunate.

In August 1860 the failure was announced of William Banks, ironmaster of Ettingshall. Mr Banks had been commercially known as T. Banks and Son, the name of the concern before the death of his father. His works consisted of two blast furnaces, some forges and rolling mills. Liabilities were estimated to be £33,000, but Mr Banks' debts were less than half that sum. Many years before, when Thomas Banks was sole proprietor, the business failed and was suspended but he paid his creditors in full. It failed again in the 1840s and the dividend paid to the creditors on this occasion was small, and the action was said to have hastened T. Banks' death. The Fryer banking family, of Wolverhampton, had a claim for £18,500 on the estate and consented to accept payment by instalment. William Banks agreed to pay £1,200 a year and subsequently paid William Fleming Fryer £18,000. He also spent a similar sum in developing the mines belonging to the furnaces. The running in of water drowned out valuable seams that had just been reached. Such was the ironmasters lot, juggling finance with the cost of mining and iron production.

Despite fluctuations in demand there was a steady increase in the number of blast furnaces. During 1869 this total equated to 172, but only half were in production. The production of pig iron in 1868 was 532,234 tons, which was 16,596 tons less than the year before. Similarly, production of coal for the same district was listed as 12,294 tons for 1868, which was less by 231,774 tons than the year before. The decrease attributed to a depression, which prevailed during 1868. It was also noted that the best seams of coal and ironstone from South Staffordshire were rapidly becoming exhausted. Yet there was some compensation; the new Cannock Chase coalfield promised to supply the deficit for many years in the future.

Iron making continued to decline as local supplies were exhausted. Failures before the bankruptcy court in 1866 included Captain Bennitt, ironmaster at Oldbury. In 1867 the Oldbury furnaces were advertised for sale. The property then comprised four blast furnaces, coke and calcining hearths, and was capable of making in 600 tons of pig iron. Oldbury furnaces and yard were situated on a strip of land placed between the Oldbury Loop and the old main line near the junction of these two waterways. Tramways crossed the old main line to mines on the southern bank. There were also mines to the north at Roway Lane Colliery. Oldbury furnaces were later worked by the Onions family and finally closed during the 1870s. The Great Western Railway redeveloped the site as a goods depot and railway interchange basin.

Other iron makers went on to to found successful businesses in providing certain types of finished iron. James Solly, brother of Neal Solly, after a period of receivership went on to found the Great Bridge Iron & Steel Co. Ltd, which took over his Great Bridge Works, alongside the Walsall Canal. The new company was floated with a capital £50,000 in 2,000 shares in 1866. James Solly the previous proprietor was engaged to act as managing director.

Another successful venture was run by Hingley & Smith at Hartshill and was located beside the banks of the private Pensnett Canal. A valuation produced in April 1868 describes the site as comprising four acres with a frontage of six boats' lengths to canal. The works included forges, rolling mills, carpenters shops, smith shops and stables. Many of the mills, as was common at this time, were open sided and made of wood, each with a slate roof and cast-iron pillars for support.

There were three forges, and associated with each were groups of puddling furnaces:

Richard Clarke's Valuation 8 April 1868
Original Held at Dudley Records Office

Forge No.1   a single puddling furnace, a single puddling and ball furnace, and two groups of four puddling furnaces.

Forge No.2   two puddling furnaces, one puddling furnace, four puddling furnaces, two puddling furnaces and two puddling furnaces.

Forge No.3	four puddling furnaces and stores, four puddling furnaces, which work to two heating furnaces then to guide mill.
Mill Nos 1 & 2	three mill furnaces, two mill furnaces, three bulldog, or cinder, kilns of red brick, low-pressure beam engine cylinder 20in x 5ft 6in. 9in guide mill with set of three high bolting rolls and three high strand rolls, low-pressure beam engine 36in cylinder x 5ft 9in stroke.
Helve Forge	20in forge train with one pair of forge rolls to roll 4in, 3 ½in, 2in widths. High-pressure beam engine by T. Holcroft with 24in cylinder x 6ft stroke.
Helve Forge	Mine crusher or ball dry rolls. 20in forge train with pair of 6in and 4in bar rolls; 5in and 2 **1/2**in billet rolls, pair of 7in and 8in bar rolls, pair of 9in and 12in bar rolls.
Helve Forge	Boiler plate shears by D. Rowley, low-pressure beam engine by Boulton and Watt, 48in cylinder x 8ft stroke, driving gear, 18in merchant mill with one set of hard rolls, small vertical steam engine 6 ½in cylinder x 12in, high-pressure steam engine with 12in cylinder, 6in merchant bar and slitting mill with pair of bolting rolls from 5in to 3 ½in.

Diversification in the local iron industry produced a number of successful firms. Hill and Smith, of Brierley Hill Ironworks beside the Dudley Canal, did iron and wire fence and gate making for parks enclosures and railway embankments. Hill and Smith commenced business in 1826 and were inventors of flat bar continuous fencing. They rolled iron and their mills would produce up to 130 tons per week. The mill and fence manufactory was placed close to the canal. The iron was taken to the cutting up or press shops, of which there were two, each containing ten sets of shearing and punching machines driven by steam engines of 50hp. It was cut into lengths. In order to reduce the cost of punching, Hill and Smith put down a machine by which iron for twelve hurdles could be punched out at the same time. Punched up iron was laid onto tramway tracks and taken round to the blacksmiths shop to be worked up. These shops contained forty fires, each fitted with a steam blast. There were machines for bending and twisting hurdles. Next to the blacksmith shop was the finishing shop where the gates and fencings were generally put together. The assembled fencing was then taken by tramway to a large shed adjoining the railway siding and stored ready for shipment. Ancillary plant included a hurdle blackening plant complete with dipping tanks.

Hill and Smith also made wrought iron sheep folding hurdles and hurdles made to Gillett's patent that had a wide market in the agricultural community. There was a department for making wire netting, where fences were made of woven wire. Specialist machines were installed for weaving the wire netting. There were also departments for heavy forgings and for iron roofs.

The local chain industry benefited from both rail and canal transport. Chain making began as a blacksmith trade and involved the forging of links of iron together to make chains of different lengths at the hearth. Chain had variety of uses that varied from the heavy pit chains for colliery use and anchor chain for naval purposes to the small-linked chain, or trace, that was employed in making horses' harnesses. Strength was considered

Glede Ovens, Old Hill. Glede was a small type of coke, which was produced from coals in the Old Hill area and which was popular with local industries such as chain making. The ovens shown were located at the Haden Hill Colliery near Waterfall Lane. (Sandwell Archives)

essential. Some smiths like John Brown took exceptional pride in their work as the following notice shows:

To Coal and Ironmaster
I JOHN BROWN of Coseley in parish of Sedgley, County Stafford, Blacksmith and Chainmaker, begs leave to inform all persons concerned in mines, that chains used in drawing coals, stone and other heavy materials are manufactured at my shops at Coseley, in the best most expeditious manner and the toughest materials, and also all kinds of ironwork used in steam engines, and I beg leave to add that a competitor of mine, who calls himself the best chain maker in England, lately challenged to work me in the manufacture of a chain for a wager. The challenge was accepted, we produced our chains of equal length, in weight, and a public trial was made of them on 21st inst at Coseley in the presence of several hundred persons, the chains being fixed end to end was fixed to two trees, and then forcibly extended by a lifting jack till one of them failed; the end found my work superior to his, for my chain sustained but little injury by this extension and his broken in two places. All orders thankfully received and expeditiously executed by,
John Brown, Coseley September 281801
(*Aris's Gazette*, 12 October 1801).

Chain making continued to be carried on around Coseley and Tipton, but the principal district for chain was located around Cradley, Cradley Heath and Netherton. Several chain makers set up works close to or beside the Dudley No.2 Canal where they specialised in the making of not only chain but also anchors. The best-known chain maker in this district was the firm of Noah Hingley & Son. The chain part of this works was established in 1837, whilst Noah Hingley introduced the manufacture of anchors in 1848.

Their works were located at Netherton. Hingley's had collieries at Dudley Wood, Old Hill and Gawn and also mined their own ironstone, which was mixed with imported ores to produce their brand of Netherton Crown brand iron. Pig iron was made at the Dudley

Noah Hingley, Chain Works, Netherton.
The making of chains and anchors became a speciality of certain firms in the Cradley and Netherton district. The firm of Noah Hingley became the best known of all the local chain makers. Their extensive works lined the Dudley No.2 Canal at Netherton. (Dudley Archives)

Wood Furnaces, which Hingley purchased from the New British Iron Co. These furnaces were amongst the oldest furnace plants then in work and they were closed down when the Old Hill Furnaces came up for sale. Old Hill Furnaces had been erected during 1848 for T. & I. Badger and had subsequently passed to David Rose in 1863 and were taken over by Hingley during 1871. These furnaces were improved to make up to 18,000 tons of hot-blast pig per annum and were served by an internal tramway system that connected furnaces, mines and the canal basin on the Dudley No.2 Canal. When the Great Western Railway line from Old Hill to Netherton was completed in 1878, railway sidings were provided for the Old Hill Furnaces. The two blast furnaces consumed 36,000 tons of ironstone and limestone and 26,000 tons of coal per year. The furnaces were 52ft high and 15ft in the bosh and had nine tuyeres each. Firebricks lined the hot-blast stoves and the blast was provided by an engine of the Boulton & Watt type.

The Netherton Ironworks was also placed alongside the Dudley No.2 Canal and occupied much of the offside bank from Bishton's Bridge to Primrose Bridge. At the heart of the Hingley property was the New Works, which comprised the original works. The New Works at Netherton had engines to drive various trains. One drove a forge train 22in, with four sets of bar rolls capable of making iron from **1/2**in to 6in round. There were puddling and ball furnaces, four re-heating furnaces and the mill had a steam-driven saw. On another part of the ironworks steam engines were used to drive helves and furnish power for three forges, also a 4-ton steam hammer. There were puddling furnaces and ball furnaces and eight reheating furnaces, and train rolls, producing iron from **1/4**in rounds and squares up to 4in square. Another engine drove a mill connected with puddling and balling furnaces and six reheating furnaces.

Construction of the Netherton to Old Hill Railway provided a new goods station and interchange basin at Withymoor for the Great Western Railway. It was a link that was to have considerable benefits for Hingley's and improved the transport arrangements for the carriage of Lancashire and Yorkshire pig iron for working up to the best quality of wrought iron needed to make chain. Netherton Crown brand became a well-respected brand. In addition to the high quality iron (Netherton Best brand) used in the making of chain, cable and anchors, they also produced boiler stays and iron plate. The Best Yorkshire brand was used to make boiler stays and bolts. Wrought iron plate made at Netherton was used for gas holders, boilers, water tanks, ships, boats and barges, railway wagons, locomotive tenders, and colliery wagons and tubs. The adjacent works of H. & T. Danks, boilermakers, no doubt benefited from the supply of boilerplate iron.

six

ENGINEERING
AND INNOVATION

Railway construction brought new business to the Midlands. Black Country ironworks benefited through the supply of rail and galvanised iron. Foundries turned out a variety of cast irons for railway needs. Stampers, brassworkers and glassmakers all benefited through the demand for lamps and signals. Local tube makers made the weldless tubes required for locomotive boilers, Birmingham button makers received a host of orders for uniform buttons and there was also a demand for whistles from Birmingham manufacturers.

Invention and innovation encouraged new industry. The gas industry technology saw considerable improvement after 1850. Larger gas making plants started to be made to supply the needs of public lighting and industry. Yet despite an increased need for gas coals, canal-borne coal to supply the local gasworks went into decline. Although heathen coal was a suitable gas making coal, other coals from local mines produced a gas that made a weaker light than coals from Derbyshire, Flintshire, Nottinghamshire and Yorkshire. The development of the railway network enabled the carriage of gas coals to the midlands and gasworks came to be built with railway connections or railway sidings provided to supply existing works. Local coals continued to be used to heat the retorts and boilers, and this fuel was often carried by waterway.

Another crucial factor was the limited coal resources in the local coalfield. By 1860 coal reserves throughout South Staffordshire had been depleted with particular respect to the thick coal seams. Some people even considered that the Black Country had squandered the reserves of coal through wasteful mining techniques. Good coal had become expensive and inferior fuels more common. As early as 1862 C. Siemens read a paper to the Institute of Mechanical Engineers, where he described a regenerative furnace suited to local fuels. Inferior quality fuel was converted into crude gas through a separate furnace or gas producer. The gas was then used to heat the furnace. Waste gases were passed through the brick regenerators, which retained heat and made the furnace more efficient. Several local glassmakers, such as Chance Brothers, Lloyd & Summerfield and Osler had adopted these furnaces, and another use was for heating and welding iron tubes.

Gas making continued to increase. There were various milestones in the gas industry that accompanied improved technology and a wider use of gas. The adoption of gas for heating enabled the domestic and industrial use of gas cookers and gas fires. Gas was also used to heat furnaces for many trades, or provide the fuel for gas engines. The development of the gas industry also generated a considerable demand for metalwork. Gas lamps were made from cast iron, whilst iron tubes were needed to convey the gas from the works.

Manufacture of town gas was a heavy manual job for many of the workers associated with the trade. The first retorts had single openings and were known as 'stop enders'. Coal was loaded into the retort by hand. It was barrowed to the floor in front of the retorts and shovelled through the mouthpiece. There were banks of retorts that were all held in place by firebrick surrounds. The retorts were heated and allowed the gas to escape through ascension pipes leading from the mouthpiece. After a period of time the coke was drawn out. It was a process fraught with problems. Remaining gas in the retort had to be burnt off before opening the retort door. Once it was safe to do so the hot coke was raked out and loaded into barrows and taken to boats or a stacking place for land sale.

Retort mouthpieces came in different sizes ranging from 14in to 25in. They might be circular, oval or D-shaped. Local firebrick makers supplied the clay retorts. They included firms like Mobberley & Perry, Harris & Pearson and E.J. & J. Pearson, all of which were located in the Stourbridge and Brierley Hill districts, whilst companies like Tangyes made a variety of gas plant, including retort lids and ascension tubes. Tangyes also supplied more specialised plant such as exhausters and mechanical self-propelled loading and discharging machines for the retorts at the larger gas making plants. Windsor Street New Retort House had a Tangye loader. Thomas Piggot and the Horseley Co. also provided gas plant and amongst the specialities were wrought or cast-iron gasholders.

Parliament made concessions to general utilities in 1870 with the passing of an Act that enabled local authorities to build gasworks, waterworks, etc. Birmingham Corporation set about taking over the mains and works within its boundaries and acquired the assets of both Birmingham gas companies during 1875. Adjacent local authorities decided to erect their own gas making plants, taking over in some cases the customers (and mains) of the former Birmingham & South Staffordshire Co.

Birmingham gas supply until 1875 was in the hands of the two companies, which owned the following works:

Birmingham Co. Gasworks 1875
and their Dates of Opening

Birmingham Gas Light & Coke Co.

Fazeley Street, Birmingham (1836)
Windsor Street, Aston (1848)

Birmingham & Staffordshire Gas Light Co.

Swan Village, West Bromwich (1825)
Adderley Street, Aston (1842)
Saltley (1857)

Each individual gas company has an element of uniqueness that was born out of the way gas was made and how the company operated. Some were formed through private finance, others with money supplied by municipal undertakings. As the demand for gas increased to supply industrial and domestic needs, more public undertakings were established. The Solihull Gas Co., formed in 1869, initially served a decidedly rural area. Land was purchased in Wharf Lane beside Solihull Wharf, on the Warwick and Birmingham Canal. It was commenced as a small works that originally included a small retort house, purification plant and a gasholder. The Solihull Gas Co. increased the capital from £7,000 to £15,000 through a new share issue made in 1885. At the time the gas was required to supply only forty-nine lamps and the annual consumption of coal to make the gas only amounted to 660 tons, which was carted by road from the Great Western Railway station. The additional funds were used to build a new retort house, purifier, boiler house and a house for the manager.

At Soho Foundry, Smethwick, William Murdoch had developed the first 'D'-shaped retorts in 1789 and one of his original gas holders remained for many years in the foundry yard, long after Boulton & Watt had quitted the site and even into the years W. & T. Avery had this foundry. Gas was first supplied to Smethwick by the Birmingham & Staffordshire Gas Light Co. When Birmingham Corporation purchased that undertaking in 1875, gas supply was continued but a clause in the Birmingham Gas Act enabled outlying districts to erect gasworks. Smethwick opened their new works in 1881 and in 1892 and 1898 made further expansions and, in addition to Klönnes regenerative furnaces, four beds of inclined retorts were built. Both furnaces and inclined retorts were amongst the most up-to-date gas making technology of the time.

Some works such as Cradley, Dudley and Sedgley had no canal connection and were conducted on a relatively small scale. Cradley Heath Gasworks was built in the borough of Rowley Regis and stood in a valley between Staffordshire and Worcestershire, with the River Stour running beside its walls. These works were established in 1854 by a private concern managed by William Bradley. During 1871 the Cradley Heath Gas Co. was incorporated to purchase the works. Dudley Gasworks was constructed during 1820 and ranks amongst one of the earliest in the district. Built on the hillside above Dudley Canal Tunnel, these works received all coal supplies by road. Sedgley Gasworks was similarly situated on a hillside at Lower Gornal and was owned by Sedgley District Council. The supply of gas from these works was contracted out to the private Sedgley Gas Co., established in 1875 by George Hancock, who acted as manager for the works.

Rowley Regis had a small canalside works owned by the Rowley Regis and Blackheath Gas Co. Ltd. Stourbridge Gasworks was erected in Amblecote during 1835 and purchased by the town in 1895. The retort house and other plant were established close to the end of the Stourbridge Town Arm and railway sidings were constructed in 1858 to serve the interchange basin. Gas from these works was pumped through to a diffuse area that included Amblecote, Blakedown, Churchill, Clent, Lye and Wollascote.

Walsall comprised an ancient borough and a thriving market town noted for the manufacture of saddlers' ironmongery and saddlery. Surrounding it on three sides to the south, west and north was the Foreign of Walsall that included a number of villages and hamlets such as Birchills, Blakenheath, Bloxwich, Caldmore and Pleck, and with it some two-thirds of the combined population. Gas was first supplied from 1826 by a private gasworks erected in Lichfield Street, on land now occupied by the Arboretum. Between

Wolverhampton Gas Works, through the Great Western Railway Arches.
The flight of twenty-one locks at Wolverhampton that enabled boats to pass between the 473ft level of the Birmingham Canal and the Staffordshire & Worcestershire Canal traversed both through industrial landscapes and fields. The railway arches shown marked the boundary between the two. (Black Country Museum)

Swan Village Gas Works.
The Swan Village Gas Works, near West Bromwich, had a long working life that spanned three different periods. Established by the Birmingham & Staffordshire Gas Light Co., these works were improved and rebuilt by Birmingham Corporation during their tenancy of the site and improved and rebuilt again by West Midlands Gas Board during the 1950s. (Local Studies Department, Birmingham Library)

1849 and 1850 the corporation erected a gasworks in Wolverhampton Street and the old one in Lichfield Street was dismantled. During 1859 the Birmingham & South Staffordshire Gas Light & Coke Co. Ltd also bought the right to supply Walsall with gas and this right was acquired by Birmingham Corporation in 1875. These rights were purchased from Birmingham under the Walsall Gas Purchase and Borough Extension Act of 1876. Under these powers a new gas making plant at Pleck was constructed. Wolverhampton Street Works continued to supply gas through to the year 1895, when the site was adapted for electricity generation purposes.

Wolverhampton's first gasworks at Horseleyfields remained in use until the late 1890s when production ceased and staff were transferred to the Stafford Road Works. The Wolverhampton Gas Co. made considerable improvements and enlargements, erecting new retort houses, gas holders and purifiers on vacant land between the canal and railway.

By-products of the gas industry also came under close scrutiny by chemists eager to develop the waste products, and even works of the size of Solihull were able to dispose of some of its by-products to a ready market. Coke had always found a saleable use in metalworking and iron smelting and gas tar was also collected for coating surfaces. The ammonia-rich gas water had been considered waste, but scientists came to look at the distillation products of gas tar and the value of gas water. Two new aspects of the chemical industry were developed as a result: tar distillation and chemical manures.

Coal tar became a valuable source of home-produced organic chemicals. 80 per cent of crude tar reappeared after distillation as pitch and creosote. These products were consumed as road tar and tarmacadam. In the early days of tar distillation many small firms existed, each of which distilled a few thousand tons a year of coal tar. Such firms were in competition and led a precarious existence. They fell behind other countries with research. Various chemical works established along the length of the BCN.

The original process of tar distillation involved the pumping of coal tar into large iron or mild steel pots that held from 10 to 40 tons. Each pot was heated by direct fire, which sometimes led to accidents on site. As crude tar was heated the lighter products including water boiled off, followed progressively by oils of higher boiling ranges. All of these distillates were condensed and run into a receiver. Generally, when the temperature reached 350°C, the heating was stopped and the liquid residue was run out to leave the still ready for a new charge. The residue left comprised pitch that was either broken-up for sale as solid lumps or was blended hot with select distillate oils to make road tars and fuels.

One of the first local tar distillers was John Clarkson Major at Monmore Green, Wolverhampton, whose chemical works was established during 1856 on a canalside site, near Ettingshall, to treat tar and later gas water. It was a partnership that was originally composed of Major and Turner and in addition to the Monmore Green works owned another tar works at Boughton near Chester. The Springfield Chemical Works, owned by Lewis, Demuth & Co., started refining tar about 1864. There was a basin that joined the Titford Canal below the bottom lock on the Wolverhampton level. Their site comprised some 20 acres where a group of retort sheds and tanks were distributed. Distillates from the retorts were collected and stored in the tanks. These included petroline, naptha and pitch, which were then sold for other purposes. The pitch element was a useful preservative, whilst

Robinson Tar Distillery, West Bromwich.
Robinson's 1924 catalogue included the following photograph, which shows the extent of their Tar Distillery at Ryders Green beside the Walsall Canal. The many chimneys are interspersed between a host of stills and storage tanks. An extensive boat dock is also shown to the right of the main factory. (Local Studies, Birmingham Library).

naptha was a fuel used in lamps. Robinson Brothers founded the Ryders Green Chemical works in 1869. They had tar from the various gasworks transported to their works by boat. The tar was used to make chemicals such as creosote, which also went out by boat.

Other local tar distillers included J. Spencer Balfour, who established the Cannock Chase Chemical Works at Brownhills beside the Anglesey Branch and John Bethell & Co., who had a naptha, creosote and patent coke works beside the Balls Hills Branch, Brickhouse Lane, West Bromwich. Bethell's tar distillery remained in use until 1887 when the stock of tar and oil stills, boilers, and drying and cooling pans was advertised for sale.

Most tar distillers had canal boats and would contract with the gasworks to take tar or liquor for a period of years. Lewis Demuth & Co., Springfield Chemical works, for example, had a contract with West Bromwich Corporation to collect all tar from gasworks for three years from July 1894.

Ammoniacal liquor, or gas water, was a liquid, which separated out and floated on top of the tar. It was rich in ammonia and sulphocyanides. It was first produced in small amounts, but as gasworks began to adopt more sophisticated means of purifying the gas with scrubbers, larger quantities of liquor were made. Gas water was treated with sulphuric acid to make ammonium sulphate, which found particular use as chemical manure. Sales of ammonium sulphate could fetch between £12 and £14 per bag and several firms became keen to produce it. The Galen Chemical Co. was set up at Ettingshall, in 1864,

Whimsey Bridge, Oldbury.
Whimsey Bridge was the name given to the bridge that carried the road from Birchfield to Oldbury over the canal deviation completed in 1821. (Bournville Village Trust/Connurbations).

specifically to deal with gas water. The manager of the plant was Alfred Payne, who had previously worked for Sturge Brothers, in Wheeleys Lane, Birmingham.

Chance Brothers, Galen, William Hunt and J.C. Major were all competitors for the available gas water and had boats to collect gas water from the local gasworks. Galen succeeded in getting a supply from Moxley Gasworks during 1868. The percentage of ammonia was measured according to 'twaddle' content and Payne arranged for payments for the liquor to be made according to strength. All other gas water customers appear to have made a flat payment. The contract with Moxley remained in use until 1872 when J.C. Major agreed to take the liquor.

The Galen Chemical Works were placed near to the Bilston & Sedgley Flour Mill, whose owners often objected to the smells emanating from the works, and especially hydrogen sulphide gas, which was a waste product of gas water treatment. It also seems that other compounds were manufactured at Ettingshall. Albright & Wilson's letter books record the supply of calcis muriate (calcium chloride) that was collected by boat from the Oldbury Phosphorus Works. The original Galen Chemical Co. was wound up during April 1871, but the works were taken over by Bailey Brothers, who continued the works under the name of the Galen Chemical Co. until about 1886.

A number of canal carriers also specialised in the carriage of gas works by-products. William John Yeomans was an Oldbury carrier who conveyed tar and gas water by canal.

Edwin Wilkes of Rowley Regis was a general carrier who had at least one boat, which was equipped to carry gas water between Birmingham, Shrewsbury and Warwick. Perhaps the best-known bulk liquid carrier was William Clayton.

Clayton had moved to Birmingham in about the year 1858 and had set up as a general canal carrier at Park Wharf, Adderley Street, beside the Warwick and Birmingham Canal and close to the newly erected Saltley Gasworks. He made a speciality of carrying gas works by-products and several boats amongst William's large fleet of boats were vessels modified to carry chemicals such as tar and ammoniacal liquor or creosote between the gas works and the chemical works. William Clayton & Co. had a contract to supply creosote to the Great Western Railway. In June 1885 they approached the BCN for a reduction of the tolls on creosote from the Springfield Works of Oldbury; Robinson Brothers of Ryders Green and Bethel Brothers of Golds Green to Bulls Bridge on the Grand Junction Canal. No reduction was granted, however.

Thomas Clayton succeeded his father William on his death to run the family firm. During 1889 Thomas Clayton merged his carrying business with Fellows, Morton & Co. to found the largest canal carrying company in the country. The specialist gas products traffic was subsequently segregated from Fellows, Morton & Clayton, when Thomas Clayton moved his fleet of tar and liquid carrying boats to a new base at Oldbury, located in the heart of the chemical manufacturing district.

Production of acid and alkali also continued to provide important canal revenue. Several new chemical works were established in the Black Country during the 1830s and 1840s and came to rival the established Birmingham chemical factories. Some like the Rowley Regis Alkali Works and the Swan Village Chemical and Ammonia Works had brief existences. Plant at Rowley Regis was offered for sale in February 1844, whilst during October 1847 a dismantling sale was held to dispose of F. & C. Hill's buildings, sal-ammoniac furnaces, vitriol lead chamber, stills and retorts. Two canal boats were offered for sale at the same time.

Wolverhampton attracted a number of manufacturing chemists. In addition to Major & Turner, by 1860 other manufacturing chemists included William Bailey & Son, Gibbons & Wills and James Wildsmith at Horseleyfields, and Bradburn & Co., Commercial Road, Wolverhampton. There was also W. Ridyard, of the Lower Bradley Chemical Works, Bilston, William Ward of Victoria Chemical Works, New Street, West Bromwich and William Hunt at the Alkali Works, Leabrook, Tipton.

William Bradburn & Co. specialised in the making of artificial manures and relocated to Wednesfield where they set up a manure works between the Wyrley & Essington and Bentley Canals. James Wildsmith and George Gaunt became Wildsmith & Gaunt manure merchants at Shakespeare Street, off Walsall Street, their brief partnership ended in the mid-1860s. William Bailey built up an extensive chemical plant that produced a range of pure substances suitable for the photographic and other trades. His works had direct access to the Birmingham Canal through a basin made under the towpath. Next to Bailey's chemical works was Gibbons, Wills and Gibbons artificial manure factory. William Ridyard came to enlarge his operation to include chemical works in Oxford Street, Bilston and Baggot Street, Birmingham. William Ward concentrated on the making of dry soap and washing powder, but also traded as an oil merchant and a refiner. The Ceres Works, placed beside the Wolverhampton lock flight was another supplier of artificial manures.

Carriage of salt and other basic ingredients were often influenced by canal tolls or railway rates and this affected decisions to send by railway or canal. Costs were critical and careful negotiations frequently ensured the continued use of canal transport. Arrangements were not just confined to local waterways; long-distance transport involved negotiations with all canal companies along a particular route. Chance Brothers, glassmakers at Spon Lane and chemical makers at Oldbury entered into a time bargain arrangement made with the Grand Junction Canal. A two-year agreement, from September 1857 to September 1859, enabled Chance Brothers to bring brimstone from London to Spon Lane at 14/8 per ton. Nitre was carried at 16/8 per ton. Soda ash was taken from Oldbury to London at 16/8 per ton. Chances' Oldbury chemical works manufactured a variety of products They collected a large fleet of boats, which traversed the canals collecting and delivering a variety of by-products and chemicals, which included ammonia, empty carboys, gas water, muriatic acid, nitric acid, purple ore, salt cake, sodium sulphide, spent oxide and waste acid.

Muriatic acid is better known as hydrochloric acid. It was produced as a waste gas hydrogen chloride, until a method was devised to condense it. In aqueous solution, it was both volatile and corrosive. Once the hydrogen chloride gas was collected for industrial purposes, hydrochloric acid became a useful product. Hydrochloric acid was used to produce bleaching powder, sodium bicarbonate and was also used to treat metals in the same way as sulphuric acid. Hydrochloric acid was of particular use in the pickling baths associated with cold strip rolling, where the acid produced a clean, grease-free surface.

William Hunt carried on with considerable success at the Leabrook Works, near Wednesbury. Hunt built up an important business by water and in particular did considerable trade with John Corbett, salt manufacturer at the Stoke Works. Hunt built up a business that came to rival Chance Brothers. Their works lay beside the Walsall Canal opposite the Patent Shaft & Axletree, Monway Works. Hunt, too, owned a fleet of boats and carried similar traffic to Chance. In March 1898 the chemical business of Chance was merged with Hunt to establish Chance & Hunt.

The production of alkali was important to the making of soap. The common process was to mix animal fat, or tallow, with alkali in various proportions to make yellow or mottled soap. The alkali manufacturing process requires salt. In 1866 Atkins, Chance and Hunt were major alkali manufacturers in the district. It was recorded that their three works used about 12,000 tons of salt annually, which was brought principally by canal from the Worcestershire salt works located at Droitwich and Stoke Works. If it is assumed that each boat carried between 28 and 30 tons of salt, more than 400 boatloads would have been needed. That is, at least two boatloads of salt were delivered weekly to each of the three works.

The salt producing companies generally owned their own narrow boats. They delivered salt to the chemical works and loaded up with coal for the return journey. The salt extraction process required a lot of coal. Some was needed for the boilers to drive the pumping engines, but the majority was used to heat the vast number of saltpans, which heated the brine. Coal was carried from mines throughout the Black Country. Dudley Canal records for the 1830s and 1840s mention traffic to the Droitwich Salt Works, which were then reached either via Hanbury Wharf on the Worcester & Birmingham Canal or the Droitwich Canal via the River Severn. The development of the British and Imperial Salt Works at Stoke Works, on the Worcester & Birmingham Canal during the 1830s led to a new demand for coal in that district. The two works at Stoke Works faced each other on either bank of the canal and made both salt and alkali. In addition to coal there was a requirement for limestone that arrived by boat originally from quarries near Dunhampstead, but was supplemented by limestone from other locations. The building of the Droitwich Junction Canal (1853/1854) enabled direct movement of coal and salt between the Worcester & Birmingham Canal and the principal salt works in Droitwich, such as the Patent Salt Works. The 1850s was also a time when John Corbett came to gain control of the salt works at Stoke Works.

In October 1883 the Droitwich Salt Co. applied for a reduction of the toll on salt that passed along the Droitwich Junction Canal, Worcester & Birmingham Canal and Birmingham Canal Navigations to the Leabrook Chemical Works. There was keen competition in the supply of salt for chemical manufacturing purposes and the Droitwich Salt Co. wanted to retain the trade. It was estimated that at that time the tonnage of salt was equal to 5,000 tons per annum. Another tonnage rate equal to 10,000 tons of slack was derived from the return traffic. An agreed rate of 1s 3d per ton of salt allowed Droitwich boats, which carried up to 30 tons, to be charged for 27 tons. Droitwich Salt Works also had rail sidings and the possible loss traffic to rail induced the canal company to agree to reduce the toll to 1s 1d. A reduction was also agreed for John Corbett who owned the salt works at Stoke Works. At that time he paid 1s for 24 tons carried in a 28-ton boat.

Salt was also produced in Cheshire and Staffordshire. The Staffordshire salt works were mainly located around Stafford Common, where Chance and Hunt had a rail-served salt works, and there was another works with wharf access to the Staffordshire & Worcestershire Canal at Baswich.

Each salt works produced three basic types of salt. Best quality salt was collected for domestic use, being put together in blocks of white salt. The second quality was the industrial salt that was sent to the chemical works or for other uses such as to Doulton's works at Rowley and Smethwick. Salt-glazed pottery was used in sanitary ware and a large amount of this pottery was manufactured in the Midlands. A poorer quality was defined as agricultural salt and was sold as fertiliser.

The manufacture of sulphuric acid used either sulphur (brimstone) or pyrites and there was traffic in both. Iron pyrites, drawn from Staffordshire mines, were processed in works such as Chance's and there would have been traffic in these along the Trent & Mersey and Staffordshire & Worcester Canals. Later other metal pyrites were imported from Portugal or Spain through ports such as Gloucester and brought up to the chemical works by carriers. Copper pyrites produced copper as a by-product and by 1866 a copper works had been established at Anchor Bridge to refine this metal. The firm was originally known as the Staffordshire Copper Extracting Co. Ltd, but by 1872 had become the Tharsis Sulphur & Copper Co. Ltd.

In 1866 the Leabrook, Oldbury and Soho chemical works were producing 20,000 tons of sulphuric acid and 10,000 tons of hydrochloric acid annually. Approximately 12,000 tons of pyrites and 40,000 tons of coal were needed. During October 1883 James Fellows, as agent for the Severn Canal Carrying Co., applied for a reduction of toll on 4,000 tons of pyrites imported into Cardiff Docks for Oldbury. The agreed toll of 1s per ton was based on 32 tons charged as 29 tons. The reduction, on this occasion, was not agreed. Acid made elsewhere was also carried onto the BCN. The Union Acid of Manchester carried acid in carboys to West Midlands industry.

Yellow phosphorus was required for the making of Lucifer matches. J. & E. Sturge grasped the new business opportunity and went into the making of yellow phosphorus during the 1840s. Arthur Albright was a partner in this firm from 1842 and it was under his careful management that phosphorus was made at the Selly Oak Chemical Works. The essential ingredient was bone ash imported from South America, which was treated with sulphuric acid to extract the phosphorus. During 1850 plans were initiated to build a new phosphorus works at Oldbury and production transferred there in 1851. It was a location that was useful for the canal network, where bone ash and coal were delivered by boat and sulphuric acid from the nearby chemical workings of Chance Brothers. The Sturge partnership was dissolved 1854 with Arthur Albright retaining Oldbury Phosphorus Works. In 1856 the firm became Albright & Wilson.

Albright & Wilson's chemical works were built between 1850 and 1851 beside the Houghton Arm. Construction materials such as bricks and timber were brought in by canal boat. Other goods were also probably carried to the site by canal. They included various iron goods supplied by Smith & Hawkes Eagle Foundry, Broad Street and structural ironwork by Lloyds Foster Old Park Ironworks, Wednesbury.

Yellow phosphorus used in match making had several disadvantages. It would ignite and workers were subject to phosphorus disease, a serious affliction that destroyed bones and shortened lives. Albright chose to adopt a new process invented by an Austrian chemist, which made red, or amorphous phosphorous, and did not catch fire on exposure to air. It presented less dangerous health hazards. Arthur Albright gained the British rights to the process and patented a manufacturing method.

At first most of Albright's traffic came and went by canal. Local carriers were regularly used, but they also had a few open day boats owned by the company. During November 1855 Arthur Albright had cause to complain about the service they received from the Grand Junction Canal Co. There were several days when the Grand Junction steerer failed to call and on other occasions refused to take certain traffic. There was a consignment of 7 tons of sulphur potash in casks, which should have been delivered to Hickling & Co. in Birmingham. Albright & Wilson were left to send the order by one of their own boats. Later other consignments were ignored and were taken by cart to the LNWR at Spon Lane.

Albright's works were gradually enlarged. The Lower Works was a new part that extended towards the Titford Canal. A short branch called the Jim Crow Arm served the Lower Works and joined with the Titford Canal. During the mid-1870s trustees of J. Fellows carried gypsum in bags to different destinations, and often to Saltley Dock, on the Birmingham & Warwick Junction Canal, where it was presumably sent on by rail wagon along the metals of the Midland Railway. The Severn Carrying Co. also carried gypsum and brought loads of phosphates to either the Upper or Lower Works.

Their bulk traffic was phosphates and limestone. The phosphate traffic fluctuated between canal and railway and up to 7,000 tons could be conveyed each year. The phosphate rock arrived by sea and was landed at a British port and then forwarded by suitable transport. The cost was foremost in deciding whether the goods were taken by canal or railway. Often it was a combination of both. Until 1884, Albright and Wilson's works had only a canal connection and goods had to be transhipped into a canal boat for the final leg of the journey. Phosphate traffic by rail had to be transferred at interchange basins such as Swan Village. This basin, which belonged to the GWR, also handled limestone traffic for Albrights, which had come from Minera near Wrexham. Another interchange basin kept busy with their traffic was the LNWR basin at Spon Lane. They transhipped lime from the Buxton lime quarries, which had travelled via the LNWR or MR to get there. Rail connections improved from 1884 with the construction of the GWR Oldbury Branch from Langley Green that passed beside the phosphorus works and Chance's alkali works. A rail connection was provided into Albright's works that enabled rail wagons to be sent direct to their works and consequently led to a reduction in canal trade.

Albright & Wilson's boats appear to have been generally of the open wood or iron type and several were replaced in 1898. For long-distance work they continued to rely on commercial carriers. During the 1890s, for example, Fellows Morton & Co. carried waste black to Gas, Light & Coke Co.'s Shoreditch and Beckton gasworks in London. W. & S. Foster of Tipton carried manganese ore from London to Oldbury. The Shropshire Union Co. supplied boats for local journeys to Wednesfield.

Up to and including the late 1890s a significant proportion of rock phosphate was taken all the way from the port of arrival to Oldbury by canal. The choice of carrier depended on where the vessel docked. Anything from 100 to 200 tons of phosphates could be landed at a time and it was up to the carrier to get it to Oldbury as speedily as possible. Each carrier had to compete with rail traffic and only won the business if they were capable of moving the load speedily. Phosphates that arrived at Liverpool were carried by the Shropshire Union Co. Loads landed at Cardiff and Avonmouth were brought by the Severn Canal Carrying Co., and Fellows Morton & Clayton loaded in London. Other Albright & Wilson traffic was waste to tip on BCN beside the old Tividale Colliery and also to Netherton.

Glue manufacture was an industry derived from animal products that required bulk boiling in vats. Coal was an important requirement and works for glue making were sometimes canal features. R. Bindley glue, gelatine and size makers, Smethwick, produced a range of adhesives, which included concentrated ground glues for joiners, painters and decorators as well as other glues of varying qualities for fixing veneers, joinery or fixing emery onto grinding wheels for edge tool work.

With the completion of the Cannock Extension Canal only minor extensions and alterations were made to the local canal network. A short section of Telford's feeder from Titford Engine House towards Spon Lane was widened and made navigable to a basin near Rood End railway sidings on the Stourbridge Extension Railway. Improvements were also made at Norton Springs on the Cannock Extension Canal where a short branch, little more than a basin, was made, to serve Conduit No.3 Colliery and the Norton Springs Tramway. The same Act of Parliament that approved the building of the Cannock

Extension Canal and the Littleworth Tramway sanctioned Norton Springs Tramway. The line was to continue north towards Heath Hayes as a narrow gauge tramway. Contractor John Boys was engaged to make the tramway in 1870 and 1871 but work was abandoned and all equipment sold off. The route was eventually incorporated into the LNWR Five Ways mineral branch railway that was opened in 1894 to Coppice Colliery, otherwise known as the Fair Lady Pit. The only canal improvement was the long arm or basin that became known as the Norton Springs Branch, which was lined on both sides by tramway lines that brought coal down from Conduit No.3 Colliery to load into boats.

The 1880s and 1890s were times of rationalisation and improvement and the Birmingham Canal Navigations benefited through the able assistance of George Jebb. Mr Jebb had first accepted the post of engineer to the Shropshire Union Canal, which was then owned and vested in the LNWR. It was an association that led Jebb also to take on the role of engineer to the Birmingham Canal, which was controlled by the LNWR. George Jebb was able, through sheer skill and ability, to bring plant and equipment up to date and maintain the waterway efficiently. His involvement in BCN affairs was all the more remarkable as traffic on the Birmingham Canal increased at a time when other canals experienced a fall-off in trade.

These last two decades of the nineteenth century are noted for the many changes throughout industry brought about through developments in engineering. The legacy of pioneers such as Isambard Kingdom Brunel, Robert Stephenson and James Nasmyth had borne the greatest fruit and students and followers of these great men had adopted their ideas and through innovation had brought in many improvements.

New trades grew out of modified working practice. New skills and working methods were honed as invention led to new types of machines being developed. The town's people of Birmingham were particularly adept at grasping new ideas and new trades flourished there. The continued demand for coal and metal ensured a continued role for the canal and transport along it.

Steam engine manufacture required the provision of both a brass foundry and iron foundry to cast the essential parts, and fitting shops for erection. Canalside locations were frequently considered useful locations for the placing of a steam engine works. Goscote Foundry, placed near the Wyrley & Essington Canal, had been used to cast steam engine cylinders from the start of the nineteenth century and was later employed in the repair and manufacture of steam engines, especially after 1853 when Edward Thomas Wright had the lease. York's foundry near Pelsall also produced parts for steam engines, as did the Pelsall Foundry established by Joseph Wilkes.

Engineering skills continued to be honed, and improved manufacturing techniques led to more efficient and compact engines. The making and maintenance of steam engines was an essential service to keep the wheels of industry moving. Firms located in the Black Country and Birmingham provided improved stationary steam engines. Simpson and Shipton, originally of Manchester, produced a reciprocating engine that was used to drive James Shipton's sawmill at Old Factory Wharf, Wolverhampton. J.A. Shipton had the use of the Oak Farm Foundry near the end of the Stourbridge Extension Canal, but by 1856 had transferred to a new engineering site adjacent to Albion Flour Mill. A short-lived business was the Oxford Works, Trinity Street, Oldbury, which was placed beside the private Chemical, or Houghton, Arm that was erected about 1852 for steam engine making. The Oxford Works comprising a range of one-storey shops covered with galvanised and corrugated iron roofing that included smith shops, iron foundry and a brass shop was offered for sale in 1857, some five years after the firm had commenced.

Some firms had longer existences. May & Mountain of the Suffolk Works, Berkeley Street, Birmingham, were built alongside a basin that joined with the Worcester & Birmingham Canal. They had fitting shops, and an iron and a brass foundry that was used for the construction and repair of steam-driven plant. George and Jonah Davis operated from three separate premises, but had their headquarters at the Albion Foundry (Toll End). Davis was numbered amongst the most prolific Black Country stationary steam engine makers, supplying engines for both industry and civil undertakings. A beam engine, built by G. & J. Davis, can still be found in the former South Staffordshire Waterworks, Sandhills pumping engine house at Lichfield. Rowland William Brownhill of the Birchills Foundry, Walsall, was another accomplished engineer who included steam engines in his range. He is also credited with the invention of the first coin payment gas meter.

Birmingham's ammunition trade grew out of the supply of precision caps. Firms like George Kynoch had their roots in this trade. It was, however, a very dangerous occupation to enter and explosions with sad loss of life were not uncommon. Knowing the precarious nature of the job, it is a surprising fact that this work was originally carried out in Birmingham town centre until public opinion caused its removal to the outskirts. Kynoch's moved to Witton where they built up an ammunition making trade.

Early forms of ammunition included powder and ball. The firm of J. & E. Walker, Gospel Oak Ironworks, included amongst their make cannon balls, yet this was a trade that went into decline when more modern forms of ordnance were devised. The new shells and bullets had elements of copper and brass in their cases. The demand for copper and brass sheet increased. Three main manufacturers came to be established in the Birmingham area: Birmingham Small Arms Co., Kynoch's and the National Arms & Ammunition Co. Kynoch's took over the old steam mill in Water Street for rolling sheet. The BSA had rolling mills in Adderley Street beside the Birmingham & Warwick Junction Canal.

The National Arms & Ammunition Co. had four separate works, which included Holford Mills, near the Tame Valley Canal at Witton. Their brief existence came to an end in 1888, leaving the BSA and Kynoch's to compete for the trade. Copper and zinc ingots were regularly purchased for casting into alloy or the correct composition. This then passed through the breaking down rolls, was annealed, pickled and rolled and re-rolled until the correct thickness was achieved. Finally the sheets were cut down to sheet or strip of a required width. Coal, acid and metals were amongst the raw materials brought to the mills by canal or road cartage.

Strip and sheet were then drawn and machined into cartridge or shell cases. Such was demand for shell cases that other rolled metal manufacturers assisted with demand, particularly in times of conflict. The Kings Norton Metal Co. beside the Worcester & Birmingham Canal was one of several local firms engaged in the rolled metal trade who supplied metal for this use.

The Victorian era was a time of innovation and invention. New ideas seemed to come to the fore at regular intervals and the patents office was frequently inundated with proposals for variations on existing machines and methods or totally new concepts. Out of this vast array of paper documentation came some very good ideas and principals. British industry benefited as a result. Within the West Midlands, honed engineering skills led to improvements in steam engine design, new machines to make pins, nuts and screws, and the gas engine. The steam engine had been developed to increased efficiency with double and triple expansion systems utilising the power of the steam on two or three occasions. The gas engine was, however, more compact and found ready use in a number of engineering applications and became a favourite for cycle and bedstead makers.

Metallic bedstead making had become a staple trade in Birmingham, but cycle making was a new industry, which during the 1890s would blossom after the invention of the safety bicycle. Early bicycles were large and basic machines. They included the 'penny-farthing' and the 'tricycle'. Although Coventry is justly associated with the development of the safety bicycle and bicycle making in general, Birmingham had many more cycle component makers. The metalworking skills in forging and stamping parts, making tubes, spokes and wheels were all derived and adapted from existing trades, which existed around the town of Birmingham.

Thomas Smith had works in Adderley Street, beside the Birmingham and Warwick Junction Canal. It was a metalworking business that had been built up at the old Saltley Mill, in 1848, and transferred to the canalside works. Thomas Smith decided to retain the name Saltley Mill, and it is a name that can be seen on the premises to the present time. Smith produced both penny-farthings and tricycles there.

Starley's safety bicycle was a considerable improvement on the early bicycles and was quickly adopted by cycle makers and the public in general. New firms quickly set up in business. Their need for components rapidly increased. Stampers and piercers, tube makers and cycle chain makers all reaped the benefit. The demand for weldless tubes in steel was particularly important and a number of new firms came into existence to supply the cycle trade.

It was a propitious moment as the black iron trade was in decline. Tube drawing firms frequently replaced previous industry on a canal site. As demand increased more firms were established, but then came the crash. So many cycle making and component companies had been formed that the market was oversubscribed. The demand simply did not match production and both cycle companies and their suppliers came on hard times and bankruptcy followed bankruptcy in the same fashion as the serious iron trade depression of 1857–1860.

The Concentric Tube Co. had works on the corner of Love Lane and Dartmouth Street, which backed onto the Digbeth Canal. The premises had a long and previous history as Armitage's chemical works, but had been converted into tube drawing and rolling mills about the year 1889 for making steel tubes, only to be offered for sale in 1898 following bankruptcy. Sites in Birmingham were at a premium and a London copper rolling firm, Delta Metals, acquired the 'Dartmouth Works'. They installed new plant that included the first metal extrusion plant in the country. The method of extruding non-ferrous metal into rods became an important tool for local industry and extrusion presses were later installed at several local firms.

Walsall Canal, Pleck.
This postcard view shows the Walsall Canal looking from the area known as the Pleck towards Walsall. This area around Rolling Mill Street Bridge was noted for the Alma, Cyclops and Walsall Tubeworks that lined the waterway there. (Ray Shill collection).

New Brotherton Tube Works, Wolverhampton.
Drawbenches were an essential part of the tube making process where strips of metal were drawn through a die to form the tube. In this view a group of benches is shown for the production of welded tubes suitable for gas or water purposes. (Reproduced from *Wolverhampton & South Staffordshire Illustrated*).

The Credenda Tube Works at Smethwick also acquired a canal site beside the Engine Arm at Smethwick in 1889. This property had belonged to the Birmingham Plate Glass Co., which had been sold to Chance Brothers in 1873. They had tried their best to make the making of plate glass there a success, and had even invested in new plant during 1888. The investment proved to be a waste of money and Chance's decided to close the works in 1889. Half of the site was taken over by Credenda to make solid drawn steel tubes.

Most tube drawing benches utilised chains to draw the tube out, but Credenda decided to adopt a different method and purchased benches from Armstrong Whitworth that were of the double-ended screw type, worked by a centrally placed steam engine. The innovation proved not to be a success. Credenda was taken over by the Star Tube Co. in 1896 and in 1897 merged with Climax Weldless Tube and St Helens Tube to form Weldless Tubes Ltd. They later shortened their title to Tubes Ltd, which became the bedrock of the twentieth century firm TI. Meanwhile, other tube makers continued to be established. Amongst their number was the New Brotherton Tube Works beside the Commercial Arm in Wolverhampton.

Another concept, which came about during Victorian times, was compressed air as a means of power. Steam engines were initially used as compressors and a company was formed in Birmingham to pump compressed air through mains to works where engines were converted to use compressed air rather than steam. The works were established beside the Birmingham & Warwick Junction Canal at Bordesley and had coal delivered by boat to fuel the boilers there. This commercial venture did not meet with success. The company had difficultly maintaining pressure and eventually abandoned the scheme, much to the annoyance of the firms who had signed up with them.

There was another side to compression technology that could be used for refrigeration. Local engineer W.H. Haines, whose father had been associated with iron smelting at Willingsworth and iron working at Sheepwash ironworks, became a specialist in steam engine engineering. William Haines was brother-in-law to the carrier Joshua Fellows. When Fellows, Morton & Co. took over the disused gasworks site in Fazeley Street, Birmingham, in 1880, the land was used for three purposes. Part was rebuilt as warehouse accommodation for the canal trade, another part was given over for William and his brother, Alfred, to set up an engineering business. The third part was adapted as an ice factory by a company titled the Patent Transparent Ice Co. There was a need to preserve food and it was common to collect ice, in winter, and store it in specially constructed icehouses. Concern was often felt about the source of the ice and its quality. With the new refrigeration technology it was possible to make ice from a known and purer supply. W.H. Haines was retained as manager for the ice company and although the firm itself had but a brief existence, the ice factory had a much longer existence in private hands.

Brick making in the second half of the nineteenth century benefited through increased mechanisation and improved kiln design. Works were distributed throughout the Black Country and certain districts around Birmingham. Yards in Birmingham were particularly noted for the adoption of new and improved kilns such as the Hoffman type. Canals served brickworks in this district, including works at Lapal, Kings Norton and Millpool

Hill. Workers employed in these works were usually men. Black Country yards by contrast tended to have smaller kilns arranged in banks. The brick makers were commonly women, assisted by girls.

Wood & Ivery owned the Albion Brickworks, West Bromwich. They had a ten-hole Baker & Co. (of Oldham) patent fuel kiln that consumed smoke and saved on fuel use. Clay was taken from the adjacent marl pit for treatment. The pit as described in 1876 required gunpowder to bring down the blueish rock that formed the material for brick making.

The soft rock was put into a wagon and drawn up an incline from the marl hole to the mill. Here the broken rock was mixed with hot water and ground down by revolving iron rolls and rotating knives to produce a mouldable clay. Brick making was conducted in a square low-roofed room, known as a stove, which had many openings to the outside air. A network of flues under the floor enabled the stove to be heated from below. Here the bricks were made and allowed to dry. Women, assisted by girls, formed the bricks from the rich brown-coloured clay. They worked quickly as wages were based on completion of an agreed daily amount. Men, and some boys, performed the tasks of carrying the clay to the stove and wheeling the bricks to the kiln as well as loading and stacking the finished products.

A great pile of the clay lay on a rough bench by the women's side. They took hold of a lump of it, and patted and punched it. Four pats and the lump of clay took shape as a rough oblong, and it was flung into an oblong box, which acted as a mould. The interior of the box was dusted to prevent the clay from sticking to the sides. A wire knife cut off the surplus clay from above the edge of the mould and the unpressed and unbaked brick was shaken out. With a mechanical and practised swing the box was dusted and shaken to remove the superfluous dust, filled with the roughly shaped clay, shaved with the wire knife at the top edge and then shaken free of its contents. So it went all day long – dusting, shaking, filling, shaving and emptying without pause. The brick was then taken to a hand press on a screw pattern. A boy put in and took away the bricks. A girl standing on a platform above him set the bar, which worked the screw to and fro. Wood and Ivery also had a Pollock and Pollock brick making machine and raw bricks, whether machine or handmade, were left to dry. A day was required for drying the raw bricks, after which they were taken to the kiln. There were groups of kilns on the site. Each kiln would hold 40,000 to 50,000 bricks for one to fourteen days. The blue bricks made here were of quite a durable nature.

Wood & Ivery's were quite a large undertaking, many works operated on a smaller scale. In 1873 Thomas Walton of Park Lane, Tipton, brick maker, entered into an agreement to work the brickworks and marl pits at Dudley Port. William Hopkins originally occupied these works. Hopkins also worked the adjacent blast furnaces. Plant included kilns, slopes and machines. The tramway from the marl pit passed under the Sedgley Turnpike Road to brickworks near basin to wharf beside the BCN old main line. The basin was leased to the Grand Junction Canal Co. A set of schedules included within the lease provides useful information about the works.

Above:
Black Country Brick Works *c.*1945. This panoramic view of the Black Country shows a brickworks and associated marl pit. Material for brick making, which was usually marl, but could be almost solid rock, was dug and quarried and then brought to the brick making sheds in wagons drawn up an incline. (Bournville Village Trust/Conurbations)

Right:
Stourbridge Canal Brickyard. There was a time when canalside brickyards were a common site throughout the Black Country. Gradually the yards have closed. This yard was placed near Moor Lane and the stacks of bricks are clearly seen from the canal bank. The top of the long kiln is also visible, which appears to be the continuous type. (Ray Shill 1975).

Circular Brick Kiln.
Some brickyards used kilns that were loaded with a single charge of bricks that was then left for several days to complete the firing process. Early kilns of this type were rectangular in nature, but gradually they were replaced by the more compact circular kiln. Banks of these kilns were placed around the drying and moulding sheds of yards engaged in making house bricks and firebricks. (Ray Shill collection).

Dudley Port Brickworks Lease Schedule 19 July 1873 (Dudley Local History Centre Coseley MS 88950)

First Schedule
Boilers – cylindrical boiler.

Clay Mill – a brick building, a pair of kibbling rolls, shafts, pinions and fittings, two hoppers, wet clay pan, mixer and other fittings. Driving gear to clay mill with driving wheel, crab, cam ring etc.

Drying Stoves – 40 yards x 9 yards, with flues under floor, tiled roof, eight principals – building is damaged by subsidence.

Engines – a high-pressure vertical engine with a 16in cylinder. A donkey engine on iron standards with force pumps.

Incline – strong wooden frame with winding drum for incline bank, strong timber fixing, overhead gear, pulleys and fixing. Wood-built incline and supports from hopper to top mouth of tunnel under turnpike, a wrought iron railway.

Kilns – three eight-hole kilns, brick built, forty-eight sets of fire bars.

Pumps – main pumps under Sedgley Road for pump rods from Jacky pit in marl hole.

Second Schedule

Pair of smooth clay rolls, attached to revolving mixer, wet clay tubs, round chain, clay wagons for marl hole incline, rails and sleepers leading from kilns down to LNWR railway sidings with sleepers.

New drying stove.

New round kiln for blue bricks with flues and fire grates, 17ft diameter.

Certain clays proved suitable for pottery and sanitary ware. The firm of Doulton's had potteries at Rowley Regis and Smethwick that used local clays. Their clay mines were located at the Saltwells and a tramway brought the clay down to the Dudley No.2 Canal for transfer by boat to either the Rowley pottery or Smethwick pottery.

Flint glass making in the Birmingham district saw considerable decline after 1850. Several works closed. Harris's Islington Glassworks in Sheepcote Street was sold in 1861 and converted into a bedstead factory. Park Glass and Chandelier Works was disposed of in 1879 and the land was subsequently developed by Barker and Allen as a rolling mill for nickel silver and other non-ferrous alloys.

Innovation led to important improvements for the plate glass makers. The Birmingham Plate Glass Co. was established at Smethwick in 1836 to compete with the established business at Newcastle upon Tyne and St Helens and remained in business until the late

Chances' Glass Works, Spon Lane.
The largest glassworks in the Midlands was located at Spon Lane. Here Chance Brothers conducted the manufacture of sheet and plate glass and glass for lighthouses. Spon Lane glassworks received its supply of coal, limestone and sand via basins placed alongside the old main line between Spon Lane and Steward's Aqueduct. (Bournville Village Trust/Connurbations).

1870s. At nearby Spon Lane R.L. Chance had taken over the British Crown Glassworks in 1824 and made considerable improvements to the site setting up plant to make rolled plate, crown and sheet glass. Chance had previously made crown (window) glass in London and amongst his early customers there was Trentham Hall that received glass by canal boat. The move to the Spon Lane site was particularly advantageous for transport by water, lying beside the old main line of the Birmingham Canal. Sheet glass came to replace crown glass from 1832. Robert Lucas Chance and James Hartley perfected a process based on Bohemian sheet glass. The essence of this method was the blowing of cylinders of glass that were opened out into sheet.

Chance's Spon Lane works required considerable quantities of coal to heat the various furnaces, and coal was brought by boat to the works. In 1865 an account written for the British Association visit to Birmingham reckoned that some 3,000 tons of coal were required each week, which would amount to 120 boatloads if all were sent by canal. Some 200 tons of sand, 85 tons of alkali (sodium carbonate) and 67 tons of chalk or limestone were also needed on a weekly basis.

New developments in the coal industry included improved mechanical haulage and more efficient steam engines to drive winding and pumping plant. A better understanding of mining techniques had led to the employment of more capable mining engineers and careful studies of the mineral seams had given a better understanding of where to find coal and how to mine it. The dangers from flooding, gas and roof falls were ever present yet engineers and mine owners were becoming better equipped to deal with the problems.

The developments on Cannock Chase had opened up a new coalfield for exploitation, but elsewhere on the South Staffordshire Coalfield mining was still carried on despite dwindling resources. Mines in this area were reworked to extract the ribs and pillars of thick coal. The square work system had left a considerable amount of coal to support the roof and with time and pressure the ribs and pillars had been forced down into a mass that could be reworked. Shafts were reopened and the miners returned to get what they could.

Elsewhere the hunt was on to reach the hidden measures. Geologists had suspected that coal might exist under the red sandstone rock at the extremities of the South Staffordshire Coalfield. This suggestion turned to fact, when the Sandwell Park sinking found thick coal. A public company was formed to finance this venture and after considerable difficulty managed to establish a successful mine beside the Great Western Railway at West Bromwich. The first coal was raised during 1877. A significant part of the coal mined was sent along a rope-worked tramway to a loading wharf beside the old main line of the Birmingham Canal, near Smethwick.

Sandwell Park Colliery was followed by other new colliery ventures at Hamstead and Walsall Wood. The sinking at Perry Colliery proved less successful when the sinkers found water rather than coal. The shaft was later adapted by Birmingham Corporation to supply water to the town and subsequently, when Elan Valley water became available to the people of Birmingham, Perry Well was used by the Birmingham Canal Navigations to supply water to Perry Barr Locks.

Colliery development continued in the Cradley, Dudley, Halesowen and Old Hill districts as mines tapped the more difficult strata. These included mines such as Haden

Black Country Colliery.
Pit headstocks, pumping engines and steam winders were once an integral part of the Black Country skyline. This view of the pit bank of a mine near Rowley Regis, suggested by some as being Rowley Hall Colliery, dates from the 1890s. Lines of narrow-gauge tramways pass hither and thither complete with trains of pit tubs. (Sandwell Public Libraries)

Hill. The Haden Hill Colliery, as described by the Colliery Guardian in 1897, comprised two plants. The old mine had been commenced by a Mr Barr in 1834 to mine a 10-yard seam and brooch coal. Later workings at the No.2 pit had commenced in 1865 with two winding shafts 263 yards deep. The No.2 pit was located at a distance from the canal but was served by a surface tramway that brought pit tubs down to the canal basin (Dudley No.2 Canal), near Waterfall Lane Bridge. Coal was mined by the by square-work system. The stalls were 10 yards wide and ribs of coal left 8 to 10 yards thick. In the course of a few years the workings were re-entered to take away pillars and ribs as far as was practical. Haden Hill No.2 colliery was kept dry by a steam pumping engine made in 1865 by John Withinshaw of 33 Broad Street, Birmingham. A Lilleshall & Co. winding engine powered surface and underground rope haulage.

Water remained a handicap to mine workings and a mines drainage scheme was instituted in the Old Hill area to keep the district dry. This scheme came into operation during 1870 and local mine owners were charged a levy to pay for the operation of the engines. Credit for the idea belongs chiefly to one man, Edward Bindon Marten, who put forward the concept of mines drainage based on observations he had made. Edward gave lectures on the subject from 1865. The crux of the idea was the fact that private mine pumping engines might raise water from the pits they served but this water was then pumped into streams and waterways and often found its way back into the mines.

His concept was to manage water more effectively. The core of his ideas was to form the basis of the Old Hill Mines Drainage.

Underground mining districts were divided into areas known as 'pounds' and the Old Hill district was concerned with the Cradley and Old Hill pounds that included mines north of the River Stour. The new Old Hill Drainage Authority took charge of three pumping engines in private hands, at Prince of Wales Colliery, Buffery Colliery and Cobbs Engine at Windmill End. Cobbs' engine house is still a landmark feature beside the Dudley Canal. The survival of this structure was helped through the purchase of the engine house from the owner Sir Horace St Paul in 1871.

A wider scheme, South Staffordshire Mines Drainage, received parliamentary approval in 1873. This act sanctioned the incorporation of the Old Hill district and created four more districts at Bilston, Kingswinsford, Oldbury and Tipton. The 1873 Act had two objectives:

1. The repair of the watercourses, so as by efficient surface drainage, to prevent water percolating from them into the mines.
2. The efficient pumping of water out of the mines themselves, so as to effect a proper mine or underground drainage.

The Act also provided for the appointment of commissioners, some of which were to be elected and others were *ex officio*. Funds for the venture, to include the purchase of existing pumping plants, construction of new plant, repairs of watercourses and other maintenance, were derived from two separate rates. A general drainage rate was charged for surface drainage work and a mines drainage rate was to subsidise all underground pumping. Each rate was directly connected to the amount of minerals raised.

A group of arbitrators was also appointed to assess rates for all mine owners and grant exceptions as required. They were the most important functionaries under the Act. They reported to the commissioners. Surveys and plans were made by them of the surface drainage area and they made suggestions of how the surface water might be disposed of. Underground they made plans and sections of all working and exhausted mines, especially noting the ribs and barriers left in place to prevent the flow of water.

During the first year of operation, 1873/1874, both commissioners and arbitrators were occupied in assessing the area. Once the rates were decided the problems of rate collection began. Rates were constantly disputed by mine owners, who determined to pay as little as possible.

The best-laid plans that gave rise to the original Act did not prevent many other problems once the scheme was in operation. Each district was semi-autonomous and responsible for its own finances. The Bilston and Tipton districts, which were effectively combined from 1881, experienced the most problems and incurred a considerable debt. The main cause of the debt was the cost of pumping, which increased with further mine closures and stoppage of private pumping engines. New plant and engines had to be purchased to keep levels down. They were the subject of a chancery case in October 1888 that resulted in a permanent receiver being appointed for that district and three Acts of Parliament were required to guarantee finance for the Tipton district from the loan commissioners.

Drainage commissioners worked a number of engines across the South Staffordshire coalfield and these delivered water into the Birmingham Canal. Prior to these times the Birmingham Canal had received, and paid for, water from a number of private mine pumping engines.

Principal South Staffordshire Mines Pumping Engines

Bradley	delivered water to Wednesbury Oak Loop (473ft)
Buffery	water sent to Dudley No.2 Canal (453ft)
Deepfield	delivered water to Wednesbury Oak Loop (473ft)
Herberts Park	delivered water into Walsall Canal (408ft)
Moat	delivered water to Wednesbury Oak Loop (473ft)
Rough Hay	delivered water to Walsall Canal (408ft)
Stow Heath	water conveyed to Bilston Gasworks basin, main line (473ft) along 1,300-yard-long cast-iron main
Waterfall Lane	delivered water to Dudley No.2 Canal (453ft)
Windmill End	delivered water to Dudley No.2 Canal (453ft)

New developments in the iron industry included the Bessemer process, which carried on the oxidation of carbon content within the metal to make mild steel. Steel making by the crucible process had been long established in the West Midlands, but manufacture of steel by this method was both long, time consuming and dependent on charcoal as an essential ingredient. The new methods of mild steel manufacture promised increased production. Staffordshire pig iron was unsuitable to be made into steel through its phosphorus content. The Patent Shaft had Bessemer converters at their works at Wednesbury, but were denied the use of local iron. There was a particular need for steel, in their case, as it proved more suitable than iron for the railway axles and wheels made there. High-quality iron such as hematite pig iron had to be imported from other parts of the country to be converted into steel by the Patent Shaft Bessemer converters. The furnaces around Whitehaven and Barrow produced suitable iron, which was either sent by coastal vessel to Ellesmere Port and narrow boat to the Midlands, or by railway wagon direct to the sidings, which served the Patent Shaft site. Other iron was sent from Yorkshire and even Scotland.

Surviving Patent Shaft company documents mention payments to some of their suppliers. Entries in the directors' minutes for 1879 record specific purchases for different types of pig iron. They included iron from Awsworth Iron Co. (Ilkeston), Airside Hematite Iron Co. (Leeds), C. & T. Bagnall (Grosmont), Barrow Hematite Steel Co. Cumberland Iron Mines and Steel Co. (Millom), Glendon Iron Co. (Finedon, Wellingborough), Lonsdale Hematite Iron Co., Staveley Coal & Iron Co., Wigan Coal and Iron Co., Whitehaven Hematite Iron Co. (Cleator Moor) and the Workington Iron Co. A proportion of this iron would be used to make steel, whilst other iron went to other uses such as the important structural ironwork making plant at Old Park. The company also retained iron blast furnaces at Old Park that made pig iron from local and other ores. The Barborsfield Co. (Bilston), the Earl of Dudley (Brierley Hill and Tipton), Thomas Turley (Coseley

Moor) and Willingsworth Iron Co. all sent their own special types of Staffordshire 'mine' and 'cinder' pig iron.

Another requirement was for axles and tyres that were provided by Bolton, Iron & Steel Co., Brown, Bayley & Dixon (Sheffield), J. Brown & Co. (Atlas Works, Sheffield), Charles Cammell & Co. (Cyclops Steelworks, Sheffield), Taylor Brothers (Clarence Ironworks, Leeds) and Vickers, Son and Co. (River Don Works, Sheffield). Thomas and Charles Wells also provided steel from the nearby Moxley Iron & Steelworks.

The Patent Shaft & Axletree Co. organisation was then quite extensive with three manufacturing plants at Brunswick, Monway and Old Park, and several collieries that supplied coal by boat via the Tame Valley and Walsall Canal to the Monway Branch that served the Brunswick and Monway. Monway and Old Park had belonged to the Lloyd family who had in 1818 leased the estate from the heirs of the Parkes family. John Lloyd arranged for a tramway to be built from the Monway Branch Canal to Old Park, where blast furnaces were erected and later also became the site of the structural ironworks owned by Lloyds, Foster & Co. The Monway Works were acquired by Lloyds, Foster, whilst Patent Shaft & Axletree carried on a modest operation of railway wheel and axle making at Brunswick.

Brunswick Works had built up a reputation for making good quality railway wheels and axles on a restricted site at the end of the Monway Branch. An essential part of railway making was the fitting of a metal tyre around the perimeter of the wheel. It was on the tyre, or tire, which the wheel ran along the rails and it was the tyre that was worn down and replaced when needed. Tyre making remained a manual process that required brawn and strength. The following extract from the Engineer describes this process at Patent Shaft:

Standing gazing at the welding of a tire by six brawny Vulcans, as they swung ponderous sledges, and rained rapid and measured blows upon the seam to be united, one could not help being struck with surprise that so costly a work of manufacturing supererogation should continue to be practised in an establishment, which seemed to possess in so high a degree, the elements of progress. Nor was our surprise less when we watched the well-known process of building a tire. Here was the roman lictor's bundle of rods the later however wedge shaped – all being beaten, at immense toil and cost, into a compact mass as it was possible to secure by such a process.
(The Engineer, 22 September 1865).

Lloyds, Foster made some important engineering structures, and it was they who installed Bessemer steel making at the Monway Works. The supply of components for the Blackfriars Bridge brought Lloyds, Foster to the brink of administration. The Patent Shaft & Axletree Co. decided to amalgamate with Lloyds, Foster in 1866 and took over the works, mines and other assets of the latter firm. It was a move that was to prove a success. Careful management kept the firm profitable and sometimes difficult decisions had to be made. Pig iron making by the company was discontinued by the early 1880s and the furnaces were pulled down. All iron was then purchased from other suppliers.

Faced with a declining local iron industry and an increasing demand for steel in Midlands industry, ironmasters became determined to find a means to use local pig iron in the making of steel. Alfred Hickman led the way with experiments at the Monway Works in 1882 that adopted a new method of lining the interior of a converter with a type of limestone called dolomite. The phosphorus was removed with the slag, leaving mild steel.

The success of these experiments led Hickman and others to set up a new company, the Staffordshire Steel & Ingot Co., at land adjacent to his own furnaces at Spring Vale in 1884. The method became known as the 'basic process', the steel as 'basic steel' and the phosphorus-rich slag was called 'basic slag'. The earlier method produced what became known as 'acid steel' and 'acid slag'.

Alfred Hickman had a long association with the iron and steel trade. He was born in 1830 and was baptised at Tipton on 2 August 1830. Alfred Hickman was the son of George Rushbury Hickman and Mary Haden, who had married at Tipton Parish Church on 18 June 1822. Alfred had two older brothers; George Haden and Edwin, and there were sisters Frances and Sarah. George Rushbury Hickman was manager of the Moat Colliery, Tipton and later was associated with Bilston Brook Furnaces. Alfred Hickman was educated at King Edward's School, Birmingham and at the age of sixteen joined his father in business at Bilston Brook. Alfred also built up a trade as an iron merchant. When George Rushbury Hickman retired, both George and Alfred took over the management of the two furnaces at Bilston Brook and from 1857 were also associated with the Stonefield Furnace. The great crash in the iron trade of 1857 did little to help the traders that survived the chaos. G.H. & A. Hickman filed a petition for bankruptcy during 1860. George went on to run the Groveland Furnaces and was briefly assisted in this venture by Alfred, who during 1866 purchased the furnaces at Spring Vale. These furnaces had been worked by George Jones and his son John, but following the receivership of John Jones, Spring Vale Furnaces were sold to Alfred Hickman.

Three furnaces survived near to the private branch canal to Sparrow's Bilston Ironworks and Bilston Quarries. Hickman started to acquire land that included the Ladymoor Colliery and Spring Vale Colliery estates. The steel and ingot works was erected on land between the furnaces and Bilston Quarries. The new plant included rolling mills, and an extensive railway system came to be laid down that connected with the LNWR Stour Valley Railway and the Great Western Railway.

The Staffordshire Steel and Ingot Iron Co. was formed in 1882. The prospectus listed directors as Alfred Hickman (Spring Vale Furnaces), George J. Barker (Chairman of Chillington Iron Co.), William B. Harrison (Brownhills Colliery), Percy C. Gilchrist (Metallurgist) and Edward Bilby (Metallurgist). This company was formed to make steel by the Thomas Gilchrist process, under licence, with the aim of converting common Staffordshire cinder pig into a metal of high quality suitable for best boiler plates, stamping sheets, tinplate, hoops and boiler tubes.

Politically, Alfred was chairman of Wolverhampton Chamber of Commerce (1883/4) when he tried to achieve a reduction of railway rates, which he believed were crippling business. Alfred favoured cheaper conveyance and improvements of water communication to London, Liverpool and Gloucester. He was appointed to the Commission of Light Railways and assisted with the preparation of the Light Railways Act. He was elected as Conservative Member of Parliament for Wolverhampton West in 1885–1886 and

Tipton Green Blast Furnaces. Iron smelting was carried on at the Tipton Green furnace site from 1809 when the original furnaces adapted the different canal levels to their advantage. Tipton Green furnaces were rebuilt from time to time and were eventually replaced by a bank of tall iron-cased furnaces, which received much of their minerals by rail, but still retained canal communications. (Sandwell Public Library).

1892–1906 and assisted with the Railway Regulation Act, Coal Mines Regulation Act and Workmen's Compensation Act. He was knighted in 1891. In business, his interests, in addition to the Bilston works, included the Haunchwood Collieries, near Nuneaton, and ironstone mines in Oxfordshire. The Staffordshire Steel and Ingot Co. had three Bessemer converters that were capable of making 300 to 400 tons of steel per week. With the aid of cogging mills and rolling plants boiler plates were produced at Bilston to the order of Lancashire & Yorkshire engineers. Steel was also rolled thinner for tin plate use. Steel bars, billets, blooms and sections were also produced.

The Patent Shaft went on to make steel by both the acid and basic processes. Reorganisation at their works during the 1890s created four main plants. The Brunswick Iron & Steel Works to include steel cogging, bar and plate mills, and plant for both basic and acid steel making, and the Brunswick Wheel Works occupied the land nearest the main road at Leabrook. The Monway Iron and Steel works specialised in the making of weldless steel tyres, and iron and steel plates. Monway had four open-hearth acid steel melting furnaces and two basic open-hearth furnaces. Old Park Bridge Yard was the fourth site and included a boiler yard and foundry. The department was laid out for bridge and roof building and was capable of making the largest bridges of the day. The Benares Bridge, across the Ganges, was made there in 1885. It comprised seven main spans of 356ft x 25ft x 35ft and nine spans of 114ft. Made entirely from steel, the weight of Benares Bridge amounted to 6,500 tons. Railway bridges were made for lines across Britain and many large bridges were sent to India, Japan, South America, Egypt and South Africa.

Mild steel making was also adopted by other manufactures. The Lilleshall Co. installed a Bessemer plant at their works at Oakengates, whilst the Earl of Dudley considered the use of basic open-hearth furnaces at Round Oak. The Earl of Dudley, through his agents, had built up a considerable industrial empire that included the Coneygree Furnaces, New Level Furnaces, Castle Mill Engineering Works, Round Oak Ironworks and a number of coalmines, limestone mines and fireclay mines. Richard Smith had laid out Round Oak Works in 1857 for the making of bar iron. The plant was sensibly arranged with mills and puddling furnaces arranged in careful and neat order around the site with narrow-

Springvale Steel and Ironworks, Stewarts & Lloyds.
Alfred Hickman learnt the trade of iron making whilst working for his father and later in partnership with his brother, George. Hickman developed the old Bilston site, acquiring adjacent mineral properties, building up iron making there and adding a steel making plant. Stewarts & Lloyds further improved Hickman's works for the steel tube trade. (Wolverhampton Public Libraries).

Mars Ironworks, Ettingshall.
The working up of iron through puddling and rolling led to a number of successful independent iron working ventures placed along the waterway. George Adams' Mars Ironworks was placed alongside the banks of the Birmingham Canal near Wolverhampton where they produced quality bars and sheets for the coopers, horseshoe, rivet and welded tube trades. (Ray Shill collection).

Round Oak Ironworks.
In many ways Richard Smith, agent to Lord Dudley and Ward, created an industrial masterpiece when he designed the Round Oak Ironworks at Brierley Hill. These works were carefully laid out, arranging the mills and furnaces in an ordered fashion, unlike their competitors whose existing works had furnaces, forges and mills arranged haphazardly about. (Dudley Archives)

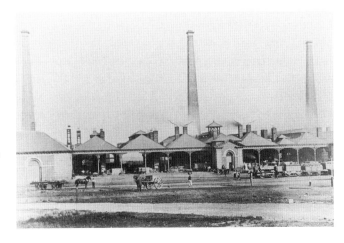

Darlaston Iron and Steel Works, Engraving Published with Griffiths' Guide to the Iron Trade 1872.
The extensive iron and steel making plant at Darlaston was developed by Samuel Mills and passed to the Darlaston Steel & Iron Co. during 1864. This company had mines, blast furnaces and extensive ironworks. (Ray Shill collection)

gauge tramways bringing ingots of iron from the furnaces or canalside pig iron store yard into the works. Standard-gauge sidings from the extensive private railway also served the Round Oak Works, bringing coal from the mines and taking away finished goods.

The closure of the Old Level Works had enabled the Earl's agents to take over this site and transfer the bar iron department there. New puddling furnaces, steam hammers, forge trains and mills were installed leaving the old Round Oak Works available for redevelopment as a steelworks. Round Oak Steelworks was put into operation during 1895 and comprised five Siemens open-hearth furnaces that made steel by the basic Bertrand Thiel process. Steel ingots were reduced in a cogging mill where angles, channels, tees and rounds were made. There was also a chain and anchor works that made chain cable and gear for the British Admiralty and comprised steam hammers and end-welding fires.

The properties of aluminium as a pure metal or alloyed with others came to be appreciated towards the end of the nineteenth century. Initially aluminium was extracted from its ores by chemical means. One process adopted in the Midlands had been perfected by a Nottingham-born engineer and inventor, James Webster. Mr Webster moved to Birmingham where he set up in business as an engineer and machinist about the year 1857. Webster was quite innovative and inventive and presented a number of patents applications during the 1860s and 1870s. Three important stages in his life were the production of metallic paint, making of steel and the refining of aluminium.

Webster's essay into metallic paints led to a factory being established in Oozells Street, Birmingham. He then moved into the realms of steel production and devised a new type of steel converter for the Globe Steelworks, at nearby Freeth Street. The fortunes of this company were as brief as those in making metallic paints and Webster moved on again to set up the Crown Works at Solihull Lodge to refine aluminium.

This business was transferred ten years later to a new site beside the BCN old main line at Oldbury to take advantage of the proximity to Chance Brothers' chemical works. New methods of aluminium production, made possible through the availability of cheaply made electricity, led to the abandonment of the chemical process and the relocation of the industry to the districts where hydroelectric power was available.

Local industry had often benefited from foreign orders, but these began to decline as trade tariffs were imposed and competition increased. It became more common in newspapers during the 1890s to find closing down and dismantling sales. The complex of works, which belonged to R. W. Winfield, in Cambridge Street, Birmingham was split up during 1898 following a legal action. Winfield's works had come to form an entire ring around Gibson's Basin with premises in Cambridge Street, Baskerville Passage and Attwoods Passage.

The rolling mills, wire mills and brass tube mills occupied the length between the basin and Cambridge Street. Facing Baskerville Passage was the Cromwell Works, which was an engineering works used to make cycle and gun components. Another long building was the Bedstead Works, which occupied a strip of land between Gibson's Basin and Attwoods Passage. Either side of the lock was the cased tube department and brass foundry department, whilst facing another part of the private basin and Attwoods Passage was a department engaged in the supply of gas, water and electric-light fittings, as well as some wrought ironwork. The sale left the rolling, wire and tube mills in the hands of Winfields Rolling Mills Ltd and the brass foundry department under the ownership of J. & A. Tonks.

The canal was a hidden world, reached only by the private arm from Newhall Street and the lock under Cambridge Street. Once boats came out of the lock they had to be pulled around by hand or poled either into the Gibson Arm or under the bridge in Attwoods Passage into the Baskerville Basin, which served Easy Row Wharf, Bolton's Rolling Mills and Timber Yard, and Nettlefold & Chamberlain's Screw Works. This basin too was hidden from the hustle and bustle of Broad Street, being surrounded by many buildings. Today this vast space comprises Centenary Square, the Hall of Memory, a car park and Baskerville House!

Another firm to succumb at this time was the Great Bridge Iron & Steel Works with forges and sheet mills. They specialised in the making of finished iron. The complexity of finished iron manufacture is illustrated by list of makers detailed in Appendix 2. Finished iron works converted local and other pig iron into angle iron, bars, hoops, plate, rods, strip or sheet. The sheer number of works listed amply demonstrates the volume of traffic generated for the local canal and railway networks, both with the supply of raw materials and the disposal of finished products. In many instances these products were simple intermediates to be worked up further to make a particular product. Fortunately a buyer was found for the works and production was continued.

Bar iron might be made to a number of different sections, but was often round or square. Hoop iron was suited for tying cotton, baling or for the use of the cooper when making barrels. The blacksmith to fashion and shape horseshoes used another type of bar iron. Some iron might be stamped into shape to form bicycle parts, tricycle parts, stirrups, spurs and bits. Strip iron was keenly sought for a variety of uses that included the making of boiler tubes, gas piping and bedstead parts. Sheet iron was left either flat or corrugated and was popular for roofing once galvanised or tinned. This type of product was common in the Wolverhampton and Bilston districts, where several works were engaged in the trade. Sheet iron might also be used for stamping out nails and tacks. Rod iron had long been utilised for nail making, but rod iron was also used for wire production.

Competition on the metal trades remained acute. Closures and takeovers were common in the district. Most notable amongst the closures were the Chillington Iron Co., New British Iron Co. and the Pelsall Coal & Iron Co., which had generated significant canal revenue. Chillington's main base of blast furnaces, collieries and ironworks was situated at Wolverhampton, but they also came to operate furnaces and mines at Bentley (near Walsall), ironworks at Caponfield (Bilston) and Leabrook (Walsall), all of which relied on the canal for transport of materials. The vast New British Iron Works site was principally rail served but they also had developed canal interchange facilities with their metre-gauge private railway at Lion Colliery Basin on the Dudley Canal. The New British Iron Co. also retained long-established ironstone mines at Heath, Wolverhampton and the Green, Darlaston, and these two mining estates sent ironstone by boat to the furnaces at Corngreaves. Pelsall had been established by Richard Fryer, but was considerably enlarged by Davis and Bloomer. Boaz Bloomer Senior, and Junior, made the greatest efforts that led to the making of three separate ironwork plants and a modern pair of blast furnaces lined up alongside the banks of the Wyrley & Essington Canal. The Bloomers had also arranged for the sinking of new mines, (Pelsall Nos 8, 9, 10 and 12) and from 1865 had a railway connection made from the London & North Western Railway.

The Pelsall Coal & Iron Co. was formed in 1873. They specialised in the making of strip and bar iron of greater width than any other works in the district. Initial success led to heavy losses from 1886 as demand for their bar and strip dwindled. A liquidator was appointed in 1891 and the ironworks was sold off during 1892. Only the profitable No.12 mine remained in use after sale to the nearby Walsall Wood Colliery Co.

Chillington's assets were mostly sold off during the years 1885–1887 and only a core business, the making of edge tools, was retained. The New British Iron Co. works was disposed of piecemeal during the years 1894–1897 with the ironworks and furnaces and some collieries passing to the Corngreave Furnace Co. and the remainder of the mines to Shelagh Garrett.

With the closure of most of the blast furnaces, contractors came in to remove the slag mounds for road making. John Freakley of Dudley Port and George Element of Oldbury became actively engaged in the slag trade. Slag was brought to a cracker for crushing and the broken slag taken away by boat or railway wagon. Freakley dismantled Coneygre, Corngreaves, Goldsgreen and the Pelsall mounds whilst Element took away slag from Willingsworth.

George Element had a large family that included sons Samuel and Thomas, who later established a separate carrying business for coal and rubbish. Coal contractors were to become a significant force in canal affairs during the twentieth century as firms abandoned their own boats in favour of the cheaper option of employing a contractor.

seven

DAWN OF A
NEW CENTURY

The year 1901 heralded the end of Victorian times, but local industry was still served
by waterways completed in the nineteenth century. Calls were made for improvement,
and these might have been made had the people of the day possessed the vision for
improvement as those in other European countries. The investment required was not
forthcoming despite different schemes being proposed to widen the Worcester &
Birmingham Canal to the Severn or improve canal navigation to the Mersey.

Canal operators were left to work with what they had. Engineers for the local waterways
were generally restricted to modifying and improving water supply, and maintenance was
continued, but trade was still limited to what could be carried in a narrow boat hold.
Canal boatmen worked as they always had, moving coal around the system to supply the
works. There was still a merchandise trade and an important railway interchange trade.
Yet as the canal trade moved into the twentieth century, local industry was also in a state
of change.

Wrought iron making was in decline, as mild steel came to find increasing use throughout
the industry. This was also a time of mergers, where firms combined, closing some plants and
enlarging others. Production was often moved outside the Midlands. New industry came
in to fill the vacuum left. There was an increasing demand for steel tubes to make bicycles
and motorcycles. The fledgling motorcar industry added a new demand for engine castings,
axle assemblies, assorted metal parts and wood for carriage work.

The three large steel making plants, which were the Patent Shaft, Round Oak and Spring
Vale Steelworks, were to have long-term prospects and utilised the canal particularly for
the movement of fuel. Black Country mining continued to decline despite the best efforts
of the South Staffordshire Mine Drainage Authority. Principal supplies now were sought
from the Cannock Chase, Warwickshire and Leicestershire Coalfields, even if traffic was
confined to the single boatload. Day boats continued to line up alongside the colliery
wharves awaiting their next load. Longer distance family boats were there too with their
attendant crews waiting for a load of coal to take back to a distant coal merchant's wharf,
factory or mill.

Boat people would chat and find amusement amongst themselves at these times of
enforced wait. For when they were on the move there was an urgency to complete the

journey as soon as possible. Time was money and their payment for delivering the load was the same no matter how long it took. Stoppages, ice and delays at the locks were a constant trouble, and yet despite these handicaps journeys were generally completed in a measured time. Boatmen on the day and family boats were well aware of the time taken to complete the journey.

The Wolverhampton and Bilston districts, once noted for the many corrugated galvanised iron and tinplate works, saw a steady decline in these factories after 1900. Gospel Oak Works and Tupper's collection of works around Bradley all closed down, with many facing demolition.

Gospel Oak had had various owners since the establishment of the blast furnaces by William Bancks, John Read and John Dumaresq during the closing years of the eighteenth century. The ironworks that was developed on the site has already been noted. Change's, following the association with Morewood and Walker's, concentrated on the production of galvanised corrugated sheets at their works near Tipton Old Church, Summerhill. As the nineteenth century drew to a close the Gospel Oak Iron and Galvanised Iron & Wire Co. had charge of the Gospel Oak Ironworks as well as the Mitre Galvanising Works in Wolverhampton and the Regents Canal Bridge Iron Roofing and Tank Works at Limehouse, London. Their occupation was comparatively short lived and Gospel Oak Works changed hands again passing to the Tipton Iron & Steel Co. By 1896 they were recorded as have seven rolling mills and twenty puddling furnaces that were capable of making some 300 tons of finished iron per week. Sheet iron continued to be made but the market supplied included not only roofing but also catered for cut nail and hollow ware. Despite extensive alterations made by the new owners to make iron for the wider market, the Gospel Oak Works was sold in 1901 and the buildings demolished.

Tupper's had begun as Tupper & Carr with works on either side of Berkeley Street, Birmingham and beside the canal arm originally constructed to serve the gasworks. They subsequently moved to the Black Country and set up premises chiefly around Bilston alongside the old main line, or Wednesbury Oak Loop. Their chief works were the Regents Ironworks, Batmans Hill, Pyramid Ironworks, and the Britannia Works and Boat Dock. Here they conducted rolling, annealing and corrugating of iron as part of their general business of galvanised roof builders and tank makers. The Batmans Hill Works was the largest plant. It extended south from Cross Street (or Tup Street) Bridge along the banks of the canal. Enclosed within this space were galvanising works, sheet mills, a forge and a hoop mill. There were also two canal basins. Tupper's empire was offered for sale in 1911. In addition to the Bilston works, they had the Capponfield Ironworks and the Britannia Bar Ironworks at the Albion. Following the sale, J.B. & S. Lees purchased the Britannia Bar property, sold off the equipment and machinery and demolished the existing buildings to enable an expansion of their Albion Ironworks.

Ironworks closures had a domino effect on the canalside industry in the Black Country. The works that existed frequently supplied others nearby in the working up of chain and the canal played a part in the short-distance transport of materials between works. As firms went out of business, or relocated, those that depended on their services were forced to bring in material from further afield at increased transport cost. The difference in cost was sometimes the same as the gulf between profit and loss. The result was further closures.

Throughout the 1890s and 1900s this course of events was played out several times, and with closures came the inevitable demolition, and gaps started to appear in the previously unbroken line of firms and factories.

The Wednesbury Oak Loop from Deepfields through to Bloomfield was heavily industrialised and ironworks, furnaces and mines lined its banks throughout. The character began to change after 1890. Most of the mines had closed and a wilderness of wasteland had formed between Tipton and Bilston. The demolition of the Gospel Oak Works was followed with the sale and demolition of William Barrow's & Sons, Bloomfield Works. Barrow's works had witnessed the birth of Hall's improved puddling process and by 1900 was capable of producing 900 tons of finished iron per week. Their fifty-nine puddling furnaces, seventeen mill furnaces and eight rolling mills turned bar and sheet iron for a wide market. But in 1903 the works was offered for sale. It was closed, demolished and the underlying coal worked by the Blooms Smythies Colliery Co. Ltd.

Batmans Hill works had a more fortunate existence and by 1918 was in the hands of the Bilston Manufacturing Co., who made hardware. At Summerhill, Millington's ironworks had belonged to a group renowned for production of good quality bar and sheet iron sometimes referred to as the 'marked' bar houses. The others in this select group included the Earl of Dudley, William Barrow & Son, New British Iron Co., Chillington Iron Co., Noah Hingley & Sons, Plant & Fisher, Brown & Freer, T. Wright & Co. and W. & J.S. Sparrow. For some forty years they had the power to dictate the price of iron for South Staffordshire and for much of the British iron trade. William Millington founded the Summerhill Works that were established alongside a private canal basin. Competition from the steel trade finally forced the closure of many bar iron works. Those at Summerhill were no exception. They were closed before 1895 and demolished. Only Charles Lathe's foundry remained nearby. The Moat Foundry, Summerhill, had been set up by Lathe about 1880. Located near the Wednesbury Oak Loop, Moat Foundry was used for the production of general iron goods. By 1920 pottery kilns had been erected as the firm embarked on the making of 'Claco' furnace pans in addition to founding.

Another works closure from the 1890s was that of the Hope Iron and Tinplate Co. that made sheet iron. Their plant had been adapted to make galvanised and tinned sheets for tin box manufacture. Hope had been established by the Lowe family who traded under the Hope name. These works lay beside the Wednesbury Oak Loop to the south of Summerhill and the original Gospel Oak Furnaces and Ironworks. Company finances suffered after the death of Mr James Lowe Senior and a receiver was appointed during 1885. Despite a ruling to pay creditors 10s in the pound, the Hope survived but a few years before demolition.

Changes in the iron trade might have been one of marked decline, but the local non-ferrous trade was perhaps in greater demand. Allen Everitt's Kingston Works were copper and brass rollers, making boiler tubes amongst their range of products. They had moved their operation from their canalside location in Adderley Street, Birmingham to a new site in Smethwick taking over part of the former Plate Glass Co. works along with a basin, which joined with the Birmingham Canal and a siding that connected with the London & North Western Railway. Orders for boiler tubes included the Admiralty and locomotive makers. Manning Wardle & Co., Leeds was ranked amongst their customers and Everitt's had shares in their company. When Manning Wardle's orders reduced, Everitt disposed of their shares and reinvested in Kerr Stuart of the California Works, Stoke on Trent, who had become good customers.

The site included casting shops, rolling mills and tube drawing mills for both copper and brass. They also owned collieries (previously operated by the Dudley Colliery Co.) at Mud Hall, Sledmore and Tansley Hill, which supplied coal for the melting and annealing furnaces, muffles and boilers at Smethwick. Tramways brought coal down to the Dudley Canal for transfer by boat through the Netherton Tunnel and the new main line to the Kingston Works.

Everitt's Smethwick works were reconstructed as a result of George Bean's survey. Improvements included the installation of new rolling plant. Metal rolling up to the end of the nineteenth century had been restricted to passing the metal between a pair of rollers that either 'broke down' the heavier gauges or rolled to a finer thickness. Then the more economical three- and four-high mills were designed. In 1910 George Jones of Lionel Street, Birmingham, were contracted to supply a three-high mill to Everitt's. Another innovation was the provision of hydraulic tube drawing plant at Smethwick as a replacement for the tried and tested mechanical method. Unfortunately the hydraulic plant proved troublesome and Everitt's experienced both operational problems and breakdowns with this plant leading to inevitable delays in production.

During the First World War production was changed to the rolling and making of cartridges for the War Office. In December 1914 production was set up for 3,000 thirteen-pounder cases per week. After the war production reverted to civilian occupation. The post-war years proved difficult for the brass and copper rollers. Economies were made and, for Everitt's, the expense of working mines was dispensed with during 1922, when their collieries were sold to H.S. Pitt. Everitt's remained independent until 1928, a time when industry had generally fallen on hard times. They were absorbed into the giant ICI empire.

The name of Vivian was usually associated with the Swansea copper industry, but there was a Birmingham equivalent that was H.H. Vivian & Co. Ltd. Their works was first established in 1860 to produce brass and copper tube strip and wire. The original works were located on Whitmore's Arm but later transferred to a site beside the Icknield Port Loop. Vivian's works as described in 1929 comprised three sections. There was a tube mill for the making of brass, copper and cupro-nickel tubes; a rolling mill for hot- or cold-rolled brass, copper sheets, nickel silver sheets and strip, and thirdly a wire mill for making brass, copper and nickel silver wire rods, tape, strip and sections. Machinery was driven by electricity supplied by the City of Birmingham Electricity Department. There were four departments in the tube mill, one for heavy and one for smaller copper tube, one for brass tube and one for condenser tubes. Some muffles were coal fired others gas fired. The hot and cold rolling mills, originally driven by a beam engine, were converted to electric drive. The wire mills, in addition to wire and rods produced copper tape. The muffles in the mills and wire department were gas fired and burned producer gas made in a central producer plant. Coal continued to be brought by boat to the gas producer plant, which was situated alongside the canal. An electric hoist was used to raise coal from the boats to an upper charging platform.

Barker and Allen's mills were erected in 1896 on land acquired in Spring Hill, formerly the Park Glassworks when James and Samuel Allen had charge of the business. Barker & Allen made nickel silver sheet and wire. Like most rolled metal manufacturers component metals were heated together in the casting shop. Ingots of nickel silver then went to the ingot plane shop before being passed through a series of breaking down and finishing rolls. Longer and thinner ingots were cast and rolled into strips for making wire. These strips were slit and then taken to wire drawing benches.

In Birmingham the demand for metallic bedsteads lessened after 1910, through foreign competition and a change in public taste. Birmingham had so many bedstead factories placed around the city and all had benefited from the supply of beds to British and Foreign customers. In fact, the export market was so considerable that some firms like Hoskins & Sewell and Peyton & Peyton had London offices. Hoskins & Sewell's main factory was located in High Street, Bordesley, but sent beds out by canal from Fazeley Street. Crosbie, Marriner was one of the bedstead firms that had a canalside location. Their Globe Foundry was placed alongside Whitmore's Arm. Several Birmingham bedstead makers sought out canalside locations when building new factories. John Hoyland Ltd built a factory in Western Road during 1890, whose property extended back to the Winson Green Loop. Whilst alongside the nearby Icknield Port Loop, Frazer Brothers, W. Hulse and William Robinson all had bedstead works. J. Troman took over a site in Bolton Street that was close to the towpath of the Birminghan and Warwick Junction Canal and the Birmingham Bedstead Co., Sampson Road North, established a factory beside a private arm of the Warwick and Birmingham Canal. Elsewhere in the Black Country Thomas Perry & Sons of the Highfields Foundry, Bilston built up an important bedstead trade to complement boiler making, the making of rolling mill plant and structural ironwork. Another firm was J. & H. Brookes who had a factory at the end of the Cape Arm, Smethwick.

Evered's of the Surrey Works became prominent bedstead makers during the twentieth century. The firm began with Richard Evered who set up as a brass caster in London in 1809. Richard Evered II came to Birmingham in 1860, where he founded the Surrey Tube Works at 43–44 Old Bartholomew Street. Property was acquired in Smethwick during 1866 and the Surrey works were transferred there. The new site bordered the canal alongside Brindley's original flight of locks (1769).

The Surrey Works made general brass foundry, but specialised in the supply of plumber's brass foundryware. A bedstead department was added from 1885 and during 1894 the bed making side of the business was enlarged through the opening of a new cot and mattress department. In 1884 freehold property in Devonshire Street, Birmingham, called the Barnett Works, was opened to supply brass cabinet castings and stampings. The Surrey Works came to occupy an extensive site bounded by Lewisham Road and the canal. The property was divided into a number of shops and departments. A sand casting department produced plumber's brass foundry and castings for metallic bedsteads. There was a strip casting shop where spelter was mixed with copper to make brass, in another part modelling, chasing and painting was conducted. There was also a tube drawing shop where cased tubes (brass on iron) were made and tempered.

Women workers found regular employment in the case tube lacquering shops and capstan shops. There were also press and plating shops. Techniques such as bronzing, dipping and nickel chrome plating were all required to produce a final finish. Evered's were successful in the bedstead trade and despite a recession in the trade after 1920 absorbed a number of firms into their empire. These included British Chromium Plating Ltd, James Clews & Son (brass founders) and the former bedstead making firms of Fisher, Brown & Bayley, F. Andrews & Co. Ltd and William Robinson Junior.

The increasing population of West Midlands towns eventually led to better standards of living. Local councils took on more and more responsibility and established certain undertakings for the benefit of all. Many roads were poor, but there were also the better-maintained turnpikes. Each turnpike was looked after by a trust that had originally built it. A toll was charged for all traffic and the tolls provided the money for the upkeep of the road as well as a dividend for those who had invested in the trust.

As towns developed they took on the obligation for the maintenance and building of roads within their jurisdiction. Road stone was carried along the Birmingham Canal almost from the start. There is a note in the Birmingham Canal Proprietors Minute Book, dated 12 August 1776, concerning a Mr Bingham who was required to pay tonnage on 'Rowley Ragg', which had been navigated at an improper time and hindered three boats loading coal.

Quarries at Rowley and Sedgley were important suppliers of stone to towns in the Black Country as well as Birmingham. Several quarries were established at Rowley where the celebrated Rowley Ragg was obtained. As far as canal traffic was concerned there were two important quarries, which brought stone down to the canal. The first was the Hailstone Quarry located high on the hills above Blackheath. A tramway brought stone down to the Dudley No.2 Canal to a basin close to Doulton's Pottery. Jones and Fitzmaurice and later R.W. Fitzmaurice worked hailstone. They owned their own canal boats and brought stone into their depot beside the Oozell Street loop in Birmingham. The second was Darby's Hill Quarry, which was served by a tramway that brought stone down to the Old Birmingham Canal at Tividale. Other stone was brought from the Hartshill district near Nuneaton where quarries operated by Abel, Jees and Mancetter sent stone down to the Coventry Canal for transport by boat.

Birmingham Corporation once had four stone breaking depots for the supply of macadam for their roads. They included Holliday Street Wharf alongside the Worcester & Birmingham Canal and Sheepcote Street, which was built beside the BCN. Each year the Public Works Department contracted for stone. Records show that quarries such as Hailstone were suppliers, but there were others such as the quarry masters at Hartshill.

Flourmills retained a steady canal trade not only for the supply of flour but also for the production of cattle and other animal feed. The means of grinding flour had changed. A new method of grinding corn by iron rollers had been pioneered in Hungary during the 1840s. It was a method that operated on the principal of gradual reduction and produced high quality flour. From 1880 British millers had slowly adopted this method.

Various systems and techniques were available. The Albion Flour Mill, Wolverhampton, which has recently been renovated for new housing, had a separate existence as a mill until the year 1887. Milling was improved during the early 1880s with the combination system of Hind & Lund of Preston that employed stones and rollers powered by a steam engine. The plant as described in 1887 mentioned five pairs of French stones, one pair of grey stones, break rolls, dusting reels, bran rolls and finishing rolls.

Evered's Surrey Works as Seen from Bridge Street, Smethwick c.1900.
The Surrey Works received copper and spelter (zinc) by boat to be melted and mixed to form brass.
The brass was then employed in the making of gas fittings, plumbers' brass foundry and bedsteads.
(Reproduced from *Birmingham Arts and Industry Magazine*)

Rolling and Tube Drawing Mills at the Surrey Works.
Evered's built up a considerable business in bedstead manufacture at the Surrey Works. Brass, or brass
cased, tubes formed an essential part of the bedstead frame. Here workers are seen engaged in tube
making. (Reproduced from *Birmingham Arts and Industry Magazine*)

Rowley Regis Stone Crusher. Ragstone was quarried extensively in the Rowley Hills and broken down into pieces suitable for road making. The broken stone was loaded into tramway wagons and ferried down to the old line of the Birmingham Canal near Dudley Road Bridge. (E. Blocksidge)

Albion Mill, Walsall. The Albion Mill façade carries a foundation stone dated 1849. This mill was constructed beside the Walsall Junction Canal and faced the road from Walsall to Wolverhampton. As in many mills of this period, grain was ground into flour by millstones driven by a steam engine. The more efficient roller process eventually replaced this method. (Ray Shill 1983)

The Eagle Mills, Snow Hill, Birmingham were established sometime before 1815 by Samuel Badger, who had previously carried on the trade of hay, straw and corn dealer at Ann Street. Joseph Henry Parkes acquired the mills in about 1880. They then stood some four storeys high and included granaries, storerooms and offices. The premises adjoined Honduras Wharf that was still retained for the timber trade. Parkes installed new machinery. A system of revolving fans and sieves removed the flour dust from the middlings and grist and the roller system pulverised the wheat by successive crushings. Broken wheat was passed onto fresh sets of rollers until a fine white powder was produced. By this method the Eagle Mills were able to produce some 600 sacks a week.

Similar improvements were made at Rayner's Old Steam Mill, Snow Hill and the Old Union Mill, Holt Street. At the New Union Mill a change of ownership and investment in new plant led to the New Union Mill being renamed City Central Mills.

Canalside Flourmills 1901

Mill	Owner	Canal
Albion (Walsall)	Smith Brothers (Walsall) Ltd	Walsall Locks
Bilston	Barlow & Son	BCN main line
Bloxwich	Thomas Pratt & Co.	Wyrley & Essington
Brownhills	Joseph Haddon & Albert Grimes	Wyrley & Essington
City Central (Birmingham)	Walter Brown & Son	Oozells Street Loop
Eagle (Birmingham)	Joseph Henry Parkes	Birmingham & Fazeley
Midland (Birmingham)	Watson, Todd & Co.	BCN main line
Old Steam Mill (Birmingham)	William Rayner & Son	Birmingham & Fazeley
Old Steam Mill (Wolverhampton)	John Norton Miller	BCN main line
Oldbury	Harry Tyndall Nock	Oldbury Loop
Old Union (Birmingham)	Old Union Mill Co. Ltd	Digbeth Branch
Union (Wolverhampton)	Union Flour Mill Co.	BCN main line

Gas making continued to adapt to the needs of a changing industry, and there was an increased demand for gas-fired furnaces. Gas offered a more steady control than coal or coke-fired heating. The supply of gas-heated furnaces for enamelling, glass making, metal annealing, and porcelain and pottery manufacture led to several firms entering this market. Population increase and new house building also made additional demands for gas. Birmingham Corporation was at the forefront of exploring new methods of gas making. They also decided to go ahead with a new gasworks at Nechells that was completed between 1900 and 1901. Another gasworks was contemplated near Erdington, but this was not built. The Nechells Works were situated on the opposite side of the canal to the Saltley Works. The Nechells site had one working retort house fitted with inclined retorts and space for a second retort house that opened later. Birmingham Gas Department managers visited Europe to examine ways of improving gas production. They decided to install a bank of coke ovens at Saltley before 1914 that was fired by a Mond gas producer. At Windsor Street, it was decided to install Woodall–Duckham vertical retorts.

If a single engineering development was responsible for changing gas production, the vertical retort must be a serious contender. The principle involved the feeding of coal at the top of the retort through hoppers, this passed through the heart of the retort and the combustion zone that released gas and allowed coke to fall to the bottom of the retort where it was discharged into coke cars or wagons. These were towed out to the stacking ground where the coke was allowed to cool for sale or heating the retorts.

Woodall–Duckham was a London-based company formed originally in 1909 and with H.W. Woodall and A. Duckham listed amongst the directors. Woodall–Duckham Vertical Retort and Oven Construction Co. Ltd (1911) was formed two years later to market the new design of retort. They came to specialise not only in the provision of retorts, but also Peale Davis tar plants and Becker coke ovens. Manufacture of components was in the hands of associate companies, which included Gibbons Brothers, Newton, Chambers & Co. and Thomas Vale & Sons. Vale & Sons were builders and contractors based in Stourport, and Newton Chambers owned the Thorncliffe Ironworks and collieries at Chapeltown near Sheffield. They were iron makers, iron founders and engineers. Gibbons Brothers Ltd had the Dibdale Fireclay Works at Gornall. Benjamin Gibbons had established the firm in 1834, which developed not only into mining fireclay and the making of fireclay goods, but also established a construction and engineering business. The fireclay found at Dibdale was equal in quality to that found around Stourbridge and the Delph and coal drawn from their own mines reduced production costs. The engineering trade was responsible for the construction of gas making plant and complete retort houses. When the vertical retort was devised, Gibbons Brothers were in an ideal position for promoting the product. W.P. Gibbons, managing director of Gibbons Brothers, and W.N. Drew of Newton Chambers were both appointed to the Board of Woodham–Duckham Vertical Retort and Oven Construction Co.

Vertical retorts had certain advantages over the earlier system and in particular dispensed with the hard labour of hand charging. As gasworks across the county came to adopt the vertical retort system, Woodall–Duckham, Gibbons Brothers and Newton Chambers profited through the steady flow of orders for their work.

The demand for gas continued to sustain a number works in the West Midlands and there were few closures at this time. Perhaps the only one of note was Aldridge, which was a small works built alongside the Daw End Canal. The chief supply was for lighting and this was taken over by the Walsall Corporation with the inevitable closure of Aldridge Gasworks. Some twenty-nine public works remained to carbonise coal for the making of town gas, coke and useful by-products:

Birmingham and Black Country Gasworks, 1912 (also see appendix 4)

Owner	Location
Bilston Gas Co.	Ettingshall, Wolverhampton
Birmingham Corporation	Adderley Street, Birmingham
Birmingham Corporation	Nechells, Birmingham
Birmingham Corporation	Saltley, Birmingham
Birmingham Corporation	Swan Village, West Bromwich
Birmingham Corporation	Windsor Street, Birmingham
Brierley Hill District Gas Light Co.	Delph, Brierley Hill
Brierley Hill District Gas Light Co.	Kingswinsford
Cannock Chase Gas Co.	Church Street, Chasetown
Cannock, Hednesford & District Gas Light Co.	Cannock
Cannock, Hednesford & District Gas Light Co.	Hednesford
Coleshill Gas Co. Ltd	High Street, Coleshill
Cradley Heath Gas Co.	Cradley Road, Cradley Heath
Dudley Gas Light Co.	Spring Gardens, Dudley
Fazeley Gas Co.	Fazeley, Tamworth

Halesowen Gas Co.	Great Cornbow, Halesowen
Henley in Arden Gas, Coal & Coke Co. Ltd	High Street, Henley in Arden
Knowle & District Gas Co.	Dorridge
Lichfield Gas Co.	Queen Street, Lichfield
Ogley Hay & Brownhills Gas Co. Ltd	Brownhills
Oldbury Gas Co.	Dudley Road, Oldbury
Rowley Regis & Blackheath Gas Co.	Powke Lane, Old Hill
Sedgley Urban District Council	Lower Gornal, Dudley
Solhull Gas Co.	Wharf Lane, Solihull
South Staffordshire Mond Gas	
(Power & Heating) Co.	Dudley Port, Tipton
Smethwick Corporation	Rabone Lane, Smethwick
Walsall Corporation	Pleck Gasworks
West Bromwich Corporation	Albion Gasworks
Willenhall Gas Co.	Clarkes Lane, Short Heath
Wolverhampton Gas Co.	Stafford Road, Wolverhampton

A gas producing plant was installed at the Winnington Works, Northwich and aroused keen interest in engineering circles. Gas from this process was suitable for powering a new type of internal combustion engine, known as the gas engine. These engines were becoming popular at this time and replacing steam engines in various establishments. The Power Gas Corporation was formed to manufacture and sell producer plants based on the Mond pattern. About 1900 Edmund Howl, pump maker of Tipton, approached Dr Mond with a plan for a plant in the Black Country. Howl's proposal led to the formation of the South Staffordshire Mond (Power & Heating) Co., in 1901, to supply producer gas throughout the Black Country. The plant was supplied and erected by the Power Gas Corporation Ltd, of Parkfield Works, Stockton on Tees, and Mr Humphrey was the consultant engineer.

The Act of Parliament giving the company powers to distribute gas to firms and factories in the Black Country received Royal Assent in 1901. The plant went into

Mercer's Coal Wharf, Staffordshire & Worcestershire Canal.
The coal wharf was an essential part of the canal trade. Here coal boats would deliver coal from the local collieries to be sorted, graded and stacked. The coal was then sold for both domestic and industrial consumption.
(Ray Shill collection)

production during Easter 1905 and comprised eight 20-ton producers, of which four were worked and four kept in reserve. Fuel for the producers was initially supplied as rough slack from nearby mines. But the yield was unsatisfactory and the company resorted to purchasing larger coals, such as 'peas' and 'beans'. Eventually a reliable source of coal was obtained from the Exhall Colliery, near Hawkesbury Junction on the Coventry Canal. Dr Mond purchased a controlling interest in this colliery to ensure a continuous supply. Exhall fuel yielded about 80lbs of ammonium sulphate per ton of fuel!

Some of the first customers were the South Staffordshire Mine Drainage that used Mond gas to heat boilers and later drive gas engines for pumping purposes. Gradually a customer base was built up and a network of mains laid throughout the district. Such was the demand that, in 1912, further 30-ton producers and ancillary plant were installed. Increased electricity generation and availability of compact electric motors led to the decline in the use of gas engines and by 1920 output of Mond gas became principally directed towards furnace work. Sales of ammonium sulphate also declined, but the demand for tar was on the increase. The tar from the producer plant had been difficult to dispose of and tar distillers had paid a low price. After the First World War a plant was installed at Tipton to distil the tar and extract the valuable constituents.

By-products from the gas industry, in general, were regularly under scientific scrutiny. By the start of the nineteenth century a process had been developed to include the separation of sulphocyanides from ammoniacal liquor. One company, British Cyanides, came to specialise in this process. From 1904 sulphocyanides were collected by canal boat from certain gasworks to be delivered to the Cynanide Works, beside the Jim Crow Arm on the Titford Branch. The British Cyanide Co. Ltd built up a fleet of boats that included the *Peter* and *Tiger*.

Coke might be conveyed from the gasworks by road, rail or canal. The following list records canal traffic in October 1902:

Coke Carried on the BCN, October 1902

From Local Gasworks

Carrier (or toll payer)	Gasworks	Destination	Amount in tons and cwt
Alfred Hickman	Stafford Road	Spring Vale	636t 00cwt
Alfred Hickman	Windsor Street	Spring Vale	307t 15cwt
Alfred Hickman	Nechells	Spring Vale	1,390t 5cwt
Bradley, T. & J.	Stafford Road	Capponfield	325t 15cwt
Chance & Hunt	Windsor Street	Leabrook	19t 5cwt
Fanshaw & Pinson	Stafford Road	Capponfield	32t 00cwt
Fanshaw & Pinson	Autherley Junction	Capponfield	21t 00cwt
Jones, T.P. & Co.	Kiddermister	Tiger Works	21t 10cwt
Lloyd & Lloyd	Windsor Street	Coombswood	21t 10cwt
W. Roberts	Stafford Road	Tipton	436t 15cwt
W. Roberts	Windsor Street	Tipton	546 15cwt
Sankey & Sons	Stafford Road	Bordesley	17t 15cwt

H.B. Whitehouse	Stafford Road	Priorsfield	565t 10cwt
Willingsworth Iron Co.	Nechells and Saltley	Willingsworth	101t 15cwt
C. Wilcox Ltd	Windsor Street	Tividale	12t 15cwt
Total carried	2,832 tons	toll £89 7s 8d	

Access to the Birmingham Canal was readily available to manufacturers who did not have wharf access by a system of public wharves. Several had weighbridge accommodation and were manned by company staff to take account of the goods passing between the canal and road wagons. The public wharves were placed in strategic locations and adapted from company land at bridge crossing places or where road access was available. Some had long periods of use, like the Crescent Wharf, others were more recent and had been formed as the need developed. Snow Hill Wharf, for example, had been a timber wharf for John Iddins. When he died the BCN had purchased the wharf from his widow.

Coal merchants and dealers also frequently rented space at public wharves as a base for their business. Aston and Bloomsbury wharves were placed alongside the Birmingham & Fazeley Canal. Aston Wharf was located beside the Lichfield Road and near Cuckoo Lane Bridge. A weighing machine office, three coal dealers and a coal merchant were recorded there in 1901.

Birmingham Canal Wharves 1900

Aldridge	Daw End Branch
Alma	Wyrley & Essington Canal
Anglesey	Anglesey Branch
Aston	Birmingham & Fazeley Canal
Bell	Rushall Canal
Birchills	Walsall Locks
Black Delph	Dudley No.1 Canal
Blackcock	Daw End Branch
Bloomsbury	Birmingham & Fazeley Canal
Bodymoor Heath	Birmingham & Fazeley Canal
Bone Pit	Dudley No.2 Canal
Bordesley Basin	Digbeth Branch
Broad Lane	Wyrley Bank Branch
Brookfields	Soho Loop
Can Lane	Wolverhampton Locks
Chester Street	Birmingham & Fazeley Canal
Churchbridge	Churchbridge Locks
Crescent	New Hall Branch
Darlaston Green	Walsall Canal
Darnford	Wyrley & Essington Canal
Devils Elbow	Wyrley & Essington Canal
Dudley Junction	Old Main Line, Birmingham Canal

Dudley Wood	Dudley No.2 Canal
Dunton	Birmingham & Fazeley Canal
Engine	Engine Arm
Erdington	Birmingham & Fazeley Canal
Fazeley	Birmingham & Fazeley Canal
French Walls & Handsworth	Engine Arm
Gosbrook	Wolverhampton Locks
Hardings	Wyrley & Essington Canal
Haywood	Dudley No.2 Canal
Hednesford	Cannock Extension
Holloway Bank	Tame Valley
Horseley Fields	Wyrley & Essington Canal
Icknield Port	Icknield Port Loop
Landywood	Wyrley Bank
Langley Green	Titford Branch
Leabrook	Walsall Canal
Leacroft	Cannock Extension
Lichfield	Wyrley & Essington Canal
Little Bloxwich	Wyrley & Essington Canal
Longwood	Rushall Canal
Minworth	Birmingham & Fazeley Canal
Moat House Bridge	Wyrley & Essington Canal
Newtown	Lord Hay's Branch
Norton Green	Cannock Extension
Ocker Hill	Ocker Hill Branch
Oozell Street	Oozell Loop
Perry Barr	Tame Valley Canal
Pothouse Bridge	Old Main Line, Birmingham Canal
Princess End Wharf	Old Main Line, Birmingham Canal
Redcap	Wyrley & Essington Canal
Silvester	Cannock Extension
Smethwick	Engine Arm
Snow Hill	Birmingham & Fazeley Canal
Stone Cross	Tame Valley Canal
Toll End	Tipton/Toll End Communication
Twenty Fourth Lock	Wyrley & Essington
Walsall	Walsall Canal
Waterloo	Main Line, Birmingham Canal
Watling Street	Anglesey Branch
Willenhall	Bentley Canal
Wyrley Grove	Cannock Extension
York's Bridge	Wyrley & Essington

There was a constant demand for boats to supply the many aspects of the canal carrying trade. Traditionally narrow boats were made of wood and comprised a long open hold up to 70ft in length and 7ft wide. They were made with oak sides and elm bottoms, although sometimes other woods were used. Iron boats were also made, but their numbers were a fraction of those constructed in wood. Some boats had a cabin at one end, which reduced carrying capacity but provided living space for the boatman and his family on longer journeys.

Boatyards and Boatbuilders 1912

Boatyard	*Canal*
Boatbuilders	
J. & B. Aston, Toll End, Tipton	Walsall Canal
Eli Aston, Iron Boat Dock, Alexandra Road, Tipton	Toll End Communication
Bowaters, Brookfields Boat Dock (Edward Yeomans Manager)	Birmingham Heath Branch
Chambers & Marsh, Timber Merchants, Freeth Street, Oldbury	Oldbury Loop
J.W. Cornwall, Springfields, Dudley	Dudley Canal
John Crannage, Moor Street, Brierley Hill	Stourbridge Canal
John Freeman & Son, Bumble Hole Road, Netherton	Bumble Hole Arm
J.T. Gill, Greets Green, West Bromwich	Walsall Canal
Charles and Thomas Hendley, Sutherland Dock, Heath Town	Wyrley & Essington Canal
George Hale & Son, Birmingham Road, Oldbury	BCN old main line
Harris's Boat Dock and Boiler Yard, Bumble Hole Road	Bumble Hole Branch
Daniel Hewings, Upper Green Lane, Walsall	Birchilld Canal
Joseph Hollowood, Brickhouse Lane, Great Bridge	Walsall Canal
Mathew Hughes & Son, Selly Oak Wharf, Harborne Lane	Dudley No.2 Canal
John Lovekin, Rotten Park Street, Birmingham	Icknield Port Loop
T. & E. Lowe Ltd, Powke Lane, Old Hill	Dudley No.2 Canal
F. Mason, Canal Street, Moxley	Walsall Canal
Monks, Harborne Lane, Selly Oak	Dudley No.2 Canal
John Morris, Bush Farm Dock, Albion, West Bromwich	Izon's Turn
James Nicholls, Upper Green Lane, Walsall	Birchill Canal
Peabody & Co., Upper Green Lane, Walsall	Wyrley & Essington Canal
Thomas Pearsall, Upper Green Lane, Walsall	Birchill Branch Canal
Rogers & Son, Bromford Dock, West Bromwich	Izon's Turn
H. Rollinson, The Brades, Tividale, Oldbury	BCN old main line
Joseph Steadman & Son, Pothouse Bridge, Bradley	Wednesbury Oak Loop
Edward Tailby, Stonehouse Dock, Holly Lane, Aldridge	Daw End Canal
Edward Taiby, High Street, Selly Oak	Worcester & Birmingham Canal

Edward Tailby, Albion Dock, West Bromwich	BCN new main line
Joseph Tedstill, Alma Dock, Heath Town	Wyrley & Essington Canal
Webster & Son, Swan Lane, West Bromwich	Balls Hill Branch
W. Worsey Ltd, 53 Plume Street, Aston	Dowlers Arm (private)
W. Worsey Ltd, Icknield Port Road, Birmingham	Icknield Port Loop
W. Worsey Ltd, Toll End Dock, Tipton	Toll End Communication

Canal Carriers

Thomas Bantock, Millfields, Bilston	BCN new main line
George Element, Brades, Oldbury	BCN old main line
Fellows, Morton & Clayton, Park Wharf, Duddeston Mill Road	Birmingham & Warwick Junction
Fanshaw and Pinson, Heath Town	Wyrley & Essington Canal
Price & Son, John Street, Round Oak, Brierley Hill	Dudley No.1 Canal

Private Firms

Biggs Boat Dock, Ten Score Bridge	BCN main line
Bromford Boat Dock	Birmingham & Fazeley Canal
Chance & Hunt, Chemical Manufacturers, Oldbury	Valentia Arm
Chance and Hunt, Chemical Manufacturers, Leabrook	Walsall Canal
Fishers Boat Dock, Old Hill	Dudley No.2 Canal
Fishers Boat Dock, Spon Lane	Spon Lane Locks
Harvey's Boat Dock, Brownhills	Cannock Extension
Hambletts, Brickmakers, West Bromwich	BCN new main line
Hewins Boat Dock, Daw End	Daw End Branch
Alfred Hickman, Spring Vale Steelworks & Furnaces, Bilston	BCN main line
W.H. Jones, boat dock, Old Hill	Dudley No.2 Canal
T. Jones, Ettingshall	BCN main line
T. Jones, Heath Town	Wyrley & Essington Canal
Matthews Boat Dock, Oldbury	Oldbury Loop
J.E. Perry, Boat Dock, Ettingshall	BCN main line
Pooles Boat Dock, Millfields, Bilston	BCN main line
Pooles Iron Boat Dock, Princess End	Wednesbury Oak Loop
Reeces Boat Dock, Dragon Bason, Riders Green	Walsall Canal
Snapes Boat Dock, Pelsall	Wyrley & Essington Canal
T. Thomas Boat Dock, Ettingshall	BCN main line
Thomas's Timber Yard and Boat Dock, Summer Hill	Wednesbury Oak Loop
Tuppers Boat Dock, Albion	Walsall Canal
Turners Boat Dock, Darlaston	Walsall Canal
Turton's Boat Dock, Ocker Hill	Ocker Hill Branch

Willingsworth Furnaces Boat Dock   Gospel Oak Branch
T. Wood Boat Dock, Short Heath   Wyrley & Essington Canal

The above list quotes several industrialists as owners of boatyards. Alfred Hickman had an extensive fleet of boats to supply their extensive works at Bilston. Tupper's had works at Bilston and West Bromwich that until 1911 had been engaged in the galvanised iron trade. A constant supply of wood was required to meet the needs of the many local boatyards.

Generally the demands made on the timber trade were quite varied. In addition to building, furniture and boat building, collieries needed pit timbers to support the roof and sides of the gate roads as well as making the curbs and cogs for thick-coal working. Timber was also regularly used in making gins and the pit frames used above the shafts. Surviving records for the Blakeley Hall Colliery Co. show that Chamberlain and Marsh of the Oldbury Timber & Slate Yard supplied Oak curbs to Blakeley Hall Colliery in 1877–1878, whilst H. Turner & Sons of Darlaston Green Timber Yard and Saw Mills also supplied curbs and a pit frame of pitch pine.

Timber yards were canalside features throughout Birmingham & the Black Country despite the increased amount of timber carried by railways and the setting up of railway-served yards and timber yards in the towns. Treatment and preparation of the timber retained the old method, where stacks of wood, cut into lengths were laid out in the open air to season for a number of years. New techniques were, however, coming into the trade such as kiln-dried timber, whilst new forms of power such as the gas engines and oil engines were frequent replacements for the steam engine in the sawmill. Eventually electrically powered saws became the standard.

The carriers whose costs were competitive with the railways served the canalside timber yards. Timber was generally imported from Canada and the Baltic, although some British timber was sold from time to time. The chief source of timber was the ports of Bristol, Hull, Liverpool and London and carriers brought loads along river and canal navigation to the yards, where the respective woods were allowed to season in the time-honoured tradition.

Walsall Sanitary Inspection of Boats records survive from 1905. Generally they list the name of boat, owner and master. Occasionally they give the traffic. On 12 September 1905 three boats, *Leonard*, *Trafalgar* and *Japan* belonging to the Shropshire Union Canal Carrying Co. and carrying timber were stopped for inspection. Another boat belonging the same company, the *Turtle*, was inspected on 19 February 1906.

Some yards had long-term existences. James Shipton's yard at Old Factory Wharf, Wolverhampton, came to be owned by William Beddows. The firm of Tailby and Co. had numerous timber yards scattered around the BCN system by 1914, which were accumulated over a number of years from other proprietors. They were pioneers in the use of motorboats for carrying timber by canal. During April 1914 Edward Tailby requested permission from the BCN Co. to navigate a motorboat between his works at West Bromwich, Old Hill and Selly Oak. Permission was granted even for the use of Lapal Tunnel provided he regulated his speed to 4 miles per hour.

Tailby's came to own the Charlotte Street Timber Yard and Sawmills, which had been commenced by Joseph Shipton and had a number of different owners through to Tailby's time. They chose to convert this yard to a motor garage after 1919 and during the 1920s disposed of their yard at Bangor Wharf, Bordesley Street, to the Sumner family. The Bordesley Street Yard was another yard with a long history. David Owen had the yard that was on the corner of New Canal Street and Bordesley Street with extensive wharves alongside the terminus basins of the Digbeth Branch. One entrance to the yard was via Cotton Street and a drawbridge across an arm of the canal there. Following the death of Owen, the Bordesley Street Timber Yard was let, in 1831, to Marshall, Cox & Tibbs, and subsequently Marshalls & Sons. By 1850 part of the wharf land included a two-storey railway and road-carriage-building establishment. The carriage-building works was transferred to Adderley Park in 1855, but the timber yard remained and eventually passed into the control of Tailby. When Sumner's took over the timber yard, the buildings were cleared. Sumner's specialised in the sale of tea, which they branded under the Typhoo Trademark. A new tea-blending factory was constructed on the site of the Bangor Wharf, which formed the core of the factory.

Timber on the canals was one of the longer-lived trades to the Midlands. Narrow boats made regular trips along the Grand Junction (later Grand Union) Canal to Brentford to load up with timber brought up by Thames Lighter. Fellows, Morton & Clayton was closely associated with this traffic, whilst the Severn Canal Carrying Co. brought timber up the Worcester & Birmingham Canal to Birmingham and Black Country timber yards. The Shropshire Union Railway & Canal Carrying Co. dealt with trade from the Mersey. Traffic in timber continued through to the 1950s and early 1960s where yards such as Cox's Yard at Great Bridge, alongside the Haines Branch, and Cartwright's Yard, at Olton on the Grand Union Canal, received loads of timber by boat.

Not all canalside yards received timber by boat. Wales Ltd, bedstead makers of Oozells Street, rented part of Oozells Street Coal Wharf from the Birmingham Canal Co. for the timber required to make beds and cots. An associate company, Timberies Ltd, purchased British and foreign timber for use at the Oozells Street Works. All timber was brought to Birmingham by rail and conveyed by road to the wharf.

Timber Wharves 1910

Company	Address	Canal Link
Ball's	Belmont Row, Birmingham	Digbeth Branch
William Beddows and Co.	Union Mill Street, Wolverhamptom	BCN main line
Boys	Wolverhampton Road, Walsall	Walsall Canal
Cartwright's	Olton Timber Yard	Warwick & Birmingham Canal
Genero Cassera	Honduras Wharf, Snow Hill	Birmingham & Fazeley Canal
Chambers and Marsh	Freeth Street, Oldbury	Oldbury Loop
William Clayton Junior	Adderley Road, Saltley	Birmingham & Warwick Junction
Thomas Cox	Great Bridge Steam Sawmills	Haynes Branch
Eccleston's	Timber Yard, Pothouse Bridge, Bradley	Wednesbury Oak Loop

Fairbanks Ltd	Camp Hill Saw Mills, Sampson Road North	Warwick & Birmingham Canal
George Hale	Birmingham Road, Oldbury	BCN old main line
John Hickman	Bridge Wharf, Bilston Road, Wolverhampton	BCN main line
W.J. Hodgetts and Son	Titford Steam Saw Mills, Blackheath	Causeway Green Branch
Lowe Brothers	Lime Wharf and Timber Yard, Waterfall Lane, Old Hill	Dudley No.2 Canal
Thomas and Edward Lowe	Powke Lane, Old Hill	Dudley No.2 Canal
Marsh's	Albert Street Timber Yard, Oldbury	Oldbury Loop
Roberts and Cooper	Nine Locks, Brierley Hill	Dudley No.1 Canal
William Round and Son	Saw Mills and Offices, Castle Street and High Street, Tipton	BCN old main line
Rudders Ltd	Albion Timber Yard, Chester Street	Birmingham & Fazeley Canal
Sykes	Roughay, Darlaston	Walsall Canal
Tailby & Co.	Near Friday Bridge, Birmingham	Newhall Branch
Tailby & Co.	91 Charlotte Street	Birmingham & Fazeley Canal
Taiby & Co. (previously Aston Junction Co.)	Love Lane, Birmingham	Digbeth Branch
Tailby & Co. (previously Thomas Adams & Sons Ltd)	King Edwards Road	Birmingham & Fazeley Canal
Tailby & Co.	Bangor Wharf, Bordesley Street	Digbeth Branch
Thomas's	Boat Dock & Timber Yard, Summerhill, Tipton	Wednesbury Oak Loop
Wingates	Lodge Road, Winson Green	Birmingham Heath Branch
Worcester Wharf Saw Mills Ltd	Bridge Street	Worcester & Birmingham Canal

The brewing industry saw considerable change from the 1870s when brewing came to be increasingly mechanised. New breweries were constructed on improved lines where the process followed down the building or across the site. The brewery companies sometimes continued to own or operate maltings, but there were others who chose to specialise in the malting trade. Birmingham & the Black Country during the years 1880–1920 supported a number of independent brewing concerns. Mitchells & Butlers of the Cape Hill Brewery and Broad Street Brewery had a purpose built malthouse (No.5) located alongside Wellington Wharf on the Winson Green Loop, whilst Showells had a canalside maltings at Langley Green, on the Titford Canal and Wallis's Arm in Birmingham. Independent maltsters included Samuel Thompson & Son, who had a large maltings alongside the Engine Arm that fronted Rabone Lane. The Thompson family also had another canalside maltings at Stone Street Bridge, Oldbury, on the old main line.

Downing's owned malthouses near Spon Lane Bridge that lined the old main line there. Canalside malthouses were in the minority, however, many more were situated in town locations.

Wallis's Arm was the name given to a short branch waterway that left the Digbeth Branch above the Ashted Locks and curved around to Heneage Street Coal Wharf. Works served by this branch included the Union Glassworks and Holbrook's Vinegar Works. Holbrook's were associated with sauce and pickle and in later years vinegar was brought by boat from Stourport. Bombing during the Second World War devastated Holbrook's Birmingham works and the site was subsequently given over for development. Moore and Simpson established another vinegar works at Aston Cross, which became the factory for the House of Parliament, or HP, sauce. Tomato puree was carried by canal boat to the Midlands and completed the final leg by road. Fellows, Morton & Clayton were frequently employed in this trade and when FMC ceased trading in 1949, HP retained their wharf in Fazeley Street for the puree trade. Birmingham also had its own jam hole on the Icknield Port Loop. Canning and Wildblood, of Freeth Street, were preserve and jam manufacturers that received coal by boat to this jam factory.

Cadbury Brothers were regular users of the waterways. Their speciality was the making of chocolate, which was conducted in premises near the Old Wharf, in Bridge Street, Birmingham before a move to a new factory at Bournville, in 1879. The Bournville factory was placed close to the Worcester & Birmingham Canal but was separated from it by the West Suburban Railway. By 1883 Cadbury's had a cabin boat that was used to bring coal from Cannock Chase and timber from Gloucester. Timber was used to make chocolate boxes. Rail sidings were laid into the factory between 1884 and 1885 coinciding with the reconstruction of the West Suburban Railway for the Midland Railway Co.. Rail traffic then accounted for much of Cadbury's trade for the next twenty years. In July 1907 Kynoch's decided to dispose of the Endurance Works, Mary Vale Road. These works had been engaged in the making of ammunition and had a selection of steam and gas engines, lathes, drilling machines and presses. Cadbury adapted the vacant premises as a depot.

Popular demand for milk chocolate encouraged Cadbury Brothers to set up a pair of milk evaporating factories. The first was opened in 1911 at Knighton alongside the Shropshire Union Canal. Another was opened, in 1915, at Frampton on Severn, beside the Gloucester & Sharpness Canal. Local dairy herds supplied each factory with churns being collected from farms in the district by road. Cadbury's built up a fleet of horse-drawn and motor narrow boats for the milk trade and in 1911 were the first local firm to have a pair of boats fitted with crude-oil Bolinder engines.

Narrow boats, gaily painted in Cadbury's colours (red and green), carrying loads of milk churns became a common site along the Midlands' waterways. The boats also carried crumb, which was a coarse preparation made from sugar and milk that was bagged and placed in the hold of the boat. Cadbury boats made trips along the Grand Junction Canal to London to collect loads of cocoa beans. Cane sugar was brought into Gloucester Docks and collected by narrow boat, which made the journey to Knighton via the Severn, Stourport and Staffordshire & Worcestershire Canal. Timber tended to be carried to Bournville by rail, as was tinplate that was used to make the tin chocolate boxes. Traffic in

Mary Vale Road Depot. The Endurance Tube & Vial Co. was the first occupier of the Mary Vale factory at Stirchley. It was they who arranged for the construction of the main building. Subsequent owners were Kynoch's who adapted the premises for making ammunition. Kynoch's sold the premises to Cadbury, who eventually converted the site as a canal depot for a new trade in bringing condensed milk to Bournville for Dairy Milk chocolate. (Bournville Works Magazine)

timber changed after 1920 when Cadbury's took over the disused Blackpole works near Worcester, which became their box factory. Timber was brought by boat from Sweden to Sharpness Docks where it was either sent on by rail or canal to Blackpole. The canal traffic was loaded into barges at Sharpness that were then hauled by tug to Diglis, Worcester. Here narrow boats were loaded with the timber for the final leg from the Severn up the locks of the Worcester & Birmingham Canal to Blackpole.

Improvements made to the Bournville factory included the building of a new depot alongside the Worcestershire & Birmingham Canal in 1925. This depot was also served by the internal railway system and had sidings alongside the wharf. Cadbury's chose to dispose of their fleet of boats in 1928 and elected to have their traffic worked by other carriers. Fellows, Morton & Clayton Ltd and the Severn Canal Carrying Co. took over the carriage of goods from the Knighton and Frampton Works. S.E. Barlow brought coal from Cannock Chase.

The canal chemical trade continued to show diversity. Stalwarts of this trade remained the firms of Albright & Wilson and Chance & Hunt, but a new name was added to the list in 1920. Synthite Ltd set up as manufacturing chemists at Ryders Green alongside the pound between the first and second lock. They made formaldehyde that was an essential ingredient used to make Bakelite resin. Methanol was carried from the Albion interchange basin and carriers such as J. Toole and W. Holmes delivered coal.

Robinson's tar distillery, placed alongside the Walsall Canal, and a short distance from Synthite, made a variety of products from gas tar, which included black varnish, creosote, formaldehyde, lysol and naptha that were sold in containers and barrels up to 40 gallons in size. Fertilizers and insecticides were also produced. Robinson's owned a factory in Alma Street, Smethwick, which made the sprayer units for dispersing the liquid fertilizers and insecticides.

Steel making produced a basic slag that was broken up in a crusher and sold as phosphate-rich manure. H.E. Albert operated a phosphate works at Wednesbury that processed the basic slag made at the Patent Shaft Steelworks. Alfred Hickman Ltd also had a basic slag crusher and works alongside the branch to Bilston Meadow Colliery (near

Ten Score Bridge) that loaded boats with phosphate manure. Another manure works was placed near the Hatherton Branch of the Staffordshire & Worcestershire Canal at Longhouse near Cannock. These works were owned by the Cannock Agricultural Co. Ltd of the Longhouse Stud Farm, who made bone and chemical manures.

Adolphe Crosbie Ltd owned the Walsall Street Colour Works, at Wolverhampton, which was at the end of a long private canal, sometimes known as the Minerva Arm. They owned a large fleet of boats and made a variety of paints and specialised in the production of red oxide. Another Wolverhampton paint maker was Mander Brothers. The firm of Mander's was a long-established (1803) Wolverhampton paint and varnish maker that had a paint factory in the centre of Wolverhampton. They established a canalside colour works alongside the pound between the fourth and fifth locks on the Bentley Lock flight that also had a rail connection with the Midland Railway Walsall to Wolverhampton line. Mander's Wednesfield works was also alongside the English Lead Co.'s white lead works, which was an important paint ingredient. The lead works was offered for sale in 1905, but Mander's continued to occupy the Wednesfield works until the 1920s, when they moved to Heath Town.

Heath Town Paint Works was built as a munitions factory making phosphorus for shells and bombs under the auspices of Albright & Wilson, phosphorus makers of Oldbury. The site was chosen for its ready access to canal and railway. Heath Town Munitions Works was built between 1916 and 1917 and commenced production in 1917. Albright & Wilson Ltd sold the property in 1920.

The principle of electric lighting was refined during the nineteenth century. The passage of an electric current between separated carbon points produced an incandescent light, but the method of creating electricity of sufficient power proved too costly to be made by batteries. The invention of the magneto-machine (1853) was enough to provide sufficient power for lighting. Electric lighting was tried at Trinity House Lighthouse, Blackwall (1857). Once the concept was established a few private ventures were formed to make electricity for sale. Parliamentary committees met in 1879 and 1882 to examine the provision of electric light for public use. Their findings led to the Electric Light Bill of 1882.

A new market for electricity was the electric-powered tramcar. Street tramways had become popular for towns and cities during the 1880s when trams drawn by horses or steam locomotives became a common sight on the streets. The electric-powered trams came later, but as soon as pioneering projects such as the Manx Electric Railway started to run, commercial and municipal undertakings looked to the new form of power. Between 1900 and 1906 the national street tramway map was completely re-drawn as new tramways were constructed or old lines converted. The need for electricity increased rapidly and both private and municipal power stations were constructed to meet the new demand.

Electricity was generally provided by the turbine, which when turned by an external force gave the means of making an electric current. Fast-flowing water provided one means of turning the turbine and one of the earliest power stations located at Powick Mill, Worcester had the means to generate power through the flow of the river. A more common process was to drive the turbine blades by the force of steam. Bellis and Morcam of Icknield Street, who had already established a market making turbines for naval vessels, now benefited through the supply of turbines to the power industry. Steam was generated by coal-fired boilers and early power stations found both the canal and river to be suitable locations. Water for the boilers was drawn from the canal or river and navigable waterways provided the means to bring fuel for the boilers.

As electricity came to be used for lighting and a power source, other applications were investigated. Electricity as a provider of heat for furnaces was also adapted for commercial purposes. An early application was the extraction of phosphorus, which was promoted by the Phosphorus Co. Ltd. Phosphorus manufacture was traditionally carried out by heating chemically treated residues of bones, or mineral phosphates, in fireclay retorts. The phosphorus-rich vapour was drawn off and collected in a condenser where white phosphorus was collected. Firms like Albright & Wilson then heated the white phosphorus in sealed iron tanks to convert it into the more stable, red phosphorus. The use of fireclay retorts was an intermittent process. Like the local gasworks of the period, the furnace had to be shut down periodically to clean out the retorts ready for fresh charges. The electric phosphorus furnace provided the possibility of a continuous system, like a blast furnace.

The London-based Phosphorus Co. was formed in 1890 to develop patents presented in 1888 by J.B. Readman and in 1888 and 1889 by T. Parker and A. Robinson The share issue financed the construction of a phosphors extraction works at Wednesfield during 1891. The Electrical Construction Co. of Wolverhampton was responsible for the construction of the plant that included a furnace designed by Thomas Parker.

Thomas Parker was a pioneering spirit in the electrical industry who had been a partner in the firm of Elwell, Parker, electrical engineers. Amongst their products were early types of tramcars, which were constructed at canalside premises in Commercial Road, Wolverhampton. During 1889 Elwell, Parker became the Electrical Construction Co. and within a year had moved production to a new factory at Bushbury.

The Electrical Construction Co. was an important partner in the phosphorus works, providing the furnaces for phosphorus manufacture. It was they who had to deal with the problems of development. They gained the major share holding in the Phosphorus Co. from 1893 and eventually the registered office was transferred to Bushbury. Meanwhile production of phosphorus was conducted at the Wednesfield plant, which lay near to both the Midland Railway Station and the Bentley Canal. Manufacture of phosphorus at the Wednesfield factory was, however, relatively short lived. Members of the Albright and Wilson families undertook a lengthy battle to take over the operation and had gained positions as directors of the Phosphorus Co. by 1892. They then gradually increased their influence, which culminated in November 1896 with the shares held by the Electric Construction Co. sold to Albright & Wilson. The registered office was moved again, this time to Oldbury.

Albright & Wilson had benefited through the trials and tribulations Tom Parker and the Electric Construction Co. had experienced in developing a workable furnace. They started the first electric furnace at Oldbury during 1893, whilst Wednesfield was still in operation, but once the working of this furnace was proved, the plant at Wednesfield was shut down. From 1894 until October 1896 the Wednesfield Phosphorus Works was occupied by C.J. Banner, ironworker, and then disposed of.

eight

CANALS IN DECLINE

The electric cell and the dynamo both provided early means of electricity production. The dynamo, which proved invaluable to the electroplating industry, was worked by shafts driven by steam power. Private generation of electricity for lighting purposes began to be adopted during the 1880s. Early users included John Lysaght (Swan Garden Ironworks, Wolverhampton) who, in January 1886, lit the whole of their works, including foundry, fitting shops, bar banks and canal wharves by the new incandescent lamp.

An important contribution to the means of electricity generation was achieved when water-driven or steam-driven turbines were adapted for this purpose. Lacking suitable fast-flowing water sources, steam-powered turbine plant proved critical to the future of electricity generation throughout the Midlands. Industry was quick to adopt the technology and some progressive firms chose to adopt steam-driven power-generating plant to assist their business. With some firms, such as Albright & Wilson, the generation of electricity became essential to their manufacturing process. The provision of public lighting also became a reality when private companies were established to supply electricity for domestic and industrial use. In 1891 the Birmingham Electric Supply Co. opened their first generating station at Dale End.

Both private companies and local authorities took an interest in the generation of electricity for lighting and electric tramways. Street tramway networks were established to serve the needs of the community. They used either steam locomotives or horses for traction, but once suitable electric motors had been invented, electric traction was adopted on most street tramway systems, which also led to many new routes coming into existence. It was demand to supply electric tramways that led to the establishment of new power stations. In the Midlands most were located beside local canals where coal was carried by boat from nearby collieries.

Birmingham Corporation took over the Birmingham Electric Supply Co. operation from 1 January 1900. Their generating plants at Dale Street and Water Street became corporation property. Birmingham Corporation then enlarged the electric supply through the building at new stations at Summer Lane and Nechells. The Nechells Power Station was erected beside the Birmingham & Warwick Junction Canal. The first buildings comprised a temporary station that was erected during the First World War. In

Summer Lane Power Station, 1907. The generating station at Summer Lane was constructed on land that was formerly occupied by the General Hospital and alongside a long basin that joined the Birmingham & Fazeley Canal. This basin was adapted for the reception of coal boats, but unloading these boats involved the heavy labour of shovelling the coal out of the hold and onto a moving conveyor belt placed alongside the basin. (Local Studies Department, Birmingham Library)

Ocker Hill Power Station. A power station existed beside the Walsall Canal at Ocker Hill from 1902. A much larger station was erected on this site between 1945 and 1948 that lined both sides of the waterway. Coal for the original generating station was delivered by boat, but the new station had railway sidings to feed loading bunkers for the conveyors that carried the coal across the canal to the boiler house. (Black Country Museum)

1924 the permanent station was completed on land adjacent. Nechells Power Station became known as the Princes Power Station after the Prince of Wales (later King Edward VIII), who performed the opening ceremony.

West Bromwich, Wolverhampton and Walsall Corporations also became involved in the generation of electricity. Worcester Corporation built their first power station at Powick in 1894, which had a steam generating plant but also used the flow of the River Teme as a generating source. Small generating stations that supplied power to the tramway companies were erected at James Bridge (South Staffordshire Tramways), Downing Street, Smethwick (Birmingham & Midland Tramways) and Hartshill (Dudley, Stourbridge & District Electric Tramways). The Smethwick station was taken over by the Shropshire, Staffordshire & Worcestershire Power Co. from 1908 that substantially enlarged the station buildings and generating plant.

Birchills Power Station, Walsall.
The new power stations authorised from the 1920s were much larger structures than had been previously built and consequently a greater demand for coal came to exist. All facilities had to be improved. In this aerial view, construction of the Birchills 'B' station (completed 1949) is seen to be well underway. The original power station (1916) is dwarfed by the new generating station and associated plant. (Ray Shill collection)

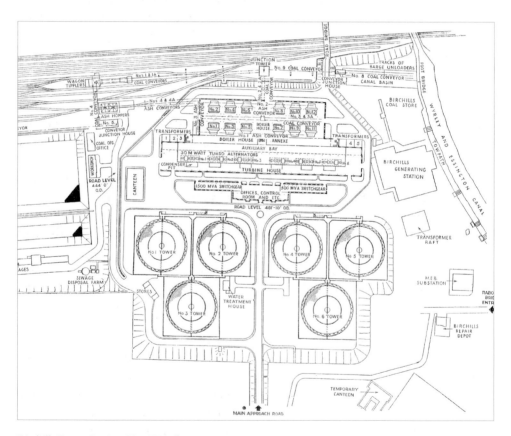

Birchills Power Station Plan, Walsall.
Boats continued to supply coal from the Cannock Chase Coalfield. They unloaded coal in a canal basin equipped with overhead telphers. Coal was then carried by the No.8 coal conveyor to the boiler house of the new power station. (Ray Shill collection)

Walsall (Birchills) Power Station had been completed in 1916 and replaced the earlier generating station at Wolverhampton Street. Situated beside the Birchills Branch Canal, coal boats from Cannock Chase Collieries avoided the passage of the Walsall Locks, as they had previously been made to do when supplying coal to Wolverhampton Street. The demand for electricity from Birchills steadily increased during the 1920s, aided no doubt by an extension order that was granted in 1924 to supply the rural districts. Electricity supply was extended to Rushall, Aldridge, Pelsall, Great Wyrley, Great Barr and Essington. An extra high-tension ring main was also laid to supply the collieries in the Essington, Great Wyrley, Brownhills and Aldridge districts. Such was the demand for coal that boats frequently lined the towpath near the power station waiting their turn for unloading.

Wolverhampton's power station was located in Commercial Road with the main generator hall and coal wharf aligned facing the Commercial Arm, which joined with the main Birmingham Canal opposite the Great Western Railway Shrubbery Interchange Basins. Like the later Birchills Station, Commercial Road Power Station was situated on the same level as the Cannock Chase Collieries.

There was a type of wooden boat used by certain Wolverhampton coal merchants known as the 'Hampton boat', which was generally wider and longer than the conventional coal boats. Some of the largest would carry up to 40 tons of coal on the lock-free section from the collieries. These and normal boats made up the bulk of the trade passing along the Wyrley & Essington Canal to Wolverhampton or Walsall.

The use of street tramways declined from 1920 following the introduction of motorbus routes. Local industry and domestic needs more than compensated for the loss and led to a steadily increasing demand during the 1920s and 1930s. Power station enlargement schemes were regularly submitted to the government controlled Electricity Authority. New (and larger) power stations were often located beside rivers when the requirement for cooling water dictated a finite supply.

Wolverhampton, West Bromwich and Walsall Corporation disposed of their stations to a new West Midlands Joint Electricity Authority in 1927. The WMJEA also took over the privately owned Ocker Hill Power Station, which was erected between 1901 and 1902 for the Midland Electric Corporation for Power Distribution. The West Midlands Joint Electricity Authority chose to close down the West Bromwich Power Station in 1931. This was located on the Ridgeacre Branch near Swan Village Gas Works and was in a comparatively isolated position for coal supply compared with the other works. They were also building a new power station on the Severn at Ironbridge that would receive coal by rail and use river water for cooling purposes. The first section of the new Ironbridge Station was officially opened on 13 October 1932. Ironbridge, Ocker Hill, Wolverhampton and Walsall stations were all classed as selected stations of the Central England Electricity scheme to supply current to the Central Electricity Board.

The 1920s were a time of depression for many industries where even the hardiest manufacturers were affected. This was also the time when commercial road transport changed in preference from steam traction to favour internal combustion. Mechanical propulsion on narrow canals had long been available using steamboats and tugs. Some schemes proved ill-fated, like the mechanical towing scheme instituted by the Birmingham & Liverpool Junction Canal Co. during 1843 and 1844 where specially designed tug boats employing a disc propeller system made by the Patent Disc Engine Co. in Berkley Street, Birmingham and steam propulsion units provided by the Vulcan Foundry at Newton le Willows, were employed to haul trains of boats between the Midlands, Nantwich and Ellesmere Port. The industrial legacy of this experiment still remains as buildings at Norton Junction, where the tugs were maintained and the various stable blocks made for the horses that towed the boats through the lock sections.

Birmingham based innovator and engineer John Inshaw of Morville Street had built and operated a pair of steam packet boats on the Birmingham Canal and later built a steam tug for the Regents Canal and tugs for the Moira Colliery on the Ashby Canal. The Moira tugs operated during the 1860s bringing coal down to Coventry. Steamboats for merchandise traffic were used by several carriers, including the Grand Junction Canal Carrying Co. and Fellows, Morton & Co. Those that belonged to Fellows, Morton & Clayton are perhaps the best known as they were built up to the year 1912. By this time, however, internal combustion engines were fitted to some boats. Edward Tailby, of the timber merchant firm, made some of the first important trials in 1907 and others copied his example, notably Cadbury Brothers, the chocolate makers of Bournville, who had a boat fitted with an engine in 1912.

Sweden's greatest gift to inland navigation was the Bolinder engine, of the semi-diesel oil type. These engines were a particular favourite of Fellows, Morton & Clayton, who installed them in their boats. Such craft fitted with oil or diesel engines became known as motorboats, which was a suitable distinction from the horse-drawn craft, once so common on inland navigation.

Problems of coal supply to the munitions and other works during the First World War highlighted the need for powered craft. A few inspired people had considered the use of motor tugs and Chance & Hunt were probably the first to use them for bringing coal boats from the collieries and were already using a tug during 1917. After 1918 others followed their example and coal contractors particularly favoured the use of tugs as these could collect loaded boats and be on the move when the conventional horse boat had to tie up and wait to be loaded. The whole character of the waterways changed when tugs went into general use. The constant stream of horse-drawn boats from the Cannock Chase Collieries was replaced by tugs hauling trains of boats at intermittent intervals. Some horse boats still made the journey but their numbers began to decline. Another experimental design was the detachable motor that could be fitted on top of the cabin of coal boats and was tried out on craft owned by Coggins & Arthur. This design appears to have had little success and could be dangerous as the revolving shaft operated near to the steerer.

Coal transport was also changing. The demand for domestic coal still led to the carriage of different sized coals for that purpose, but mines were now using coal cutting machinery that produced a smaller type of coal. In fact, crushed and pulverised coal became the requirement for power station boilers. Traffic to the main power stations at Birchills, Nechells, Ocker Hill and Wolverhampton became important revenue earners. The private power station for the GEC at Witton also increased demand.

BCN Traffic Figures Published in 1925

Comparative yearly coal traffic from Cannock Chase collieries (in tons)

	1923	1924
Brownhills	257,271t	277,453t
Broad Lane	6,437t	11,012t
Cannock & Rugeley	161,491t	157,703t
Cannock Leacroft	79,293t	89,092t
Conduit, Norton Green	204,373t	231,943t
Coppice	66,133t	64,089t
East Cannock	64,165t	71,171t
Great Wyrley	23,961t	4,799t
Littleton	53,408t	57,243t
Mid Cannock	35,965t	36,638t
Old Coppice	14,169t	12,232t
West Cannock	36,635t	29,905t
Anglesey	230,769t	245,269t

The Birmingham Canal Navigations came under a certain pressure to improve arrangements at Gorsty Hill Tunnel, which had become a bottleneck for boat movements. Traffic through the tunnel had seen horse-drawn boat numbers increase with the continued expansion of Stewart & Lloyds' Coombeswood tube works and the opening of Coombeswood Colliery for Noah Hingley & Sons. A tug was subsequently provided to drag boats through the tunnel. Eventually three internal combustion tugs were put into use for Gorsty Hill and Dudley Tunnels. Engineers quickly dismissed a suggestion for an electric tugging system at Dudley Tunnel as unworkable.

There was marked concern shown by Birmingham Canal managers as to the state of traffic. Records were regularly kept of existing trade and trade loss. The principal decline was that of coal to specific works. The mass of documentation produced for the BCN show that up to the time of the Great Strike (of 1926) coal traffic was still busy with significant annual tonnages coming from the mines both on Cannock Chase and the Old Hill district.

BCN Traffic Figures 1925

Coal Mined in Old Hill District

Buffery Colliery	55,311
Coombswood	66,354
Knowle	22,183
Netherton (Hingley)	10,630
Pear Tree Lane (Bunns)	18,951
Sledmore	2,370
Warrens Hall	45,481
Windmill End No.3	48,307

Carriage rates of both coal and merchandise could not reach the high figures reached prior to 1910. Industry was in a state of change, yet the number of firms served by water transport remained high. Metalworkers in the Midlands were a diverse lot, and many aspects of this business had shown a degree of metamorphosis to suit scientific and engineering developments. Economic conditions and competition had taken a high toll, but the war years had provided finance for the survivors. Contracts for the munitions of war as well as basic equipment for the troops provided both work and guaranteed revenue. War contracts lasted through to 1919, but then came the harsh reality of survival in a post-war world, where wage demands, renewed competition and dwindling product demand created challenges for manufacturers. To survive in business was to adapt.

Weights of Traffic 1923–1927

Year	Coal	Merchandise	Total
1923	2,515,078	2,049,652	4,564,730
1924	2,608,239	2,174,299	4,782,468
1925	2,361,668	2,001,680	4,363,348
1926	1,968,789	1,740,667	3,709,456
1927	2,206,978	1,587,502	4,094,480

Canal carrying moved into the final phase. When coalmines were plentiful in South Staffordshire many manufacturing firms chose to employ boats, if their works were at a canalside location. The development of lorries, powered by internal combustion engines, encouraged manufacturing firms to discard boats for road haulage. It was a move accompanied by an increased use of gas-fired furnaces and electrical equipment.

The firms heavily dependent on coal transport maintained a fleet of boats and paid tolls to the canal companies. For others there was a gradual shift to the coal contractors and merchants to move the coal to the works. Supply of coal came not only from Cannock Chase and South Staffordshire, but also the Warwickshire coalfield. The rise of firms wishing to enter the trade led to a few causalities. W.H. Bowater was amongst the firms that went into receivership at this time. Other coal merchants and contractors continued to provide a service to the firms that needed coal.

Iron smelters had been reduced to twelve locations and finished iron makers had also seen considerable reductions in their numbers. Yet the requirement for coal by puddling furnaces engaged in wrought iron continued to draw on local coal mines that sent out coal by boat or railway wagon.

A Select List of Canalside Ironworks (1924) as per Rylands Directory

George Adams & Sons Ltd, Mars IW, Wolverhampton
Albert Iron & Steel Co. Ltd, Witton Lane, Hill Top, West Bromwich
John Bagnall & Sons Ltd, Leabrook Ironworks, Wednesbury
John Bradley & Co. (Stourbridge) Ltd, Stourbridge

Bradley, Bar and Sheet Iron Co. Ltd, Bilston

Cleveland Iron Co., Cleveland IW, Horseleyfields, Wolverhampton

Samuel Downing & Son Ltd, Richmond Ironworks, West Bromwich

Earl of Dudley, Old Level, Brierley Hill

Excelsior Steel and Iron Co., Excelsior Works, Swan Village

George Gadd & Co. Ltd, Church Lane Ironworks, Tipton

Hartshill Iron Co. Ltd, Hartshill IW, Brierley Hill

J. Holcroft and Co. Ltd, Portfield Ironfoundry, Tipton

Johnson Iron & Steel Co. Ltd, Waterloo and Hall End Iron Works

J.B. & S. Lees, Albion Ironworks and Nelson IW, West Bromwich

London Works Iron Co., Oldbury

Lones, Vernon and Holden Ltd, Sandwell Iron Axle Works, Lewisham Road, Smethwick

J. & W. Marshall, Staffordshire IW, Green Lane, Walsall

Samuel Newton & Sons Ltd, Nine Locks IW & Steelworks, Brierley Hill

Edward Page & Sons Ltd, Roway Iron & Steel Works

E. Parkes & Co. Ltd, Atlas IW, West Bromwich

Roberts and Cooper Ltd, Bromley Ironworks

Roberts and Cooper Ltd, Brettell Lane Iron Works

Roberts and Cooper Ltd, Leys Iron Works

Roberts and Cooper Ltd, Great Bridge Iron & Steel Works

John Russell & Co. Ltd, Alma Tubeworks, Walsall

Spring Bank Iron Co., Willenhall

G. & R. Thomas, Birchills IW, Green Lane, Walsall

Tolly, Sons and Bostock Ltd, Darlaston Steel & Ironworks, Darlaston

Walker Brothers Ltd, Victoria Ironworks, Walsall

Walker Brothers Ltd, Staffordshire Galvanising Works, Pleck Road, Walsall

Iron founding was dependent on a smaller but regular supply of coal to heat the cupolas to heat to a molten state for casting purposes. Gas-fired plant was gradually replacing coal in this duty, but the canal continued to carry pig iron and casting sand to the foundry. Casting sand, or loam, was derived from a variety of locations. During the nineteenth century, Birmingham foundries had drawn on various sand quarries placed around George Street, Key Hill Cemetery and the area known as the Sandpits. The Wyrley & Essington Canal was used to convey sand from sand quarries at Ogley Hay, but some of the most important sources of sand were the quarries at Hall Green, (Tame Valley Canal), Moxley (Walsall Canal) and Wombourne (Staffordshire & Worcestershire Canal).

By 1920, supplies of sand from Moxley had ceased, but sand continued to be sent by boat for foundry use from Wombourne and Hall End. The Bratch Sand Co., Womborn, and Fred and Harry Critchley despatched foundry sand in their own boats to several Black Country foundries. Abraham Lowe of Bustleholme Sand Beds, Hall End, was also an important supplier of sand. Other contractors who dealt in sand included Frederick Lowe (of Bentley), who brought sand from quarries on the Staffordshire & Worcestershire Canal and Thomas Jones of Gorsebrook, Wolverhampton, whose principal business was the coal trade, but also used his boats to carry sand.

Charles Lathe Foundry, Tipton. The interior of Charles Lathe's foundry at Summerhill, Tipton, shows a typical casting foundry where sand or loam would be used to fashion the moulds for casting iron or other metals into useful shapes. (Sandwell Archives)

Bean's Foundry, Tipton. Bean's Foundry is a canal survivor. It stands on the site of the old Coseley Moor blast furnaces. They were developed by the Bean Car Co. to make castings for their company, which included the range of Bean cars. (Ray Shill collection)

Foundries in Birmingham and the Black Country produced a considerable range of diverse types of ironwork. Some specialised as rolling mill engineers making the chilled and grained rolls required by the rolling mill. Akrill & Co. of Golds Green foundry, George Jones of Lionel Street and Taylor & Farley Ltd, Summit Foundry, Union Street, West Bromwich came to specialise in this trade. Jones had a long history in the iron founding trade that started with the Phoenix Foundry at Snow Hill, established during the first decade of the nineteenth century. In these early days George Jones made general iron foundry for commercial and domestic use. He moved his business to take over Whitmore's Foundry in Lionel Street that was located at the end of the Newhall Branch and this was where his business stayed and prospered. Their general iron foundry trade changed to making rolls and rolling mill plant to serve the growing number of rolled metal manufacturers in the district.

Another early iron founder was the business established by Thomas Clark at the Shakespeare Foundry beside the canal at Horseleyfields, Wolverhampton. Clark, like Jones, had made general iron foundry goods, but after registration as a public company in 1909 came to specialise as chemical plant engineers.

Izons and Co., Archibald Kendrick and Edward Sheldon made hollow ware (the general name for pots and pans). Izons' and Kendricks' factories were located at West Bromwich, whilst Sheldon had the Cannon Foundry at Deepfields, Coseley. Joseph Sankey & Sons Ltd began at Bilston as iron and tinplate workers, makers of hollow ware, frying pans and sole makers of patent Neptune art-ware waiters, blank trays and candlesticks at the Albert Street Works near the canal at Bradley.

Encompassed within the name hollow ware were the enamelled and tinned cast-iron ware, coffee mills, wrought frying pans, pots, ovens and cookers. Cooker ovens and cast-iron safes came into increasing demand after 1850 and several firms started to make these goods. Sheldon started to make safes, cooking plates and ovens and from 1884 Sheldon's became known as the Cannon Hollow-ware Co. Ltd. It was a name that was later changed to Cannon Iron Foundries Ltd. Cannon subsequently diversified into the supply of ranges and gas cookers. Sheldon's could trace their firm back to 1826 and in 1926 the firm celebrated its centenary.

Another maker of gas cookers was John Wright & Co. of the Essex Works, Thimblemill Lane, Aston. Wright had come to Birmingham from his native Essex and set up a gas cooker factory at 71 Broad Street, but had transferred to a new site beside the Birmingham & Fazeley Canal during the mid-1880s. It was here that Wright established an extensive gas appliance factory, which made cookers, heaters and gas irons for the domestic market as well as annealing furnaces for industrial use. They merged with the Eagle Range Co. located in Salford Street and Catherine Street and were later to become one of the constituent companies that formed the Radiation Group. The canal continued to have a role for the supply of coal to the Essex Works.

The making of scales and weighing machine was the speciality of William and Thomas Avery at the Mill Lane Works, Digbeth. Many of the parts used in weighing machines, as well as the weights, were cast iron produced in a foundry. W. & T. Avery had the Atlas Foundry, in Charles Street, West Bromwich that was linked by a canal basin with the Ryders Green Locks. Following the purchase by Avery of the Soho Foundry in 1895 (formerly James Watt & Co.) much of the work was transferred to Soho, where coal was delivered by boat into the arm that served the Soho Foundry. Joseph and Jesse Siddons of the Hill Top Foundry also made weighing machines as part of a range of other items, which included general malleable iron foundry and hollow ware.

Metal rolling mills retained a canal trade in coal to supply the steam-driven rolling mills and to provide heat for the annealing muffles and melting furnaces. Birmingham was particularly noted for the number of rolled metal manufacturers in the town. These took basic metals such as copper and zinc to make ingots of brass for rolling into sheet and strip. They also produced other useful alloys such as phosphor bronze and nickel silver. Nineteenth century rolled metal manufacturers were contracted to supply the rolling service where manufacturers brought their metal to be rolled. This role changed and the metal rollers went into business purchasing scrap and pure metals to roll to order. The advent of electrically powered rolling mills, and gas-fired annealing furnaces reduced the amount of traffic to these works, many of which had sought out a canalside location for ease of transport.

Benjamin Mason's Rolling Mills, Wharf Street, Aston.
Independent rolling mills flourished in the Birmingham district to roll non-ferrous metal strip and sheet to supply the multitude of local industries engaged in making ornaments, buttons and cutlery. Here spoon blanks are shown being rolled at Benjamin Mason's rolling mills in Aston. (Benjamin Mason)

Rolled Metal Manufacturers Mills that Received Coal by Boat 1928

F.L. Attwood, Holt Street Rolling Mills, Birmingham	BS, LM
Barker & Allen Ltd, Spring Hill	ECB, BS, LM
Bassett & Bagnall & Co., Church Lane, West Bromwich	EA
Alfred Case, 33 Great Tindall Street, Birmingham	LCC, BS, GTR
Emery Brothers, Victoria Mills, Aston	EA, TMD
Grice, Grice & Son Ltd, Nile Street	SA
William Hadley, Sheet Rolling Mills, Smethwick	CH, AC
Hall Street Metal Rolling Co. Ltd, Western Road, Birmingham	KB, GC, LL, GHC
Heaton & Dugard, Shadwell Street	FK, SA, TEP
Hughes–Stubbs Metal Co. Ltd Albion Rolling & Wire Mills, Plume Street	TF, FS, DMS
B. Mason & Sons Ltd, Wharf Street, Aston	AC, DMS
W. Morris & Sons, Freeth Street Rolling Mills	LL
P.H. Muntz, Alexandra Works, Great Bridge	OAC
H.H. Vivian, Icknield Port Road	SB, AB, LL, DMS
Henry Wiggins & Co. Ltd, Wiggins Street, Birmingham	LCC, SB, LL, FS

Key – Coal contractors who supplied the coal
EA – E. Alderson & Son, 6 Bean Road, Dudley
ECB – E.C.S. Backhouse, Heneage Street Wharf, Birmingham
SB – Samuel Barlow, Anchor Works, Glascote
BS – T. Boston & Sons, Paradise Street, Birmingham
AB – A. Brockhurst, Oozells Street Wharf
CH – William Charles, Bridge Wharf, Wednesbury
AC – Alex Comley Ltd, 194 Corporation Street, Birmingham
GHC – G.H. Cooper, Brookfields Wharf, Birmingham
TMD – T. & M. Dixon, Birmingham and Tardebigge
TF – T. Foster & Son, 14 New Street, Birmingham
GC – Goodman & Co., 141 Great Charles Street
KB – Kimberley Beddoes and Co., Oldbury
FK – Frank Knight, Coal Merchant, Chester Street Wharf, Birmingham
LCC – Leamore Coal and Coke Co. Ltd, Birchills, Walsall
TEP – T.E. Pheasant, Bescot Road, Walsall
GTR – G.T. Rapps, Soho Pool Wharf
LL – Leonard Leigh Ltd, Wharf Street, Hockley
LM – L. Miller, Martineu Square, Birmingham
FS – Fred Smith, Harborne Road, Warley
SA – Spencer Abbott, Gravelly Hill
DMS – D.M. Stevenson & Co. Ltd, 3 Newhall Street, Birmingham
OAC – Own boats used or tolls paid by company

Heavy construction parts were supplied by Bailey, Pegg & Co. Ltd, Brierley Hill, whose works lay beside the Stourbridge Canal at Brierley Hill. Apart from general castings their work included cast-iron pipes, iron columns and gasworks plant. Their history was typical of many local firms changing from one product line to another to suit demand. Joseph Bailey and Samuel Pegg had begun in business, beside the River Thames, in London, making shells and shot, but moved to Brierley Hill in about 1820 to take advantage of the cheap iron made there. Here they continued to make shot and shells and added the making of cannons to their range before a change in military ordnance led them to seek other product lines. Another structural engineer was the firm of William Grice & Sons Ltd of the Minerva Works, Fazeley Street and River Street Works, Birmingham. They were makers of tanks, girders and columns as well as cast-iron pipes.

Samuel Thompson (Millfields) Ltd of the Millfields Foundry, Davis Street, Bilston were sanitary and general iron founders and were amongst the foundries that had sand delivered by boat. The Vono Co. began in a small way as iron founders at Groveland near Dudley Port but grew to include an engineering side and from the 1930s included the making of bedding and mattresses as part of their range. Vono's enlarged business was accompanied by the building of new works alongside Tipton New Road near Groveland. The Vono Bedstead Works occupied a large rectangular piece of land that extended from Tipton New Road to the banks of the Birmingham Canal new main line at Dudley Port.

On another side the Netherton Branch Canal was the boundary to their property. It was alongside the Netherton Branch that Vono built a modern foundry. The Vono foundry, like several of their competitors, had automated plant suited for the production of repetitive castings. These buildings remained a canalside feature throughout the twentieth century, despite ownership of the foundry changing several times. Any connection with canal transport had long disappeared, but piles of coke could still be seen stacked at one end of the site to the end of this foundry's working existence. The final association was with the tractor maker Massey Ferguson of Coventry, for which castings were made. When Massey Fergusons's American owners decided to close down the Coventry plant, the Dudley Port Foundry was also axed and by 2004 stood rusting and unused.

There was a time, particularly in Victorian and Edwardian Britain, when iron railings and gates surrounded commercial, industrial and public buildings. To meet this demand several local firms came to be engaged in the supply of these items. They included Hill & Smith and Bayliss, Jones and Bayliss.

Hill & Smith Ltd of Brierley Hill was mentioned in Chapter 5. They had a long trading existence, which continued into the twentieth century. They added the trades of constructional engineers, founder's iron and steel forgers and railway axle makers to their established business of makers of iron fencing, gates and railings.

William and Moses Bayliss established the Victoria Works at Monmore Green, Wolverhampton, during the mid-1850s, where production included brass and iron bedsteads, iron hurdles, fencing, gates, screws, bolts, and flat and round chain. They dispensed with bed making and following the demand for railway fittings made a range of patent fish bolts, chairs, spikes and other railway fastenings. Gates and hurdles remained another core part of the business. The name changed to Bayliss, Jones and Bayliss of the Victoria and during July 1893 the Monmore Works, Cable Street, was acquired from E.T. Wright & Son. They owned boats that brought coal from the local mines to supply both works. During 1925 the Anderton Carrying Co. brought loads of billets to Bayliss, Jones & Bayliss, the District Iron Co. and Coombswood Tubeworks, returning with pot clay from Dudley Port.

The firm of Rubery Brothers, Victoria Ironworks, was set up in Booth Street, Darlaston during 1884. Their property extended to the towpath of the Walsall Canal and had a private basin for their canal transport needs. Rubery Brothers made fencing and gates as well as light steel roofing and some bridgework. The firm was started by John and Tom Rubery but became Rubery & Co. in 1888, when Tom Rubery left the partnership. In 1893 Alfred Owen formed a new partnership with John Rubery. Alfred's contribution to the firm was immense. Alfred Owen had been interested in engineering since he was a child. At his instigation Rubery & Co. became early pioneers in the manufacture of the supporting frame, or chassis, for commercial and private automobiles. Rubery's version was initially made from steel section and bar. Owen was one of the first people to employ a hydraulic press to fashion a lighter, but structurally sound, frame. Rubery & Co. supplied steel chassis to automobile makers throughout the first decade of the twentieth century. In 1905 the firm's title changed to Rubery, Owen & Co. and John Rubery retired a few years later leaving the business in the hands of Owen and his family.

With the advent of the aviation industry, Rubery, Owen, were numbered amongst the first British companies to supply aircraft components. Rubery, Owen & Co. took over and absorbed a number of other companies and by the 1920s had five separate departments; aviation, metal aircraft, motor frame, motor wheel and structural steelwork. The headquarters of the group was at Darlaston where the works had been enlarged to include a large area of land between the Walsall Canal and the LMS Railway sidings.

A new business developed as a result of the increased used of electrical appliances. The public tramways might have been the principal reason for the establishment of power stations, but their number began to decline with the increased use of the motorbus. A new and greater demand arose for electrical appliances for both domestic and industrial use. The General Electric Co. flourished and during the 1920s and 1930s made extensive enlargements to its works at Witton, which had been first established there in 1902. Various departments were set up to deal with engineering, steel conduits and switchgear. There was also a moulded insulation, battery and lamp black works. Most of the working plant was driven by electricity and the company had their own coal-fired generating station on site to supply their needs. Coal carriers such as Thomas Boston & Son, Thomas & Samuel Element and Leonard Leigh regularly brought boat loads of coal to the GEC power station to be unloaded by hand. Later an overhead telpher was installed to unload the boats mechanically.

Cable Accessories Ltd (later the Revo Electric Co.), of the Britannia Works, Tividale, the Tividale Enamel Works, Groveland Brass Foundry and Eagle Foundries, Tipton, built up an extensive trade in the supply of electric light fittings and their trade name REVO can still be seen on lamp standards in different parts of the country. Lampposts were a particular speciality. These were frequently cast from iron moulded in huge moulds. William John Hayward of Tipton was amongst the coal merchants who supplied the REVO with coal. Verity's were another electrical engineers, which supplied a range of products. They operated from the old Plume Works buildings at the end of the Dowler's Arm.

Mechanical and civil engineering encompassed a wide range of firms such as Cochrane & Co. (Woodside) Ltd, iron founders and ironmasters. These works, located beside the Dudley No.1 Canal, had been started by Bramah & Cochrane and traded for many years as Cochrane and Co. They made forge and melting pig iron at their blast furnaces, but also built up a business as iron founders, cast-iron pipe makers and engineers. Cochrane's also traded a sister company at the Ormesby Ironworks, Cargo Fleet, Middlesborough. The Woodside ironworks and furnaces had collieries at Hurst and later came to operate ironstone quarries in Oxfordshire. Their operation was closed down in 1924.

At Small Heath, alongside the Warwick and Birmingham Canal, was established the Birmingham Small Arms Co. Ltd, which relied on coal transport delivered by a number of suppliers as well as in their own boats. The firm was established by a group of Birmingham gunmakers and their original product was the manufacture of guns and rifles. Such was the periodic demand for weapons that the BSA diversified into making bicycle parts, complete bicycles and motorcycles at Small Heath. In addition to their factory in Armoury Road, BSA also operated another canalside factory in Montgomery Street, next to the Lanchester factory, where motorcars were erected. Following the onset of the First World War, additional factory premises were put down, for munitions, at Small Heath that became known as the Waverley Works. These premises also had canal access to the Warwick & Birmingham Canal.

Belliss & Morcam Ltd relied on coal carriers to deliver coal by boat for their trade that specialised in marine engines and steam turbines. Spencer Abbott was listed amongst the suppliers to their Ledsam Street and Rotton Park Street works. E. Braithwaite & Co., Crown Works, Henry Street, West Bromwich used their own boats to collect coal for their works placed alongside the Balls Branch Canal. Braithwaite, later Braithwaite & Kirk, were structural engineers and supplied bridges to different parts of the world. They also constructed a number of canal boats during the depression years of the 1920s. An important engineering firm was Horseley Bridge & Engineering Co. Ltd of Great Bridge, which received sand and iron by boat along the Dixon's Branch. This firm had a reputation for the supply of bridges, gasholders and structural iron and steel work. Thomas Piggott & Co. Ltd, was also a structural engineering firm that made bridges and gas holders at their Springhill Works located beside the Winson Green Loop.

Collieries in the latter years of the nineteenth century generated a demand for structural ironwork and surface plant. These included improved screening plant for separating different grades of coal into railway wagons. Charles Wilcox of Tividale produced colliery screens during the 1880s and 1890s. Bertram and Philip Norton established the Norton, Harty Engineering Co., Central Works, Great Bridge during the first years of the twentieth century. They made a patent coal weigher as well as structural ironwork for mines and soon became competitors to Wilcox for the colliery trade. Charles Wilcox was also a tube maker and had another works for tube making at Upper Church Lane, in Tipton. Wilcox had ceased trading by 1907. A group of local businessmen, including Bertram Norton, then set up Nortons (Tividale) Ltd. Their works were called the Hecla Works and were placed alongside the Birmingham Canal old main line near Gilbert's Bridge. They produced structural ironwork but specialised in the making of colliery plant that included screens. Philip Norton continued to be associated with the Central Works and traded in competition to Bertram Norton for many years thereafter.

The increased use of acetylene gas for lighting and welding encouraged new industrial development in this field. Lockerbie & Wilkinson (Tipton) Ltd, Tipton were structural and acetylene engineers, whose works were placed alongside the Toll End Communication. Lockerbie & Wilkinson had begun, in 1906, as hardware merchants, with premises in Exeter Street, Birmingham and set up the Tipton works during 1909. Here they traded as municipal engineers making and supplying structural work such as gates and railings. The Severn Canal Carrying Co. brought calcium carbide there by boat.

The extensive Cornwall Works at Smethwick lined the main canal from Rabone Lane Bridge to the junction of the old and new main lines. It had been established by Tangye Brothers, and still continued to receive coal by boat during the 1920s. The Tangyes had come to Birmingham during 1852 when Richard Tangye obtained a position of clerk with Thomas Worsdell, engineer, Berkeley Street in Birmingham. James Tangye became foreman at the works and Joseph became the chief mechanic. George Tangye also joined the firm at a later time. Thomas Worsdell was a railway wagon builder, manufacturer of general ironwork and lifting jack maker. His works lay towards the bottom of Berkeley Street but was near to a pair of long canal basins that extended under the street to serve Tuppers galvanising works, the Suffolk Works (John Hodgkin Elliot), a limestone wharf, a coal wharf and the Berkley Street wire mills owned by John Cornforth.

Owing to a disagreement with Evans, who Worsdell had taken as a partner, the Tangyes left to set up as machinists at 40 Mount Street, where five of the Tangye brothers: Edward, George, James, Joseph and Richard, formed the firm of Tanyge Brothers. They specialised in making lifting jacks, continuing the trade of Thomas Worsdell. They invented an improved type of hydraulic lifting jack, which was to make their fortune. Premises were then leased at the rear of 61 Clement Street Parade, during 1859, which the brothers named the Cornwall Works. During 1862 land was purchased in Rabone Lane and builders erected a larger Cornwall Works on the site. James Tangye was particularly inventive. He devised a new hydraulic jack and assisted in pioneering work with the construction of a road locomotive. In 1881 James Tangye produced a design for a simplified type of steam engine. The Tangyes went from strength to strength. They went on to make gas engines and later oil engines. A large block of new shops was erected alongside Cornwall Road in 1873, and later, from 1882, other premises were added in Rabone Lane. Their range came also to include pumps, hydraulic plant and machine tools made on the extensive site bounded by the canal and Rabone Lane.

A Siemens steel making plant was installed during 1882 with the hope of gaining outside orders. The steel making venture would have generated trade for both the canal and the nearby railway. Unfortunately this aspect of the Tangye business was ill fated. Steel was only made for company use and the plant was dismantled during August 1885.

Cornwall Road ran through the property and it was in Cornwall Road that the main offices were located. The tool works were carried on under a separate title, Tangyes Machine Tool Co., Oxford Works, from 1876. They made a range of lathes, and drilling and slotting machines for the company as well as for sale to other firms.

In building the Cornwall Works, the Tangye brothers had reclaimed part of the original bed of the Birmingham Canal and had in its place arranged for the excavation of a canal basin that was carried into the heart of the engineering establishment. A system of narrow-gauge tramways criss-crossed the site and one tramway line crossed this basin by a swing bridge that was pivoted in the centre. A second long arm ran alongside the perimeter of the Cornwall Works to pass under Cornwall Road before turning east to serve the northern part of the site. A separate firm, William Warden & Sons, trading as the Phoenix Bolt & Nut Co., had a works in Dowing Street with wharf space alongside this second canal arm.

Adjacent to the Cornwall Works, and also with wharfage alongside the long canal arm, was the Woodford Ironworks, which was owned by Morewood & Co. They made galvanised iron sheeting and other ironwork. The Woodford Ironworks was closed during the 1890s and the site was taken over by the British Seamless Steel Tube Co. Ltd, who renamed the old Woodford Works, the British Mills. The British Mills later passed to Buckleys Ltd, who continued to trade there as metal merchants and tube makers. Another part of the Woodford site was acquired for the Smethwick Generating Station and the long basin provided useful moorings for boats delivering coal to the power station.

Tube makers were another group that generated significant canal traffic. During the 1920s weldless tube making continued to be a growth industry particularly to supply new the automobile and aircraft industry. A prominent firm in this respect was Accles and Pollock Ltd. Their venture at the Holford Mills, Perry Barr and their brief term of ammunition making, cycle manufacture and production of the Accles–Turrel car had failed, but the firm reorganised and transferred to Whimsey Bridge, Oldbury, to take over a disused factory and set up a tube works. The success of this venture led to the building of the Paddock Tube Works on a disused brickworks site. Paddock had a long working history and was first developed as a mine for coal and ironstone to supply the nearby Oldbury furnaces. The minerals were taken by a tramway that crossed over the canal to reach the furnace yard. When the minerals were depleted, brick clay was worked. Accles & Pollock Ltd was registered in 1910. By 1920 most of the share capital was held by Tubes Investment Ltd and it was TI who continued to have control of the firm throughout its existence. Paddock Tube Works was a canalside location placed alongside the old main line of the Birmingham Canal.

The honours of largest tube works in the district would probably be given to Coombswood, which was established during the year 1863 by Abraham Darby on an acre of land acquired from Lord Lyttelton. It was located near the east portal of Gorsty Hill Tunnel alongside the Dudley No.2 Canal. The works were taken over by Lloyd

CANAL adjoining Messrs Stewart & Lloyds Works at Coombs Wood, Halesowen.

Stewarts & Lloyds, Coombeswood Tube Works.
The Coombeswood Tube Works was developed alongside the banks of the Dudley No.2 Canal extending along both sides of the waterway from the portal of Gorsty Hill Tunnel towards Halesowen. They specialised in the making of iron and steel tubes and were heavily committed to canal transport. (Dudley Archives)

& Lloyd, tube makers of Nile Street, Birmingham and subsequently were absorbed by Stewarts & Lloyds. The works gradually increased in size spreading out along both sides of the towing path towards Halesowen. The site was never rail served although Hawn Railway Interchange Basin, opened in 1902, lay a short distance from the works. By the 1920s thousand of tons of tubes were despatched monthly from the tube works to Hawn Basin, and there was also some traffic by water in tubes to the Nile Street works. Coal was brought chiefly from mines on Cannock Chase and iron for tube making came by boat from a variety of suppliers, and chiefly Hickman's Spring Vale Furnaces, which were also part of the Stewart & Lloyd Group. Thomas Bantock brought spelter from Hawn Basin and Chance & Hunt carried muriatic acid. Stewart & Lloyd had a large fleet of boats and a number of motor tugs that were used to bring traffic to and from the Coombswood Works.

The break up of the Chillington Iron Co. concern led to the sale of their various canalside ironworks. Chillington's Leabrook Ironworks, on the Walsall Canal, were sold to Foster Brothers & Ratcliffe in November 1887, who renamed them Leabrook Tube Works. The site was converted for tube manufacture during 1888. The original partnership comprised Thomas Foster (Junior), Humphrey Foster and Ratcliffe, although Ratcliffe left the partnership in 1893 and the firm then became simply Foster Brothers Ltd. Thomas Foster (Senior) had been associated with James Russell and then with four partners set up the Anchor Tube Works in Wednesbury Old Field about the year 1850. This company failed in 1875. Thomas Foster (Senior) then went on to manage Johnson's Tube Works, Ridgacre Lane in West Bromwich. His working knowledge of tube making was passed onto sons Thomas and Humphrey who applied this knowledge to set up a successful concern. Thomas Foster (Senior) died early in the twentieth century and a third son, John, came over from Ridgacre to Leabrook bringing all serviceable plant from the Ridgacre works. Foster Brothers specialised in the making of iron and steel tubes and fittings and benefited from a number of naval contracts.

1926 was marked by a general strike, which led to the closing of the local mines in the months of May and June. Whilst industry was crippled for the want of coal, and domestic demand for coal was similarly affected, people resorted to picking over the colliery tips for what could be found. Some outcrop coal was loaded by boat to supply merchants' yards.

Outcrop Coal Loaded During the Coal Strike of May and June 1926

	May	June
Factory Wharf	1,747	1,238
Coseley Moor		690¼
Willingsworth Arm	299	1,279½
Level Street Bridge		2,835½
Bentley Wharf		613½
Bishtons Bridge		347½
Banks Bridge		134¾
Brierley Bridge		190½

Rainbow Wharf	25	600
Tup Street Bridge	29	237
Bradley Sixth Pond		250½
Porketts Bridge	26	154½
Wednesbury Oak Basin		289¼
Moxley (Tooleys)	111½	386½
Swan Meadow Timber Yard		239½
Tividale Road Bridge	84	538
Izons Turn Bridge		55¼
Total	2,321½	21,139¾

Gas manufacture continued to diversify to include a new product, water gas. This gas was rich in hydrocarbons, produced through the cracking of gas oil. Water gas plants were constructed at several local gasworks where the gas was used as a supplement to gas made by traditional carbonisation, particularly at times of peak demand. A major supplier was Humphreys & Glasgow Ltd of London. Water gas plants created a new demand for gas oil, which was generally brought, like coal, by rail.

Limestone traffic from local quarries had virtually ceased by 1920 and only the Linley mines (East Anglian Cement Co. Ltd) on the Daw End Canal continued to work, and then their produce was restricted to cement rather than the fluxing stone required for blast furnace use. The Earl of Dudley's mines at Castle Mill and East Castle were virtually exhausted and limestone was brought from elsewhere. The London, Midland & Scottish Railway quarry at Caldon Low, the Lilleshall Co. mines at Nantmawr and the Chirk Castle Lime and Stone Co., Llangollen, still supplied limestone. Several of the Northamptonshire ironstone mines were also limestone producers. Firms such as Islip Iron Co. (Islip and Lowick), Kettering Iron & Coal Co. (Ketton), Lloyds Ironstone Co. (Slipton) and the Wellingborough Iron Co. (Carroll Springs) were all associated with the trade in limestone.

Boiler making was a speciality of John Thompson, whose works were situated alongside the BCN main line at Ettingshall. John Thompson Wolverhampton Ltd was based at Millfields Road, Spring Road and Manor Road, with main offices in Millfields Road. In the 1930s there was a boiler shop, flue shop and fitting shop. During the Second World War they made mine bodies and buoys in the press shop. They also pressed out paravanes that were fitted to the front of merchant ships as a protection against mines. Boiler castings were made in the foundry. The EW shop (electric welding shop) was the place where water tube boilers were assembled. Thompson had various departments making water tube boilers, motor pressings and beacon windows, also shell boilers, pressure vessels, galvanising baths, cask washers, etc. In 1949 a new welding shop was erected on the former site of Adam's Mars Ironworks. In 1955 John Thompson formed an association company with AEI, AEI–John Thompson Nuclear Engineering, who were responsible for the design or erection of the two reactor vessels at the first commercial nuclear power station at Berkeley. John Thompson made the two reactor vessels and the sixteen heat exchangers required at Berkeley.

Car manufacture first drew on the skills of the metalworker and woodworker and production was originally limited by the supply of the many component parts. Some items were pressed, others were forged or cast in a foundry. There was a requirement for iron, steel, brass and aluminium, glass, leather and wood. The skills and craftsmanship required for the early cars was at a high level. Some of the larger factories had foundries and die stamping departments, press shops and wood yards where timber was allowed to season. Canalside car factories were few but Beans Cars at Tipton and the Lanchester Motor Co. Ltd in Montgomery Street, Birmingham both received coal by boat to their respective works. Car component suppliers were a more common canalside feature and even today castings for engines are still produced at the Bean Foundry, Tipton, even though coal deliveries by boat have long ceased.

The brickyard also provided regular traffic. Coal was delivered and sometimes bricks were despatched by boat. There was an enduring demand for bricks for building purposes and whilst supplies of marl existed, local brickworks continued to meet that demand.

Brickyards Served by the BCN 1928

J. and S. Bagott , Hurst Lane Brickworks, Tipton – bricks
S. Barnett, Rattlechain Brickworks, Tipton – bricks and coal
James Bates, firebrick and clay works, Ettingshall – bricks
Thomas Bayley, Great Bridge Brickworks – bricks and coal
B.P. Blockley, Victoria Works, Bloxwich – coal

A Pair of Stewarts & Lloyds Tugs at Bilston.
The extensive canal trade built up by Stewarts & Lloyds to serve the works at Coombeswood and Spring Vale led to the firm investing in a fleet of tugs that were used in the movement of their traffic. (Black Country Museum)

Joan II, Leonard Leigh Tug.
The last phase of coal carrying on the Birmingham Canal relied heavily on tugs powered by internal combustion engines. Unlike the horse boat trade where a single narrow boat might make the journey between the colliery and the works, tugs could handle several loaded boats and this was of particular use on the lock-free sections of the former Wyrley & Essington Canal. (Black Country Museum)

Blue Bricks Ltd, Brades Works, Oldbury – bricks and coal
Castle Brick Co., Birchills – coal
Empire Brick & Tile Co., Aldridge – coal
Forest (Walsall) Brick Co. Ltd, Bloxwich Road – coal
Hadley Brothers & Taylor, Canal Brickworks, Great Bridge – coal
Hughes Brothers, Old Hill Brick Works – coal
W. Longmore, Hopyard Brickworks, Bentley – coal
Exors of W. Morris, Radnorfield Brickworks – coal
Partridge & Guest, Powke Lane Brick Works, Rowley Regis – coal
J.W.D. Pratt Ltd, New Century Brickworks, Oldbury – coal
J. Sadler & Sons Ltd, Shidas Lane Brickworks, Oldbury – coal
Smarts Brickworks Ltd, California Works – coal
Titford Brick Co. Ltd, Oldbury – coal
B. & G. Ward, Moxley Brickworks – coal
Whiwait Brick Co. Ltd, Nechells Lane, Willenhall – coal

From 1930 canal traffic on the Birmingham Canal was in noticeable decline. Published figures for 1930 show that the total traffic carried for the year amounted to 3,160,291 tons and this figure was reduced to 2,693,009 tons in 1931. Traffic continued to decline with traffic still relatively high from the railway basins and public wharves.

Coal traffic remained in the hands of a select group of contractors and firms, who with motorboats, tugs and horse boats hauled coal from collieries. These included firms like Leonard Leigh, Mitchard, Chance & Hunt and Stewarts & Lloyds, who owned their own tug boats. Firms like Elements still employed horse boats as well as motorboats.

Industry continued to decline and adapt. Ironworks closure remained unabated and wrought iron production was particularly affected as works transferred to mild steel production. Some of the last ironworks to receive coal by boat for the puddling furnaces were the John Bagnall & Sons' Leabrook Iron Works and Noah Hingley & Sons' Netherton ironworks, whose directorships at one time included J.C. Forrest and H.J. Peart. The 1930s saw a steady decline in the use of the puddling furnace and the replacement of the steam engine by oil or electrical power. To compensate, electricity works increased in size and so did the coal traffic to those works.

With the increasing use of flush toilets the old method of collecting night soil and salvage traffic changed. Carriage of manure from public authority depots decreased, but there still was a requirement for the carriage and disposal of certain types of salvage and rubbish to tips, for which the canal boat proved to be a cheap and suitable mechanism. Thomas & Samuel Element and Mole & Wood were numbered amongst the contractors who carried rubbish by water. Birmingham Salvage Department also retained a fleet of horse-drawn boats to carry salvage to canalside tips.

Oil transport provided a steady income. Oil, in its many forms, had a variety of uses. Animal, vegetable and mineral oils had long been used for lighting and lubricating purposes. Whale oil, in barrels, was sometimes listed in cargo documentation for early nineteenth century canal carriers, but from the 1850s mineral oils such as petroleum and paraffin became the preferred choice for these purposes. Birmingham had a number of lamp makers who used the local metalworking skills to make oil lamps for both home and abroad. Firms like Joseph Lucas and James Hincks built up a lucrative trade in this respect. Railways, rather than canals, became the principal mover of oil and depots came to be set up near railway stations.

Mineral oils were imported from abroad and the American oil fields were early suppliers in this respect. In Scotland, around Lithlingow and West Calder, paraffin oil was obtained from oil shales. Prominent amongst the Scottish oil shale refiners was Youngs Paraffin Light & Mineral Oil Co. who established a lamp factory in New Spring Street, Birmingham.

Oil refining produced a range of lubricating oils and greases that supplied the needs of local industry. William Blackwell had a refinery in Victoria Road, Aston, whilst in the Black Country canalside oil refineries existed at Dudley Road, Tipton (Joseph Batson & Co.), Church Lane, West Bromwich (W.H. Keys Ltd) and Bilston Road, Wolverhampton (Gaunt & Hickman). The firm of Gaunt & Hickman had two refineries. One was located at Heath Town alongside the Wyrley & Essington Canal and another was beside the main Birmingham Canal at Monmore Green. They traded as the British Oil Works and supplied both greases and oils. Greases for locomotives and machinery were supplied as were lamp oils and lubricating oils for steam and gas engines. Another distillate product in their range was rosin.

The increasing use of petroleum products for oil and petrol engines led to a greater amount of these products being carried from the ports. Transport was generally by rail to station depots, but a new trade developed along the River Severn to inland ports at Worcester and Stourport and then by road to petroleum merchants throughout the Midlands. Shell Mex Ltd established a depot in Station Road, Langley Green during the 1920s. This was a canalside location with a wharf alongside the Titford Branch Canal. The Oldbury-based carriers Thomas Clayton, noted for the transport of tar and other liquids were frequently engaged in bringing fuel oil from Ellesmere Port to the Langley oil terminal.

The last local canal improvements were completed during the 1930s. These involved the widening of the locks and waterway along the Grand Union Canal from Braunston to Knowle. The Grand Union had been formed through the merger of the Erewash Canal, Grand Junction Canal, Regents Canal and the three Warwick canals (Warwick & Birmingham, Birmingham & Warwick Junction Canal and Warwick & Napton). The merger was also accompanied by the creation of a new carrying fleet, the Grand Union Canal Carrying Co.. Their boats worked in pairs comprising a motor and butty boat that worked between London and Birmingham (Sampson Road North). New warehouses at Sampson Road Wharf were completed in 1939 and another wharf at Tyseley opened during the 1940s.

A number of factories had been established in the Tyseley area during the 1920s and 1930s. These included the canalside factories of Wilmot Breedon, car bumper maker and Bakelite manufacturers of plastics. Nearby were the works of Abingdon–King Dick, spanner makers, MEM who made switchgear, Reynolds Tubes and a Rover Car making plant.

The open and cabin wooden design of narrow boat still provided a useful service after some 170 years of trading on the local waterways. Their basic structure, made of oak and elm planking (and sometimes other woods) held together with iron knees, metal nails and caulked with oakum to make the seams watertight, was a formula that boat builders adhered to. Boat builders still found employment making new boats and repairing others. Customers included the coal merchants, power companies and the tar boat owners. Yards were distributed around the local canal network, often on byeways and side arms, out of the way of what remained of the working waterway.

With the onset of the Second World War, the canals again came to the nation's assistance carrying goods to the works to supply the needs. Surveys were made of the working yards at the time and their ability to increase production if needed.

Spencer Abbott & Co. had offices in St Phillips Place and a boat dock at Salford Bridge. Their dock was capable of dealing with two boats under cover and one boat in the open yard. Further space was available for docking another boat in the open. The staff employed consisted of a foreman and five men. They were able to work on three boats continually, by a system of follow-up from one man to another in the several stages of boat repair. Continuous repairs were only possible to the two boats under cover; repair work in the open was only possible when weather conditions allowed men to work in the open. Repairs were carried out for Courtaulds Ltd, the West Midlands Joint Electricity Authority, Birmingham Salvage Department, National Fire Service, T. & S. Element and the Grand Union Carrying Co. Ltd. Spencer Abbott owned thirty coal boats and repairs were carried out at their own dock. Mr Allen was foreman at the dock and under his charge were five workmen. Complete docking and extensive repairs could be carried out in two weeks.

Fuel oil transport for Langley Green continued through to the 1950s. A pair of Clayton boats, a motor and butty, were commonly used in this trade. In September 1953 Vivian Bird described a journey he had made from Oldbury to Ellesmere Port. He had left Oldbury with the motorboat *Towy* and butty *Kubina* in the charge of the Berridge family. Departure time for the empty pair was 11.00a.m. on the Tuesday. Their route lay along the Birmingham Canal to Aldersley, the Staffordshire & Worcestershire Canal and Shropshire Union Canal. By Thursday the boats passed through Chester and were on the final straight to Ellesmere Port. Here they passed onto the Manchester Ship Canal for a mile-long trip to the refinery to load with 45 tons of diesel oil. Originally this short distance had been fraught with delays, waiting for the ship canal tug, but Clayton had taken out licences for his tugs to navigate the ship canal and his boat skippers received an extra 15s for taking the boats onto the congested waters of the ship canal. Some three months before Vivian Bird recorded his journey the *Towy* had made a record run leaving Oldbury at 3a.m. on a Tuesday, and returning back to Oldbury at 4p.m. on the Friday the same week to unload at the Langley Green terminal!

Following the end of hostilities, in 1945, canal traffic on local waterways resumed a steady decline. Major changes were contemplated that included the nationalisation of the transport, electricity and gas industries.

The gas industry was nationalised in 1949 and existing gasworks were taken over by regional gas boards. The West Midlands Gas Board inherited the surviving local gasworks sites, which were divided into seven divisions. The West Midlands Division was a diverse area that extended from Stoke on Trent in the north to Leamington, Kington and Hinckley. It was divided into districts that inherited both small and large undertakings. The West Midlands Division commenced a steady programme of linking up independent gas company mains as well as improving works and closing down the smaller plants.

Gasworks in Birmingham were generally left unaffected for a time and the only closure was that of Adderley Street, which received coal by road from Lawley Street Goods. Elsewhere works were selected for improvement. The Bilston Gas Works near Priestfields had an output of 1,300 million cu.ft of gas per year. Essential production in recent times included the Pluto pipeline, parts for jet engines and radar sets and the Cannon gas cooker. The Bilston Gas Light & Coke Co. had existed for over a hundred years prior to vesting day and some 60 per cent of gas was to industrial users. Gas Board engineers installed new overhead purifiers, arranged for a bank of fourteen new retorts to be erected as well as the building of a new water gas plant.

Cannock Gas Works had been built in 1865 and had eventually taken over the supply of gas previously produced by the Brownhills and Hednesford works. Cannock Gas Works was situated half a mile from the town and were adjacent to a railway station. The area was very scattered supplying Cannock, Chasetown, Huntingdon, Hednesford, Hazelslade, Bridgetown, Walsall Wood and Rugeley. The works is also connected to the Lichfield area. It was a relatively modern works having been improved during the 1940s and fitted with modern intermittent vertical retorts. At Cradley Gas Works, the total gas made in 1936 amounted to 200 million cu.ft. The plant consisted of eight 22in x 16in x 21ft horizontal retorts and an installation of four 62in Woodall–Duckham continuous verticals. There was also a Humphreys and Glasgow carburetted water gas plant with a nominal output of 1 million cu.ft per day.

Dudley Gas Works supplied a district whose largest consumer was a firm making bricks, tiles and sanitary ware, using the gas in five tunnel kilns. It was one of the oldest undertakings in the country, established under statutory powers in 1820 by the Dudley Gas Light Co. In 1929 the amalgamation took place with the Brierley Hill District Gas Light Co. and the Dudley & Brierley Hill District Gas Light Co. was formed. Dudley Gas Works was built on a site of 7¼ acres in the town centre above the railway tunnel. The plant consisted of continuous vertical retorts and two automatically operated carburetted water gas units. The town of Oldbury had been noted for the making of edge tools, which were famous throughout the world before 1850 and the first phosphorus plant for making amorphous phosphorus. Oldbury Gas Works was established in 1880. The early horizontal retorts were replaced in 1922 by continuous vertical retorts. Two large carburetted water gas plants were put down in 1939 and 1942 to meet rapidly increasing industrial consumption.

Various improvements were made to the Sedgley Gas Works. In 1912 the original hand-charged retorts were replaced with a new carbonising plant equipped with an electrically operated stoking machine, coal handling plant and generators. Further improvements were made following the promotion of the Sedgley Gas Special Order of 1932. Additional plant included a tar extractor, condensers, wet and dry purification plant and a new holder. This work was completed in 1934. Vertical retorts, and coal and coke handling plant were put to work in June 1949. At Smethwick Gas Works transport connections were improved in 1906 when a railway siding was constructed into the original canal-served site. Capacity of the gas making plant was rapidly outgrown and Smethwick had one of the first installations of Duckham and Cloudesley vertical retorts to be erected in the country. By 1913 this system had been doubled. After the First World War a monorail telpher was brought in for withdrawal of coke from the retort house and for yard stacking. A new retort house of modern design 22 was officially opened on 30 June 30 1955. It was built by the Woodall–Duckham company. It consisted of two ranges of lambent heated retorts with hydraulic extraction gear; settings were heated by mechanical producers and automatically charged.

Solihull Gas Co. took over the Knowle and District Gas Co. works at Dorridge in 1935, and in 1948 the works of the Henley-in-Arden Coal & Coke Co. Since vesting day a high-pressure main connected Solihull to Henley. A major alteration was the erection of a Woodhall–Duckham installation of twelve vertical retorts in 1936 and a further bench of twelve retorts was added in 1942 to meet the demands of government shadow factories. A water gas plant was also installed and experiments were made there to make gas from heavy oil.

South Staffs Mond Gas Works remained the only commercial supplier of Mond gas in the district. An advertisement on the side of the works advocated its economical use:

FURNACE FUEL MEANS
MOND GAS
IT IS CHEAP
EASY TO CONTROL
NO DUST OR DIRT

The gas plant also produced by-products that formed the raw material for the monsul and melanoid products marketed by the gas company's subsidiary companies. In 1936 a more up-to-date steam raising plant was installed that used coke dust and since vesting day a new producer plant was erected that was capable of making and distributing 5 million cu.ft of gas per day. Mond gas making continued at the Tipton works until 1963, when the plant was considered worn out.

Plant at the Stourbridge Gas Works included recent additions and improvements such as improved coal handling, coke handling, screening and washing. A new carburetted water gas plant was provided as well as plants for benzole and tar extraction. Birmingham Corporation's former works at Swan Village was completely rebuilt in the 1950s. The new Swan Village Works were officially opened on 9 October 1953. The reconstruction included a new retort house and coke bagging plant. Additional railway connections and sidings were constructed. There were four benches of continuous vertical retorts, capable of a daily output of 8½ million cu.ft per day. The plant was provided with complete coal, coke and ash handling plant, producer gas dilution plant and four waste-heat boilers fitted with economisers and superheaters. A new automatic water gas plant was installed on the old works site. The coke screening plant, in addition to separating coke into five sizes, could automatically bag two sizes into hundred weight and half hundredweight for yard sales. There was a powerhouse that generated power from waste steam and the main water supply was pumped from disused mine workings that were tapped through sinking two wells.

Walsall's works at the Pleck had been improved during the 1930s and was to see further improvements including a new retort house in the 1950s. Walsall's gasworks supplied the county borough of Walsall, Rushall, Shelfield, Pelsall, Aldridge and much of Great Barr.

The annual makes of 1,206,000,000 cu.ft and another 222,000,000 cu.ft are drawn from the Birmingham Division.

Coke manufacture was a key product of the gasworks that was often sent by canal boat, but gradually was sold for a number of other uses. The West Midlands area produced about 1½ million tons of coke and breeze per annum. The domestic market absorbed about 20 per cent. Sales were also made to non-industrial or small industrial markets, such as the services, Ministry of Works, local authorities including schools and hospitals, and also bakeries, laundries and dairies. About 30 per cent was sold to these markets. The West Midlands was also heavily industrialised and the largest percentage went to this market, including larger bakeries, laundries, and certain factories. Also, coke was supplied for agricultural and horticultural purposes, such as grass and grain drying, and for export to Scandinavia, for example, to Denmark. Breeze, a finer variety of coke, was in particular demand by the British Electrical Authority.

Sizes of Coke

Size No.	Size Limits	Name	Suitable Use
1	Over 1¾in No upper limit	Large	Hand firing: sectional, tubular element and shell boilers
1A	1¾ to 3½in	Large	Industrial market for large hand-fired boilers and steam raising plants

2	1 to 2in	Broken	For open fires, large domestic boilers, small central heating boilers and combination grates
3	½ to 1¼in	Boiler nuts	Closed stoves, small domestic boilers, heat storage cookers
4	⅜ to ¾in	Forge beans	Mechanical and gravity-fed stokers, and certain designs of gravity-fed boilers
5	⅛ to ¾in	Automatic stoker fuel	Mechanical and gravity-fed stokers, and certain designs of gravity-fed boilers
6	Less than ¾in	Breeze	Chain grate stokers and general industrial use

Tar was employed for a variety of purposes, which included coal briquetting, timber preservation and later the making of liquid fuels. A considerable tonnage of creosote oil was also converted to make special high-octane fuels. The Midland Tar Distillers was formed as a cooperative scheme to include Robinson Brothers, Lewis Demuth, Major and Co., Josiah Hardman and Joseph Turner. In 1929 a public company was formed that later acquired interests in other small organisations.

By the 1950s the process of tar distillation was conducted like petroleum oil in continuous-tube stills, which permitted more rapid distillation under controlled conditions of temperature and pressure. Midland Tar Distillers went on to build a new refinery at Four Ashes beside the Staffordshire and Worcestershire Canal. Four Ashes received raw material from the nine other works. Of the nine works, eight were comparatively small pot distilleries, while only the Oldbury Works had modern continuous-tube still units.

Distillation of tar produced a number of end products these included:

1. Tar acid – phenol cresol xylenol used to make plastics, synthetic resins, disinfectant drugs, insecticides and synthetic tanning compounds.
2. Coal tar bases – such as pyridene, picolines and homologues sold to produce sulpha drugs, vitamin B, other pharmaceuticals, alcohol denaturants, rubber accelerators and corrosion inhibitors.
3. Solvents – including coal tar naptha, xylole and toluole, all of which have extensive applications for paint and rubber, printing inks and insecticide sprays.
4. Naphthalene – used to make phthalic anhydride, a dyestuff intermediate.

Production of town gas was continued through to the late 1960s when most plants closed down. Natural gas from 1968 was piped into the West Midlands and a gradual programme of changeover from coal gas to natural gas commenced. The movement of tar and chemicals was one of the last cargoes carried on local waterways. At the imminent closure of the carbonisation plants, Thomas Clayton (Oldbury) Ltd gave up the trade.

Walsall Wood Colliery.
The Cannock Chase group of mines had extensive plant for raising and screening coal for both rail and canal distribution. (Ray Shill collection)

Anglesey Basin.
The Anglesey Branch canal received coal from the Cannock Chase Collieries. By 1962 all coal mining had ceased, but coal continued to be sent by road from other mines. On reaching the wharf, the lorries tipped coal into waiting boats using the chutes installed for this purpose. (Cannock Library)

The nationalisation of the electric supply industry was effected in 1948. Some local stations were improved and enlarged. Smethwick Power Station was closed by this time. The first national owners were the British Electricity Authority under whose control new power station plant included the 'B' power stations at Birchills, Nechells and Ocker Hill. Their completion led to further increases in coal by canal to these three works. Canal-borne coal continued through to the mid-1960s. The Central Electricity Generating Board then owned the power stations. They also inherited a mixed lot of narrow boats that were used to bring coal from the Cannock Chase and South Staffordshire Collieries.

Rationalisation conducted by the National Coal Board, who had taken over the collieries in 1947, led to closures and merging of underground workings. By 1969 few working mines were left on Cannock Chase and none were left in South Staffordshire. The remaining mines, Cannock Wood, Littleton, and West Cannock despatched coal by rail.

Colliery Closures

South Staffordshire
Hamstead 1965
Sandwell Park (Jubilee Pit) 1960

Cannock Chase
Brereton 1960
Cannock Chase 1962
Cannock and Leacroft 1954
Conduit 1949
Coppice 1964
East Cannock 1957
Grove 1963
Hawkins (Old Coppice) 1960
Hollybank
Hilton Main 1969
Mid Cannock 1967
Nook and Wyrley 1949
Walsall Wood 1964
Wimblebury 1962
Wyrley (No.3) 1963

The severe winter of 1962/1963 is generally credited with sealing the fate of canal carrying on local waterways. Despite every effort to keep the canals open to the Cannock Chase coalfield, long-term freezing conditions eventually defeated the ice-breakers. Water froze with every pass of the boats and went on until there was no more liquid water left in the cut. Only ice and snow remained. Coal boats broke their backs and were left as carrion waste, grey shapes amongst a stark white wasteland.

There were in fact a number of factors that combined to seal the end of the general canal trade. Coal transport remained essential till the end. Throughout the history of the

Hardy & Spicer Traffic.
The firm of Hardy & Spicer became specialist manufacturers in making transmission and drive shafts at Birch Road, Witton. During 1955 Hardy & Spicer built a new factory at Chester Road beside the Birmingham & Fazeley Canal. A push tug and narrow boat were employed in moving parts from Deakins Avenue through the bottom pair of locks of the Tame Valley Canal and along the canal to Raw Stores Wharf where a special dock for the boats was made. (Black Country Museum)

Rubbish Boat on Gower Branch.
Caggy Stevens continued to operate horse-drawn rubbish boats after most canal carrying had ceased. Here one of Caggy's boats is seen working along the Gower Branch. (Jeff Bennett)

Stevens and Keay's Tug at Oldbury.
In addition to horse-drawn boats, Caggy Stevens also used a tug for various contracts. In this nighttime photograph the tug *Caggy* is standing beside the towpath near Whimsey Bridge. (Jeff Bennett)

waterways transport in coal was integral to the carrying trade. Despite many setbacks people would find a way to carry coal from the pits, but once the pits had closed this trade finally died. Some of the last coal was sent along the Anglesey Branch with lorries loading boats by tipping their load down shoots into the hold.

Within four years of the great freeze most canal trade had ceased. The CEGB discontinued traffic to their power stations and gas tar carrying, conducted by Thomas Clayton, was discontinued. Gasworks were also closed through the conversion to natural gas. A longer-lived traffic was phosphorus waste from Albright & Wilsons at Oldbury, which was conveyed by the Coseley carrier, A. Matty, to canalside tips. Albright's phosphorus making operations eventually came to an end during 1972 and whilst they still engaged in the making of various phosphorus compounds the waste traffic, by canal, ceased.

Canal contractors such as Matty's and A. Stevens eked out living through dredging and haulage contracts. The Birmingham & Midland Canal Carrying Co. also retained boats for this business but concentrated on the leisure trade, providing boats for camping and party trips.

The final remnant of the canal age was the infrastructure. Canalside factories remained until closure. Much of this scene has been swept away by the demolition contractor and in recent times speculators have found canalside development a profitable venture. Today the canal side in Birmingham and the Black Country has been transformed by new building. Regrettably it has been a process with mixed regard for heritage and some important structures, which with care might have been saved, have been sadly lost. Notable restorations include Austin Court, in Birmingham, where the Kingston Buildings (first decade nineteenth century) were restored for the Institute of Electrical Engineers. One of the saddest losses was demolition of Shipton & Pratt's Canal Warehouse (1828) at Wolverhampton to make way for new apartments.

APPENDICES

APPENDIX ONE

Blast Furnace List
(Based on a notice published Aris's Gazette, March 1842 and Pigots and Co.'s trade directory 1841).

Furnace	Company	Total (in blast)	Make per week (tons)
BCN main line, Smethwick to Wolverhampton			
Bilston	George Jones	3 (2)	170t
Chillington	Chillington Iron Co.	4 (3)	240t
Millfields	William Riley	3 (2)	160t
Parkfield★	Bishtons & Underhill	4	
Priestfields★	W. Ward	3 (2)	160t
Priorsfield	H.B. Whitehouse	3 (2)	160t
Puppy Green	Thomas Morris	1	
Stow Heath★	William & John S. Sparrow	5 (3)	250t
Tipton	E. Cresswell	1 (1)	90t
Wallbrook	H.B. Whitehouse	2 (out)	
Wolverhampton	Dixon, Neve & Co.	3 (2)	160t
Dartmouth Branch and Ridgeacre Canal			
Crookhay	T. Davis	2 (1)	92t
Ridgeacre	E. Fowler	1 (out)	
Dudley No.1			
Netherton (Blowers Green)	M. & W. Grazebrook	2 (1)	65t
New Level	B. Gibbons	4 (2)	180t
Old Level	William Izon	2 (1)	60t
Parkhead★	Evers & Martin	2 (2)	120t
Russells Hall★	Blackwell, Jones & Oakes	2 (1)	90t
Woodside	Bramah & Co.	2 (1)	80t
Dudley No.2, main route			
Buffery★	Blackwell, Jones & Co.	3 (2)	110t
Buffery (at Bumble Hole)	Joseph Haden	1 (1)	60t
Corngreaves	British Iron Co.		
Dudley Wood	British Iron Co.	4 (2)	160t
Netherton	British Iron Co.	2 (2)	150t
Windmill End	Sir Horace St Paul	2 (1)	80t
Withymoor Branch			
Withymoor	Best & Barrs	2 (1)	80t

BCN old main line
Oldbury Loop

Oldbury	J. Dawes & Son	2 (2)	170t

Smethwick to Tipton

Coneygree (Dudley Port)	Earl of Dudley Trustees	2 (1)	95t
Dudley Port	Joseph Gill	2 (2)	100t

Wednesbury Oak Loop

Bilston (Bovereaux)	W. Baldwin and Co.	3 (2)	170t
Bilston (Stonefield)	Wooley & Co.	1 (1)	90t
Caponfield	J. Bagnall & Sons	3 (2)	160t
Coseley	George Jones	3 (2)	170t
Coseley (Deepfields)	Pemberton and Co.	1 (1)	60t
Ettingshall (Barborsfield)	T. Banks	2 (1)	80t
Hallfields	John Wilkinson & Co. (J. Dunning, agent)	1 (1)	70t
Wednesbury Oak	P. Williams & Co.	3 (2)	160t

Stourbridge Canal

Brettell Lane	J. Wheeley	2 (2)	120t
Lays	W. & G. Firmstone	3 (2)	120t

Stourbridge Extension

Corbyns Hall	Mathews & Dudley	4 (3)	200t
Ketley	Blackwell, Jones & Co.	2 (1)	90t
New Corbyns Hall	B. Gibbons	3 (2)	220t
Oak Farm	Oak Farm Works	2 (2)	140t
Shut End	John Bradley & Co.	4 (3)	200t

Union Branch

Union	Phillip Williams & Co.	3 (2)	160t

Walsall Canal, main canal

Broadwaters	Sir Horace St Paul	2 (1)	70t
Eagle	Eagle Furnace Co.	2 (out)	
Old Park	Lloyds Foster & Co.	2 (2)	160t
Toll End	Hartland & Co./Taylor & Co.	3 (2)	160t

Ansons Branch

Bentley	Countess of Lichfield	4 (1)	80t

Bilston Branch

Bilston Brook	Thomas & Henry Price	2 (2)	140t

Danks Branch

Golds Green	J. Bagnall & Sons	3 (2)	170t

Gospel Oak Branch

Willingsworth	Sir Horace St Paul	3 (2)	160t

Wyrley & Essington Canal

Birchills	E. Tyler	1 (1)	60t
Coltham	R. Mainwaring	1 (out)	
Pelsall	R. Fryer	2 (1)	90t

★Tramway to canal

APPENDIX TWO

Finished Iron Makers 1890

Key
* Denotes a tramway or railway connection to canal

F	Forge
HF	Heating and annealing furnace
PF	Puddling furnace
SF	Scrap furnace
SM	Sheet mills
BF	Ball furnace
CF	Charcoal fire
RM	Rolling mills
MF	Mill furnace
WT	Weldless tyre mill
I	Iron
S	Steel

Works	*Owner*	*Production/Plant*
BCN, Bentley Canal		
Monmer Lane	Monmer Lane Iron Co.	I & S – angles, bars, hoops, strip, sheet: SM(4), BF(1), PF(16)
Spring Bank	Spring Bank Iron Co.	I – bars, flats, bead iron: MF(1), RM(1)
Wednesfield	Wednesfield Galvanised Iron Co.	Galvanised and corrugated iron
BCN, Balls Hill Branch		
Atlas	Parkes & Parkes	I & S, galvanised and corrugated iron: F(1), SM(1), PF(12)
Brickhouse Ironworks	Robert Williams & Co.	Sheet iron: PF, RM
Richmond	Samuel Downing	I – angles and bars
Wellington	Wellington Iron Works Ltd	I – strip for loco and gas tubes, sheets for galvanising, etc.
BCN, Cape Arm		
Cape Town	W.R. Brookes & Co.	I & S – sheet: CF(1), F(1), SM(2), PF (6)
London	Patent Nut & Bolt Co.	Bolts, nuts, etc.
Monway	John & W. Marshall & Co.	I & S – for guns; stamping I & S – for bicycles, sewing machines, spurs
Stork (Soho)	Phillips, Punnett & Co.	Galvanised and black sheets
BCN, Danks Branch		
Goldshill New Ironworks	Thomas Davis & Co.	I & S – bars: PF(12), RM(3)
BCN, Dartmouth Branch		
Albert Sheet Iron Works	James Shenton	I – sheets: BF(1), PF(10), RM(4)
Crookhay	Crookhay Iron & Steel Co,	I – bars, billets, sheet, strip; S – sheet and strip: F(1), PF(16), RM(2)
Witton Lane	Roberts & Co.	I – strip for gas tube, hinge and bedsteads: F(1), MF(2), PF(13)
BCN, Dixons Branch		
Church Lane	George Gadd & Co.	I – bars and strip: BF(1), MF(2), PF(14)
Dudley No.1 Canal		
Brierley Hill	Hill & Smith	Iron, galvanised iron, fencing: F, RM
Hartshill	Hingley & Smith	I – angles, bars, rails, sections, strip: F(3), PF(36), RM(3)

Old Level PF(18)	Henry Hall	I – angles, bars, nail rods, rails: RM(2), MF(4),
Nine Locks	Samuel Newton & Sons	I – angles, bars: MF(2), PF(10)
Round Oak	Earl of Dudley	I & S – angles, bars, rods: F(4), BF(2), PF(56), RM

Dudley No.2 Canal

Corngreaves★	New British Iron Co. Ltd	I & S – angles, bars, hoops, rods, sheet, strip
Netherton	N. Hingley & Sons	I – bars, chain, hoops, rails, strip: BF/MF/PF(130), RM

BCN, Icknield Port Loop

Rotton Park Street	Birmingham Corrugated Iron Co.	Galvanised, tinned and corrugated iron sheet, bolts, nuts, etc.
Lion, Wiggin Street	Morewood & Co. (Successors) Ltd	Galvanised sheets

BCN, main line – Deepfields to Wolverhampton

Manor	Stephen Thompson & Co. Ltd	I & S and tinplate
Mars PF(34), RM(8)	George Adams & Son	I – bars, hoops, sheets, strip: F(3), BF(2), MF(18),
Millfields	W.H. Sanders	I – bars, handles for hollowware: MF(2), RM(1)
Minerva	Isaac Jenks & Sons	I & S – sheet and strip including gas strip and strip for cut nails
Mitre	Gospel Oak Iron and Galvanised Iron & Wire Co.	See Gospel Oak
Monmoor MF(13), PF(25), RM(6)	E.T. Wright and Son	I – angles, bars, hoops, sheet, strip: F(3), BF(3),
Shrubbery	Wolverhampton Corrugated Iron Co.	Galvanised and plain sheet iron
Stour Valley RM(8)	Shrubbey Steel & Iron Co.	I & S – sheet: F(1), BF(2), MF(3), HF(9), PF(14),

BCN, Monway Branch

Brunswick, Monway & Old Park★	Patent Shaft & Axletree Co.	I & S – angles, bars, rails, tyres, wheels: MF(28), PF(80), RM(9), WT(3)
Imperial	John Bagnall & Sons Ltd	See Leabrook Works

BCN, new main line – Smethwick to Tipton

Bromford	Bromford Iron Co.	I &S – angles, bars, rods, strip: F(2), MF/PF(65), RM(7)
Dunkirk	Thomas Jordan & Co.	Sheet iron: PF(9), RM(4)
Factory (Tipton)	John Stevens	Sheet iron: F(1), PF(7), RM(2)
Roway	Edward Page & Sons	I – angles, bars, strip: PF(20), SF(1), RM(3)

BCN, old main line – Smethwick to Tipton

Alpha RM(2)	Joshua Wilkinson & Son	I – bars, cable, horse shoes: F(1), PF(8),
Anchor	Batson & Radcliff	I – angles, bars, section: F(1), HF(3), PF(10)
Crown	Thomas L. Nicklin & Co.	I – angles, bars and sheets for gas tubing: PF(11), RM(2)
District	District Iron & Steel Co.	I & S – angles, bars, hoops, strip
Dudley Port	Plant & Fisher	I – angles, bars, hoops, strip: PF(20), RM(3)
Lion (Smethwick)	London Works Iron Co.	See London Works Oldbury
Park Lane (Oldbury)	F.R. Simpson	I – angles, bars, sash & shutter bars: MF(2), PF(9), RM(1)
Portfield	James & Charles Holcroft	I – angles, bars, hoops, rails, rod
Sandwell	Lones, Vernon & Holden	Coach axles and bar iron: MF/PF(23), RM(3)
Stour Valley	Patent Nut & Bolt Co. Ltd	Bolts, nuts, spikes, etc.

Tividale New	Hill & Smith	Galvanised and corrugated sheet – see also Brierley Hill
Tividale & Etna	George Wilkinson & Son	I & S – sheet iron
Woodford	Woodford Sheet Iron Co.	I – sheet and Russian roofing

BCN, Oldbury Loop

| London Works | London Works Iron Co. | I – angles, bars, strip: F, PF(18), RM |

BCN, old main line – Wednesbury Oak Loop

Bankfield	S. Groucutt & Sons	I – angles, bars, hoops, rails, sheet: F(2), HF(10), PF(22), RM(4)
Batmans Hill	Tupper & Co. Ltd	See Albion
Bilston	W. & J.S. Sparrow	I – angles, bars, hoops, rods, rails, strip: PF(24), RM
Bloomfield	William Barrows & Son	I – angles, bars, hoops, rods, strip: MF(17), PF(59), RM(8)
Bradley	Hatton Sons & Co.	I & S and tinplate: BF, CF, PF, RM (Also at Kidderminster)
Bradley	Tupper & Co. Ltd	Galvanised and corrugated iron for roofs
Bradley Field	World Galvanised Iron Co.	Galvanised, tinned and corrugated iron
Bradley Hall	J.E. East & Co.	Sheet iron: PF(10), RM(3)
Britannia	John Harris	I – angles, bars, chain: F(2), PF(11), RM(3)
Capponfield	William Molineaux & Co.	I – bars, billets, hoops, sheet, strip
Deepfields	George Tinn & Co.	Sheet iron: F(2), MF/BF(12), HF(6), SM(5)
Ebenezer	E. Birch & Sons	I – bars, thimble iron
Ettingshall	Ettingshall Iron Co.	Sheet iron: F(1), PF(10), RM(4)
Factory	Bilston Iron Co.	Sheet iron: BF(2), F(2), HF(10), PF(17), RM(5)
Gospel Oak	Gospel Oak Iron and Galvanised Iron & Wire Co. Ltd	Galvanised and tinned sheets and tiles: PF, RM
Regents	Tupper & Co. Ltd	See Albion
Summerhill	Hope Iron Steel & Tinplate Co. Ltd	Sheet iron: RM(4)
Summerhill	W. Millington & Co.	I – angles, bars, strip: F(2), HF(1), MF(5), PF(16), RM(4)
Wednesbury Oak	Phillip Williams & Son	I – bars, hoops, rods, strip: BF(2), MF(8), PF(18), RM(5)

BCN, Ridgeacre Branch

| Hall End, Ridgacre & Waterloo | J.T. & W.E. Johnson | I – angles, bars, sheet |

Staffordshire & Worcestershire Canal, Hatherton Branch

| Churchbridge | W. Gilpin (Senior) & Co. Ltd | I & S, axle and edge tool makers |
| Wedges Mill | W. Gilpin (Senior) &Co. Ltd | |

Stourbridge Canal, main line

Brettell Lane	Roberts & Cooper	I – bars, rods: HF, PF, RM
Brierley Hill	John Bradley & Co.	See Stourbridge
Leys	Brown & Freer	I – angles, bars, hoops, rods, sheet

Stourbridge Canal, Fens Branch

| Brockmoor | John Bradley & Co. | See Stourbridge |
| Bromley | Roberts & Cooper | See Brettell Lane |

Stourbridge Canal, Town Arm

| Stourbridge | John Bradley & Co. | I – angles, bars, hoops, strip |

BCN, Walsall Canal

| Albert | Moxley Sheet Iron Co. | Sheet iron |

Albion	Tupper & Co. Ltd	I – bars, sheet: F, PF, plate mill, SM(4), bar mill
Albion & Nelson	J.B. & S. Lees	Boiler tank and bridge plates, locomotive boiler tube, etc.
Bescot Forge*	Bescot Forge Co.	Steel bars and billets, iron bars
Bradford	J.N. Lester	Bar iron
Bulls Bridge	Thomas Jevons	I & S – sheets: PF(10), SM(3)
Bush Farm/Wood Lane	Bright & Langham	I – bars and sheets: MF(4), PF(15), RM(3)
Crown	Edward Bayley	I & S – galvanised sheets and plates: MF(3), PF(9)
Cyclops	John Russell & Co. Ltd	I & S – bars, hoops, strip: PF, RM
Darlaston	Tolly Sons & Bostock	I – bars, hoops, sheet, strip: F(1), BF(1), MF(4), PF(14), RM, SM
Eagle	Eagle Iron & Steel Co.	Sheet iron
Great Bridge	Great Bridge Iron & Steel Co.	I & S – angles, bars, sheet: F(2), merchant mill (2), SM(2)
Herberts Park	Herberts Park Iron Co.	I & S – sheet
Leabrook	John Bagnall & Sons Ltd	I – angles, bars, hoops, sheet, strip
Melbourne	John Maybury	Hammered iron
Moxley	Moorcroft Sheet Iron Co.	Sheet iron: F(1), PF(9), RM(1)
Moxley	Thomas & Charles Wells	Boiler plates, ship plates, axe iron: MF/PF(33), RM(4)
Newside & Falcon	T. & J.P. Southan	Sheet iron
St Georges	Morewood & Heathfield	Galvanised iron
Staffordshire	Greets Green Iron & Steel Sheet Co.	Sheet iron: F(1), PF(7), RM(2)

Wyrley & Essington Canal, Birchills Branch

| Bloxwich | Bloxwich Iron & Steel Co. | I & S – bars, billets, hoops, sheet: F(1), BF(1), HF(3), RM |

Wyrley & Essington Canal, main line

Beaver	Isaac Jenks & Sons	See Minerva Works
Birchills	George & Richard Thomas	I – bars, hoops, strip: F(1), MF(2), PF(13), RM
Birchills	Walsall District Iron Co.	I – bars, rods (nail and wire): RM
Cleveland	Cleveland Iron Co.	I – bars, hoop iron: PF(10), hoop and bar mill
Crown	Davies, Brothers & Co. Ltd	Galvanised sheet iron
Pelsall	Pelsall Coal & Iron Co. Ltd	I & S – angles, bars, hoops, rails, sheet: F(3), RM(6)
Staffordshire	Benjamin Bunch & Sons	I & S – angles, bars, hoops, strip: F(1), MF(4), PF(16), RM(3)
Star	David Jeavons	Bar iron: F(1), PF(7), RM(1)
Swan Garden and Osier Bed	John Lysaght Ltd	Rolling mills for galvanised and corrugated iron

Not Canal Served

| Cradley | Samuel Evers & Son | Bar iron |
| Providence (Cradley) | Joseph Penn & Co. | Bar iron: F(1), MF(2), PF(7) |

APPENDIX THREE

Collieries

(List of working collieries, 1896 (mines employing more than fifty people).

Colliery	Owner	Canal link

Cannock Chase Coalfield

Aldridge	Aldridge Colliery Co.	BCN, Daw End Branch
Ashmore Park	Ashmore Park Colliery Co.	Wyrley & Essington
Birch Coppice (Coppice)	Owen & Dudson	Wyrley & Essington
Brereton	Earl of Shrewsbury	Trent & Mersey

Cannock & Leacroft	Cannock & Leacroft Colliery Co. Ltd	BCN, Cannock Extension
Cannock Chase 1–8	Cannock Chase Colliery Co. Ltd	BCN, Anglesey Branch
Cannock Chase 9,10	Cannock Chase Colliery Co. Ltd	Littleworth Tramway
Cannock Lodge	Cannock Lodge Colliery Co. Ltd	BCN, Sneyd Locks Branch
Conduit No.3 (Jerome)	Conduit Colliery Co. Ltd	BCN Cannock Extension
Coppy Hall	E. Barnett	BCN, Daw End Branch
Coalpool	J. Hough & Son	Wyrley & Essington
Conduit No.4	Conduit Colliery Co. Ltd	BCN, Cannock Extension
Coppice (Fair Lady)	Coppice Colliery Co. Ltd	BCN, Cannock Extension
East Cannock	East Cannock Colliery Co. Ltd	BCN, Cannock Extension
Essington Farm	Essington Farm Colliery Co.	BCN, Sneyd Locks Branch
Goscote Hall	Starkey Ltd	Wyrley & Essington
Great Wyrley	Great Wyrley Colliery Co. Ltd	S &W Hatherton Branch and BCN, Wyrley Bank Canal
Grove	William Harrison Ltd	BCN, Cannock Extension
Hayes Colliery	Earl of Shrewsbury	Trent & Mersey
Hawkins (Old Coppice)	J. Hawkins & Son	S & W Hatherton Branch
Hollybank	Hollybank Colliery Co. Ltd	BCN, Sneyd Locks Branch
Hilton	Essington Farm Colliery Co. Ltd	BCN, Sneyd Locks Branch
Norton Cannock	Norton Cannock Colliery Co. Ltd	BCN, Sneyd Locks Branch
Pool Hayes	W. Bickley	Wyrley & Essington
Walsall Wood	Walsall Wood Colliery Co. Ltd	BCN, Daw End Branch
West Cannock 1–4	West Cannock Colliery Co. Ltd	BCN, Cannock Extension

South Staffordshire Coalfield

Black Lake	Black Lake Colliery Co.	BCN, Ridgeacre Branch
Blakeley Wood, Wednesbury	Thomas Price and Son	
Bournehills	Bournehills & Withymoor Colls Co.	Dudley No.2
Bromley	J. Raybould Trustees	Stourbridge Extension
Bromley Lane	H.S. Pitt & Co.	Stourbridge Extension
Coneygre Collieries	Earl of Dudley	BCN, old main line
Dairy Farm, Bilston	Mansell & Davies	
Dudley Wood	N. Hingley & Sons Ltd	Dudley No.2
Ebeneezer	Ebeneezer Colliery Co.	BCN, Balls Hill Branch
Foxyards	Earl of Dudley	BCN, main line
Grace Mary	Francis Minton	BCN, old main line
Haden Hill	W. Bassano & Co.	Dudley No.2
Hamstead	Hamstead Colliery Co. Ltd	BCN, Tame Valley
Himley Collieries	Earl of Dudley	Pensnett
Horseley	William J. Hayward	BCN, Dixons Branch
Knowle	Knowle Colliery Co.	Dudley No.2
Millfield	Patent Shaft & Axeltree Co. Ltd	BCN, Tame Valley
Mud Hall	Dudley Colliery Co.	Dudley No.2
Old Netherton	M. & W. Grazebrook	Dudley No.1
Newbury Lane	Newbury Lane Colliery Co.	BCN, Titford
Rowley Hall	W. Bassano & Co.	BCN, Titford
Saltwells Collieries	Earl of Dudley	Dudley No.2
Samson	Mansell & Davies	BCN, Titford
Sandwell Park	Sandwell Park Colliery Co. Ltd	BCN, old main line
Shut End	John Bradley & Co.	Stourbridge Extension
Wednesbury Oak	P. Williams & Son	BCN, Wednesbury Oak Loop
Woodside	Cochrane & Co.	Dudley No.1

APENDIX FOUR

West Midlands Gasworks Canal and Railway Links

Gasworks	Canal	Railway
Aldridge	BCN, Walsall Canal	Not served
Bilston	BCN, main line	GWR
Birmingham Gas Street	Worcester & Birmingham	Not served
Birmingham Fazeley Street	Warwick & Birmingham	Not served
Birmingham Windsor Street	BCN, Birmingham & Fazeley	LNWR/LMS
Birmingham Adderley Street	Warwick & Birmingham	Not served
Birmingham Saltley	Birmingham & Warwick Junction	Midland Railway/LMS
Birmingham Nechells	Birmingham & Warwick Junction	Midland Railway/LNWR/LMS
Brierley Hill	Stourbridge Canal	Not served
Cannock	Near BCN, Cannock Extension	LNWR/LMS
Cradley	Not served	Near Pensnett Railway
Dawley Brook	Not served	Pensnett Railway
Dudley	Not directly served	Not directly served
Halesowen	Not directly served	Not directly served
Lichfield	Not directly served	Not directly served
Oldbury	BCN, Oldbury Loop	Opposite GWR basin
Ogley Hay & Brownhills	BCN, Wyrley & Essington	LNWR/LMS siding
Mond (at Tipton)	BCN, Dixons Branch	LNWR/LMS siding
Moxley (original works for Bilston)	BCN, Walsall Canal	
Rowley Regis	BCN, Dudley Canal	GWR
Smethwick	BCN, old main line	LNWR/LMS
Solihull	Warwick & Birmingham	Not served
Stourbridge	Stourbridge Canal	GWR
Swan Village	BCN, Balls Hill Branch	GWR
Tipton	BCN, new main line	LNWR/LMS
Walsall (original)	Not served	Not served
Walsall (Wolverhampton Street)	BCN, Walsall Locks Branch	Not served
Walsall (Pleck)	BCN, Walsall Canal	LNWR/LMS
West Bromwich (Albion)	BCN, Union Branch	LNWR/LMS
Willenhall	Near BCN, Bentley Canal	LNWR/LMS
Wolverhampton (Horseleyfields)	BCN, main line	Not served
Wolverhampton (Stafford Road)	BCN, main line	GWR/LNWR/LMS
Workhouse (Birmingham) – private	BCN, Winson Green Loop	Not served

APPENDIX FIVE

Power Stations

Generating Station	Canal	Railway
Aston, Chester Street	BCN	Not Served
Birmingham, Dale End	Not served	Not served
Birmingham, Water Street	BCN	Not served
Birmingham Nechells Temporary	Birmingham & Warwick Junction	Midland Railway
Birmingham Nechells 'A' & 'B'	Birmingham & Warwick Junction	Midland Railway/LMS
Birmingham Hams Hall	Not Served	LMS
GEC, Witton – private	BCN	Not served
Hartshill	Pensnett Canal	Opposite Pensnett Railway sidings
Ocker Hill 'A'	BCN	Not served
Ocker Hill 'B'	BCN	British Railways
Smethwick (Downing Street)	BCN	Not served
Walsall, Wolverhampton Street	BCN	Not served
Walsall, Birchills 'A'	BCN	Not served

Walsall, Birchills 'B'	BCN	British Railways
Walsall (Pleck) SS Tramways	BCN	Not served
West Bromwich (Blacklake)	BCN	Not served
Wolverhampton	BCN	GWR opposite

APPENDIX SIX

Coal Contractors 1926

Key

CM	Coal merchant
CP	Colliery proprietor
CLM	Coal, lime, cement and builders merchants
CF	Coal factor
CPM	Coal and pyrites merchant
HS	Hauliers and steerers

Coal Merchant, Factor or Contractor	*Type*	*Canal*
Joseph Henry Allbrooke, Valentia Wharf, Oldbury	CM	BCN, old main line
E. Alderson & Son, 6 Bean Road, Dudley		
E.C.S. Backhouse, Heneage Street Wharf, Birmingham	CM	Wallis Arm
Samuel Barlow, Anchor Works, Glascote	CF	Coventry Canal
A.R. Banks, Victoria Street, West Bromwich	CF	
A. Brockhurst, Oozells Street Wharf	CM	BCN, Oozells Loop
William Charles, Bridge Wharf, Wednesbury	CM	Tame Valley Canal
S. Clarke, Old Walsall Road, Hamstead	CM	Tame Valley Canal
Alex Comley Ltd, 194 Corporation Street, Birmingham	CF	
G.H. Cooper, Brookfields Wharf, Birmingham		Winson Green Loop
J. Cooper, Aldridge	CM	
Dicken Brothers, St Vincent Street, Birmingham	CM	BCN, new main line
Henry Dixon, Dudley Road, Oldbury		
T. & M. Dixon, Stephenson Place, Birmingham	CM	Worcestershire & Birmingham
Dixon, Edwards & Co., Windsor Street Wharf	CM	
Henry Dumolo, Curzon Street	CPM	
Dunns Ltd, Peartree Lane Colliery	CP	Dudley No.1
W. Elwell and Son, Dudley Port	CP	
Thomas & Samuel Element, 285 Nechells Park Road	HS	Tame Valley Canal
Evesons (Coal) Ltd, 134 Edmund Street, Birmingham	CM	
Fanshaw & Pinson, Commercial Road Wharf, Wolverhampton	CM	BCN, main line
A. Farrington, Shrubbery House, Toll End Road, Tipton		
Field and Bradley, Blacklake Wharf, West Bromwich	CM	Ridgeacre Branch
T. Foster & Son, Railway Drive, Wolverhampton	CM	
F.M. Gateley, Soho Pool Wharf	CM	
George & Matthews, Vandyke Wharf, Bilston Road, Wolverhampton	CM	BCN, main line
Goodman & Co., Salford Bridge Wharf	CLM	Birmingham & Fazeley Canal
Goodman & Co., New Wharf, Selly Oak	CLM	Worcestershire & Birmingham Canal
George Hale, Anchor Bridge, Birmingham Road, Oldbury	CM	BCN, old main line
W.H. Hand, Unity Coal Wharf, Oldbury	CM	
W.J. Hayward, Dixon's Horseley Colliery, Tipton		Dixons Branch
William Hayes & Son Ltd, 44 Lichfield Street, Wolverhampton		
J. Hickinbottom, Hall End Wharf, West Bromwich		
T. Hickinbottom & Son, Leabrook Road, Tipton	CM	Walsall Canal
W. Holmes, Charles Street, West Bromwich		
Thomas Ingles, Meadow Colliery, Deepfields		
Kimberley Beddoes and Co., Bromford Road, Oldbury	CM	
Frank Knight, Chester Street Wharf, Birmingham	CM	Birmingham & Fazeley Canal
Leamore Coal and Coke Co. Ltd, Upper Green Lane, Walsall	CM	Wyrley & Essington Canal
Leonard Leigh Ltd, Wharf Street, Hockley	CM	

Lunt Brothers, Amblecote, Stourbridge	CM	Stourbridge Canal
Lunt Brothers, Stewponey & Kinver	CM	Staffordshire & Worcestershire Canal
Samuel Male, Lower Delph, Brierley Hill	CM	
Lawrence Miller Ltd, Martineu Square, Birmingham	CM	
T.B. Mottershead, Soho Pool Wharf	CM	
Osborne & Handley, 214 High Street, West Bromwich	CF	
T.E. Pheasant, Bescot Road, Walsall		
H.S. Pitt & Leeson Ltd, Oakfield Offices, Brettell Lane Stourbridge	CF	
E. Probert & Sons Ltd, Millfields Coal Wharf, Wolverhampton	CM	BCN, main line
G.T. Rapps, Soho Pool Wharf	CM	
John Round & Sons, Bone Pit Wharf, Netherton	CM	
Round & Downes, Whitmore Street	CM	
C.A. Sadler, New Road, Langley		
Sadler Brothers & Webster, Broadwell Wharf, Oldbury	CM	
Fred Smith, Harborne Road, Warley		
Spencer Abbott & Co. Ltd, Gravelly Hill	CF	Tame Valley Canal
S.W.B. Stephen & Co. Ltd, Rolfe Street	CM	Engine Arm
D.M. Stevenson and Co. Ltd, 3 Newhall Street	CF	
J. & S. Tonks, 279 Hagley Road, Birmingham		
John Toole Ltd, New Regent Wharf, Bilston	CF	
John Toole Ltd, Star Wharf, Heath Town, Wolverhampton	CF	
E.H. Walker, Bordesley Street Wharf		BCN, Digbeth Branch
Wilson, Carter & Pearson, 111 New Street, Birmingham	CF	
John Woodall, Hill Top		
Wolverhampton Coal & Coke Co.		
W. Worsey, Great Bridge		
James A. Wright, Deepfield Colliery	CM	
Wulfruna Coal Co., Bilston Road, Wolverhampton	CM	BCN, new main line
Tom Yorke, Tatany Wharf, West Bromwich		

APPENDIX SEVEN

Boatyards 1943
(PRO MT 52/106)

Boatyard	Location	Number of Boat Builders / Repairers
Boat Builders and Repairers		
T. Bantock	Wolverhampton	1
W. Harris	Washington Dock, Netherton	4
W.J. Hayward & Co.	Horsley Colliery, Tipton	2
Peter Keay & Son	Winterley Street, Rushall	2
W. Mosley	Parkhead, Hollyhall	1
William Poole	279 Bilston Road, Wolverhampton	2
Spencer, Abbott & Co. Ltd	Salford Bridge	2
E. Thomas	Old Birchills Wharf	3
J. Toole Ltd	Regents Wharf, Bilston	3
Warwickshire Canal Carrying Co.	Charity Dock, Bedworth	2
Worsey Ltd	Carl Street, Walsall	3

Canal Boat Repairs
(Based on PRO MT 52/106)

Boat Builder	Type	Output per Month★	Notes
Baldwins Ltd, Wilden Ironworks	Wood		Restricted
Thomas Bantock, Bilston	Iron	2	Repairs for own fleet
Samuel Barlow, Glascote	Wood	2–2½	

BCN Ocker Hill	Iron/wood	2–3	Repairs for own fleet
S.T. Chambers & Son	Wood	1	
G. & D. Crannage	Iron	2	
T. & S. Element, Gravelly Hill	Wood	2	
Fellows, Morton & Clayton, Saltley	Iron/wood	9	
George Hale & Son	Wood	2	Major repairs
William Harris & Sons	Iron	2	Yard built one new boat monthly, or two major repairs and six minor repairs
W.J. Hayward	Wood	2	Minor repairs
Thomas Hendley	Wood	1	
T. Hickinbottam & Son, Wednesbury	Wood	1	Repairs for own fleet
ICI General Chemicals Ltd, Oldbury	Wood	2	Repairs for own fleet
Peter Keay, Walsall	Wood	6–7	
LMS, Wolverhampton	Iron/wood	4	Dock for own repairs
Lees & Atkins, Polesworth	Wood	3–4	
A. Matty, Tipton	Wood	20	Includes minor repairs
T. Pearsall	Wood	1	
A.H. Price	Wood	1	
Severn Carrying Co., Stourport	Wood	2	Major repairs
Spencer, Abbott & Co., Gravelley Hill	Wood	4–8	Four major and up to eight minor repairs
Staffordshire & Worcestershire Canal	Wood	1	Intermittent repairs for own fleet
Stewarts & Lloyds, Coombeswood Tube Works, Halesowen	Wood	1	Repairs for own fleet
Stewarts & Lloyds, Bilston Springvale Steelworks,	Iron	3	Repairs for own fleet
Ernest Thomas	Wood	10	
John Toole Ltd	Wood	1	
Warwickshire Canal Carrying Co. Ltd	Wood	9	Major and minor repairs
J.A. Wright	Wood	1	Dock for own repairs
Worsey Ltd and repairs for up to six	Wood	6	One new boat a month
J. Yates, Brownhills	Wood	70–80	Major and minor repairs

*Output refers to major repairs; minor repairs or leak-stopping jobs required less time and consequently more jobs might be undertaken.

INDEX